American Life in the 1840s

For B. H. Holsinger,
a good counselor
and a good neighbor.

Carl Bode

Documents in American Civilization Series

General Editors:

HENNIG COHEN AND JOHN WILLIAM WARD

Statement by the General Editors

The Anchor Series, "Documents in American Civilization," provides primary materials for the study of the history of the United States and for the understanding of American culture. In the belief that neither history nor culture can be properly studied without consideration of a variety of sources, the editors have adopted the interdisciplinary approach in the selection of documents. In our sense, a "document" is any idea, institution, or manmade object that provides a clue to the way in which subjective experience is organized at a specific moment in time.

The purpose of the series is twofold: to show the pervasiveness of those themes which are central to particular moments in history; and to underline the significance of cultural documents in their total historical context—and thus to illuminate problems or themes that characterize American society.

HENNIG COHEN is Professor of English at the University of Pennsylvania and editor of *American Quarterly*. He is also editor of *Selected Poems of Herman Melville* (Anchor Books, A375) and co-editor of *Folklore in America*.

JOHN WILLIAM WARD is Professor of History and American Studies at Amherst College. He is the author of *Andrew Jackson: Symbol for an Age* and editor of *Society, Manners, and Politics in the United States* by Michael Chevalier.

The founder and first president of the American Studies Association, CARL BODE has written both literary and cultural history. He has published two books in the field of pre-Civil War culture, as well as a recent collection of essays, *The Half-World of American Culture*. He is the editor of, and contributor to, *The Young Rebel in American Literature* and *The Great Experiment in American Literature*. He has edited the collected poems of Henry Thoreau and a Thoreau anthology and has co-edited the Thoreau correspondence. In addition he has published two volumes of his own poetry, of which *The Man behind You* is the more recent. Born in the Midwest, he took degrees at the University of Chicago and Northwestern University. After service in the army in World War II, he taught at UCLA and then joined the faculty of the University of Maryland, where he is Professor of English. He has been on leave from his university to take up Ford, Guggenheim, and Newberry fellowships, and to serve as American cultural attaché to the Court of St. James. He is a fellow of the Royal Society of Literature. He has been president of the Thoreau Society and chairman of the Fulbright Commission in Great Britain. He is a delegate, from the American Studies Association, to the American Council of Learned Societies and a member of the national council of the American Association of University Professors. Currently he is writing a biography of H. L. Mencken.

AMERICAN LIFE IN THE 1840s

Edited with an Introduction by
Carl Bode

Anchor Books
Doubleday & Company, Inc.
Garden City, New York
1967

The Anchor Books edition is the first publication of
American Life in the 1840s

Anchor Books edition: 1967

A hardcover edition of *American Life in the 1840s* is available
from the New York University Press.

Library of Congress Catalog Card Number 67–11163
Copyright © 1967 by Doubleday & Co., Inc.
All Rights Reserved
Printed in the United States of America

For Barbara

Introduction

DAILY LIFE

The census showed over seventeen million Americans as the bustling 1840s opened. A decade later there would be twenty-three million. In the years between, a war was fought and two presidential elections were decided, immigration and westward expansion reached new heights, four more states entered the Union, and the phrase "Manifest Destiny" was coined and quickly found so satisfying that it became a national cliché. Much of this has been remarked before. In scores of books and articles the story of the Mexican War and the annals of the presidents have been recorded. Immigration and expansion also have been popular subjects for the historian.

But the daily life of the average American has not. Expansion and migration, warfare and politics, affected him of course. And yet his daily life was probably as centered on his own concerns as ours is now. Even in the South the rising threat of war over slavery failed, it may be guessed, to trouble the sleep of many men. In the rest of the country, slavery and all it portended meant as a rule even less to the individual. In the 1840s it was no harder for the man on the street to do his daily stint without worrying about war, any war, than it is today to keep from worrying about nuclear annihilation. Tomorrow we may be bombed out of existence; nevertheless, we get to work on time, buy clothes at the store, and plan our vacation for next summer.

Everyday existence bulks large in our life. As soon as we think about it we realize that most Americans of the 1840s did not spend their time playing politics or waging war. They moved instead through routines highly important to them, though not always exciting to the observer. These routines involved schooling, work, family, religion, and recreation; and if we want to understand antebellum America we must take them into account. They lack the color of war and politics, with their flashing sabers and torchlight parades, but those exciting things are not enough. As a matter of fact, in one sense they are not even *true*—that is, not typical.

The historical materials, however, for rediscovering daily life are unusually hard to find. Much of life was taken for granted and never got into print. Much that did see print was later thrown away as being of no significance. Yet the task is not impossible. The books, periodicals, and pictures of those days remain, here and there, in the great research libraries. Drawing on them we can tell a good deal about American life. True, we cannot tell enough to assure ourselves that the portrait is always accurate, the reflection full and faithful. For we still have, by definition, only those books and pictures that survive. They are the books originally intended for the largest reading public, a public mainly middle-class and upper lower-class. The poor received little attention and left little trace behind them. The Irishman in the Boston slums or the frontier wife in Arkansas failed, understandably, to buy any books and, equally important, seldom became the subject of them. The pictures are those intended for the same public—with one increasingly significant exception. The lithographs that Nathaniel Currier and his competitors had begun to publish were so cheap that almost anyone could buy them. You could often find one on the wall of a frontier cabin or a little house in town. The other limitations on our source materials are that they are more often related to an urban rather than a rural audience, though the farmer is far from overlooked; to an Eastern rather than a Western audience; and to a Northern rather than a Southern one.

Notwithstanding, we still have a rich variety of data.

Through our reading of works either published in or popular in the 1840s, and our studying of pictures, we can
recapture much of American life. We can observe the
characteristic ways in which Americans made a living. We
can see the Americans at home, in their family circle.
We can see them in the process of educating themselves,
starting with the schoolboy and ending with the wisest
American, Emerson. We can see them in the house of
worship. We can see them in their diversions, reading,
enjoying the arts and the outdoors, and relishing their
humor. We can see them as they try to comprehend themselves, explaining what it means to be an American in the
1840s. Finally, by way of epilogue in one sense and prologue in another, we can look briefly at their slavery problem. We can survey the two opposed positions on it: the
position of the small but active group of abolitionists and
the position of the numerous defenders of slavery; and a
third position, of those who tried to be fair-minded and
to weigh the evidence.

Though the printed word will be our main source of
data, visual documents, it should be said again, are also
important. Much neglected as a rule, they can furnish
insights hard to find otherwise. To show the new exuber-
ance of taste, for instance, what better way than to reproduce the page from the *Horticulturist* for July 1846 which
shows, first, a *View of a Common Country House* (doc. 11,
plate 9) with its straight lines and old-fashioned symmetry
and, second, a *View of the Same, Improved* (doc. 11,
plate 9) by adding a fancy front porch, elaborate bargeboards, and Gothic trimmings? The two pictures tell more
than many paragraphs of prose.

Probably the first of this country's concerns during the
1840s was its economic life. The ways in which the economy operated were constantly more complex but from
the standpoint of today they seem simple. The United
States was still largely agricultural; the farmer was still
the representative American man. Manufacturing, mer-

chandising, and the hand trades were growing in importance but had reached nothing like their present seven-to-
one superiority in manpower. Underlying every aspect of
the American economy and sanctioning every occupation
was the belief that work was good in itself and should be
universal.

The essence of the American way in the 1840s can be
found in *The Farmer's Companion* by Jesse Buel (doc. 1).
"Agriculture," he announces, is "the great wheel which
moves all the machinery of society." If it runs well, all
other economic activities flourish; if it fails, so does everything else. For agriculture alone feeds us. More than that,
it is the main support of our republican government, acting as the guardian of our freedom and "the parent of
physical and moral health to the state." Its very labor,
healthful and satisfying, provides the best medicine made
for man. It even allows him to continue his education.
Others must use their winter nights for work; the "agri-
culturalist, on the contrary, may devote his evenings, or
most of them, to study."

Though Buel's claims were extravagant, they suggest
how America felt about farming. This is not to deny the
mounting claims of other forms of work. The Quaker
poet Whittier celebrated the efforts of shoemakers, fishermen, and drovers, among others, in his *Songs of Labor*
(doc. 2). Edward Hazen, setting himself to the task of
vocational guidance, could find nearly ninety occupations
to describe and commend to young fellows preparing to
earn a living. Hazen explains step by step what is involved,
as he sees it, in each occupation. With so many kinds of
work to characterize he has neither the space nor the need
to praise them. The important thing about his book *Popular Technology* (doc. 3) is that it offers us a panoramic
view of the occupations open to young America. And the
lively little journal, the *Lowell Offering* (doc. 4), published by the mill girls in the early 1840s reminds us that
women had entered the labor market too.

Not the least important element in the American economy was the transportation revolution. Better transportation meant not only a busier, richer, more civilized America, it meant that the United States were coming closer to being united in culture as well as polity. W. M. Gillespie's *Manual of the Principles and Practices of Road-Making* (doc. 5) represents the revolution in its pages of careful prescription.

To see our economy in a fresh light we can turn to the first of the pictorial documents, "Town and Country" (doc. 6, plates 1–5). It is a group of five pictures organized to suggest how the economy looked in terms of rural versus urban life and how transportation was gradually connecting these two ways of life not only literally but figuratively.

Getting a living is as consequential now as it was in the 1840s. Making a home is not, however. The family as a social institution meant far more in those days. It was a firmer unit and a fuller one. Often it encompassed three generations instead of today's two. Duties were parceled out. The children, whether in town or country, usually had chores to do. The wife had the household to manage. The father had the bread to win and the family to head. And often, taking their share of the responsibilities and rewards, a grandparent, an aunt, perhaps a cousin filled out the family circle.

At base was the steadfast relationship of man and wife. How to achieve this was the subject not only of much discussion but also of some popular books, books which were the staid ancestors of today's marriage manuals. They can be represented by the Reverend Matthew Sorin's *The Domestic Circle* (doc. 8). He treats the reader like a member of his fashionable Philadelphia congregation. Books for the lower-class, rather than the middle-class, readers were rare; one of the best was J. W. Alexander's *The American Mechanic* (doc. 9). He advises the workingman on a variety of subjects, but marriage and the family are among the most notable. Sorin's tone is earnest, Alexander's light but incisive. Between them, the

authors manage to give us an inclusive view of family life
of the 1840s, its ideals and problems. Characteristically
they emphasize the duties rather than the joys of domes-
ticity.

But the family meant more than duty; it meant love.
The image of the family was bathed in sentiment; all its
associations were tender, as masses of printed matter and
pictures show. Of course Americans have always felt sentimental about home but the remarkable thing about the
1840s was the extent to which the sentimentalizing went.
Today we wonder if any periodical would publish as fervent a eulogy of "Home" as, in 1847, did the *Farmer and
Mechanic* (doc. 7). There is no place, the journal sang
artlessly, like home. Nowadays even the most womanly of
women's magazines would not print as sentimental a picture as Sarony & Major's *Married*, (doc. 11, plate 6) where
every face is honey-sweet. Nor would even a country
weekly now find space for a poem to home and mother as
fully Freudian as George Bethune's "To my Mother,"
(doc. 10) which has as its concluding couplet:

> Lean on the faithful bosom of thy son.
> My parent! thou art more—my *only* one!

The pictorial document "House and Home" (doc. 11,
plates 6–10) is designed to give us some additional insight
into the relationships within the family and also to tell us
something about American taste at the most popular, the
domestic, level. What kind of home did we want to live
in? What was our dream house during the 1840s? These
are questions that pictures can sometimes answer more
memorably than anything else, in particular perhaps the
pair from the *Horticulturist* mentioned earlier.

Education proved to be the greatest ally for an America
dedicated to progress and improvement. Most Americans
wanted knowledge in order to better themselves; a few
wanted knowledge for its own sake. During the 1840s the
public school system extended its range substantially—

elementary schools, in particular, multiplied—and in many cases raised the level of the education it was offering. Its problems then were its problems now: a citizenry readier to praise education than to pay for it; teachers of unequal abilities; inadequate school buildings; an indifferent curriculum. Perhaps the best analysis of the problems and the best prescriptions for their solution can be found in a book published at the start of the decade, Thomas Palmer's *The Teacher's Manual* (doc. 12). He considers the teacher crucial to the learning process, contrary to the folk belief that all can teach, and shows the teacher how he can get the most out of his efforts.

Education, however, meant more than the elementary schools. It meant academies and colleges. It meant books, newspapers, libraries, and lyceums. Through these different channels knowledge reached the American public. The humanities, the rudimentary social sciences, the physical and the biological sciences each attracted increasing interest. They were studied in the curriculums. They were the staple of the serious magazines as well as of the strictly professional journals. They were the subject of books and treatises. Somewhat popularized, they furnished the material for course after course of lyceum lectures.

The eagerness to know marked both the middle and the lower class. Lyceums often began as workmen's institutes and then broadened their scope. Manuals for merchants as well as those for clerks often had a chapter on reading and self-culture; so did the occasional workmen's guide such as *The American Mechanic*. The leading demand of both classes was for information on how to do things. It resulted in a multitude of manuals and technical treatises, of which Jacob Bigelow's *The Useful Arts Considered in Connexion with the Applications of Science* (doc. 16) is typical.

Beyond technology lay the more rarefied realms of knowledge. Complex though science was becoming, some of the leading scientists felt it their duty to teach the public as much as possible. The noted Swiss naturalist

Louis Agassiz, settling in America, improved his English and gave many scientific addresses, some of which were later published. A good example is his series entitled *An Introduction to the Study of Natural History* (doc. 14). Technical terms are minimal and the exposition seems lucidity itself. Another instance is the lectures of Professor Denison Olmsted. Printed as *Letters on Astronomy* (doc. 15), they not only explain the intricacies of his science, they breathe with enthusiasm for it. With patent sincerity he speaks of "this noble science." Enthusiasm for the humanities is as strong as enthusiasm for science and can be seen in such a work as *Essays on Ancient Literature and Art* (doc. 13), compiled by three gifted New England scholars. They argue ardently that the classics of Greece and Rome contained the noblest knowledge of all.

To help round out our view of the world of knowledge we have the pictorial document "Shaping the American Mind" (doc. 17, plates 11–15). Though its elements are diverse their implications are not out of harmony. We see depicted a staid private school, our greatest scientist, a stylized rendition of a new printing press, a famous scene from European literature, and a pastoral (and educational) idyl.

Knowledge has continued to be of great importance to Americans. Not so for religion. The American church like the American home had more meaning in the 1840s, to all appearances, than it has now. True, in recent years we have seen an increase in official religion—God is more frequently invoked in the Government—but the church is plainly no longer the moral and social institution it once was. In antebellum days, though exact figures are lacking, it baptized, married, and buried most Americans. Also, though this too can never be precisely ascertained, it probably indoctrinated, strengthened, and succored the majority of them as well.

The essence of religion in the 1840s can be found in the major Protestant denominations. It was positive, optimistic, open. For the reasoned approach to Christ we can go, for instance, to the thoughtful discourses of the Reverend Orville Dewey of New York (doc. 19). For the emotional impact of salvation through Christ we can go to Peter Cartwright's description of his successes as a Methodist circuit rider (doc. 20). The role of the minor sects can be discerned through a sympathetic account of visits to the Shakers by a mill girl who wrote for the *Lowell Offering* (doc. 22).

The means of salvation were much the same as they are today. However, it is evident that Americans depended on the Bible to a larger extent then than now. The Bible is still the first best seller but in the 1840s it furnished a guide to the perplexed in many a manner now forgotten. The maxim was, as Nathaniel Currier put it in one of his popular lithographs, *Search the Scriptures* (doc. 26, plate 16). The cause of American religion was further strengthened by the distribution of millions of little religious tracts. The era of the tracts is ended, but their religious anecdotes and messages, according to frequent testimony, once moved many hearts.

Into this predominantly Protestant atmosphere came the Roman Catholic Church. Catholicism had been on the American continent from the outset but it was during the 1840s that it made the first of its great steps toward national importance. The Irish immigrants in particular imported their Catholicism with them and the church took on the flavor that it still has today. Among the American intellectuals the leading convert was the Transcendentalist Orestes Brownson. His explanation in *The Convert* (doc. 21) of how he became convinced that Catholicism alone comprehended the truth aroused much interest and controversy.

Besides *Search the Scriptures* (plate 16) the pictorial document "Testaments of Faith" (doc. 26, plates 16–19) brings us further illustration of the varying roles of religion in America. We see a famous floating chapel, a lithograph of the Lord's Prayer for household use, and a primly executed panorama of an annual Quaker meeting. Each has something special to report.

As their civilization advanced, Americans found that they had more time for enjoyment. Reading for pleasure became popular. The number of literate nearly doubled during the decade, as did the value of the books manufactured. Appreciation of the arts increased. More pictures were sold, more concerts given, more sheet music printed, than ever before. This came with the conquering of the frontier and the bountiful expansion of the economy (the decade knew nothing but good times). Similarly, once the frontier stopped being an obstacle, the woods and the outdoors in general became a place for recreation. The more that people had to walk on pavements, the more they yearned for a forest path. The painter Charles Lanman could now celebrate the joys of nature in spring in his *Letters from a Landscape Painter* and be sure of an appreciative audience. One of the Lowell mill girls could expatiate on the joys of winter. Pictures of picnicking and boating could and did appear. And hunting, once a necessity, could now turn into a sport.

Under the two rubrics of social pleasures and solitary ones, the visual documents (doc. 33, plates 20–28) on enjoying ourselves are gathered. A stirring parade, a picnic of city dwellers, a maple sugar party in the country, a solitary fisherman, a lady sketching in the country, an illustration from the adventures of a buccaneer, an illustration from *Ivanhoe*, an engraving of Friedrich Schiller, an illustration from a folk tale: all these add up to an impression of a people who were broadening their avocational interests and learning, in spite of the Puritan doctrine of work, to enjoy life increasingly.

Not the least of life's enjoyments was our much-prized humor. It ranged from the tall tale, beloved of the frontier, to the satire on New York society. No single humorist dominated the decade but there was a substantial amount of humorous writing. A sample is William B. Fowle's vol-

ume *Familiar Dialogues* (doc. 32), all of which are designed to arouse guffaws and giggles. A sense of humor
was already believed to be an American characteristic.
But there were other typical traits as well, so people
thought.

What it meant to be an American, a typical American,
was fairly well agreed upon. Native observers and foreign
visitors generally felt that, for one thing, the American
was highly patriotic; in poetry, prose, and picture the evidence survives. "How glorious art thou!" the hack poet
Mrs. Sigourney (doc. 34) exclaimed to America, and
many a prose writer echoed her. The American was democratic, demolishing class distinctions with delight. He respected character and achievement but not birth; he
idolized Washington and admired the successful merchant
or manufacturer. He was a materialist, occupied with making money, and he could admit it. Yet he also considered
himself a religious man, a practicing Christian. Whatever
he did, he did with vigor; it was agreed that he was a
font of energy. His energy, however, often made him restless, sometimes made him dissatisfied, and even at times
showed him to be insecure.

Nevertheless, it was a wonderful thing to be an American; for Americans considered themselves the Chosen
People. Though this was not always said outright, the
title of a work like George Cheever's *God's Hand in
America* (doc. 39) is indicative.

The six pictures that make up the visual document
"The American Image" (doc. 40, plates 29–34) complement the printed selections which deal with the various
ways we comprehended ourselves in the 1840s. Each of the
six in its own fashion graphically reveals what it meant to
be an American. Especially through allegory and American
mythology this document attempts to convey something
on that most difficult of subjects. The over-all impression
is of a practical, vigorous, confident country.

There was in fact only one cloud on the American hori-

zon, the dissension over slavery. Most Americans tried to
ignore the possibility of crisis and war—Mrs. Sigourney
could hymn America in line after line of blank verse and
never mention slavery outright (doc. 34). There it was,
however, and it connected inexorably with the past and led
grimly to the future. William Lloyd Garrison (doc. 41)
was one of the few who foresaw the end. He knew that
universal emancipation must come and he prayed only
that his "guilty country" would not be destroyed in the
process.

Garrison was absolutely convinced that he was right.
So, on the other side, was John C. Calhoun (doc. 42).
He saw the problem chiefly in terms of political power,
which the South was in the process of losing. His speeches
often had the logic that Garrison's rhetoric sometimes
lacked; his tone was one of reason while Garrison's was
impassioned. But underneath he was as determined, even
in the 1840s, as Garrison. To understand the deeper feelings of the South, the Southern subconscious, more than
Calhoun's senatorial speeches is needed. We can find it
in the work of such an unknown as Matthew Estes of
Mississippi. His *Defence of Negro Slavery* (doc. 44) is
based on the belief that the Negro is a lower form of life.
The economic and social arguments flowing from that are
all too obvious, though it should be added that Estes reminds the white man of his responsibilities for the hapless slave.

In the pictorial document "The Two Faces of Slavery"
(doc. 45, plates 35–36) the gulf between the opposing
sides is illustrated. Slavery puts its case with vigor while
abolition speaks with restraint, but it is clear that no
common ground for agreement can exist. Considered ob-
jectively, the survival of slavery was becoming unthinkable.
One man could not continue to possess another.

Such was slavery. Yet it would be wrong to end this
look at American life on a note of discord. Americans in
the 1840s were a cheerful people: at the least, matter-of-

fact in their acceptance of difficulties; at the most, euphoric in their belief in progress and success. Their bearing was brisk.

———

At the start of this introduction we mentioned the problem of finding the materials that come closest to giving us an accurate picture of life in the 1840s. Another word ought to be said before we turn to the documents themselves, a word about the kind of material that was passed over and the kinds that were picked. Fiction, in particular, was omitted. It would have been pleasant to draw on the abundant novels and tales of the 1840s, especially for their color and flavor. But unfortunately, in a literal sense they are not true. On the other hand there is some truth certainly, sometimes a great deal, in autobiography and biography. We have drawn on them when they seem to have more to them than the history of one man, for we want a comprehensive picture and surmise that it is best achieved by using material that is either typical or essential (that is, of the essence). And there is the most truth, we feel, in selections from the works of specialists of that day, selections from the works of the authorities in the 1840s. The majority of documents here are of this kind. They are often general rather than individual because we wish to cover the broad range of American life. For instance, we reprint a significant excerpt from the works of an authority on American agriculture rather than a bit of fiction about a single farmer. Or we reprint a selection from the works of an expert on teaching rather than some pages from the biography of a single schoolmaster. It is likely that we lose in sprightliness at the same time that we gain in scope and accuracy. But the truth is what we are after, and these general documents will often bring us nearer to it than individual ones.

One thing more. These documents have been chosen partly for their rich expression of prevailing ideas. At times they will seem obvious and so no doubt will our commentary on them, but ideas are tricky and cannot be taken for granted. At any rate, for the student of American culture who is interested in conceptualization, the documents that follow are full of data.

Textual Note

The published documents are given here as they were originally printed. It has not seemed necessary to strike out commas or correct a mill girl's misspelling of "scrooge."

Acknowledgments

The documents in this volume are pictures, diagrams, and, most often, selections from books and periodicals. In this survey of the 1840s the effort has been to present contemporary materials: the pictures, diagrams, and selections from periodicals all appeared in that decade. The books were either published in the 1840s or were works still popular in the 1840s or (in two or three cases) nineteenth-century works referring to the 1840s. Nearly all the printed materials are from the Library of Congress, which for the study of American civilization is the best library in the world. The pictorial materials, except for one painting in the Corcoran Gallery, come either from the Prints and Photographs Division of the Library of Congress or from the archives of the Smithsonian Institution. In the text, acknowledgment is made for each individual picture.

In searching for visual documents I was helped at the Library of Congress especially by Dr. Alan Fern and Mr. Milton Kaplan and at the Smithsonian by Dr. Peter Welsh, Doris Esch Borthwick, and Mr. Jack Goodwin. As usual, I depended a good deal on the McKeldin Library of the University of Maryland for a variety of research purposes, and there Miss Betty Baehr was particularly helpful. Also, I received clerical assistance from Mrs. Alda Brincefield, Mr. Walter Hageter and Miss Elissa Mattheis, all of the University of Maryland.

C.B.

University of Maryland
College Park, Maryland

Contents

PART VII: EPILOGUE AND PROLOGUE: SLAVERY

PART I

Economic America

The Farmer's Companion

Even in the industrialized America of today the belief
survives that farming is a good thing in itself. It is more
than a way of making a living; it is a superior way of
life. The farm keeps a place in America's regard that
the factory-filled city has never managed to occupy.
Half-consciously, many Americans feel that better
morals as well as purer air are to be found in the country than in the city. Somehow, poverty on the farm
simply builds character but poverty in the city becomes
an invitation to vice and crime. As often as not, this
feeling of the average American is shared by the American writer and artist. Though there are certainly rural
slums as grim as any urban ones, they are not as frequently found in books and paintings. The very satires
we see on farming life are likely to be genial.

If all this is still true now, it was triply so a century
and more ago when farming was not only surrounded
with emotional associations but was the prime American
occupation. Among the various ways of making a living
it clearly came first. There were 5,420,000 "gainful
workers" at the start of the 1840s, and 3,720,000 of
them were employed in agriculture. Manufacturing,
hand trades, and construction—all lumped together in
the census figures—ran a poor second with 790,000.
The typical American worked on a farm and any look
at the economic basis of our culture must start with
farming. In *The Farmer's Companion*, Jesse Buel
(1778–1839) testified enthusiastically to its importance.
He regarded agriculture as the foundation of this country. At the same time he had some misgivings about the
way it was being conducted. He made it his business to
explain where he thought the old-style husbandry was

wrong and then to prescribe the new-style remedy. He knew what he was talking about. He had left a lucrative career as printer and editor to become, at the age of forty-three, an apostle of the new husbandry. Out of a sandhill barren west of Albany, New York, he proceeded to create a model farm. It commanded wide attention. He entered politics and became the leading spokesman in New York state for agriculture. He lectured widely and wrote for publication often. His energies made his periodical, the *Cultivator,* the most popular farm journal in the land. His manual *The Farmer's Companion* appeared in 1839, was promptly reprinted, and enjoyed a substantial circulation throughout the 1840s. Buel begins the book by making his brief for agriculture, shrewdly saving most of his criticisms of farming practices for later in the volume. Excerpts are given below from the first chapter, "The Importance of Agriculture to a Nation," and the fourth, "Agriculture Considered as an Employment."

SOURCE: Jesse Buel, *The Farmer's Companion; or, Essays on the Principles and Practice of American Husbandry* (Boston, 1840), pp. 9–16, 26–31, abridged.

The Importance of Agriculture to a Nation

There is no business of life which so highly conduces to the prosperity of a nation, and to the happiness of its entire population, as that of cultivating the soil. Agriculture may be regarded, says the great Sully, as the breasts from which the state derives support and nourishment. Agriculture is truly our nursing mother, which gives food, and growth, and wealth, and moral health and character to our country. It may be considered the great wheel which moves all the machinery of society; and that whatever gives to this a new impulse communicates a corresponding impetus to the thousand minor wheels of interest which it propels and regulates. While the other classes of the community are directly dependent upon agriculture for a regular and sufficient supply of the means of subsistence, the agriculturist is able to supply all the absolute wants of life from his own labors, though he derives most of his pleasures and profits from an interchange of the products of labor with the other classes of society. Agriculture is called the parent of arts, not only because it was the first art practiced by man, but because the other arts are its legitimate offspring and cannot continue long to exist without it. It is the great business of civilized life, and gives employment to a vast majority of almost every people.

The substantial prosperity of a country is always in the ratio of its agricultural industry and wealth. Commerce and manufactures may give temporary consequence to a state, but these are always a precarious dependence. They are effeminating and corrupting; and, unless backed by a prosperous agricultural population, they engender the elements of speedy decay and ruin. . . .

Great Britain has now become ascendant in commerce and manufactures, yet her greatness in these sources of power and opulence is primarily and principally owing to the excellent condition of her agriculture; without which she would not be able to sustain her manufacturers or her commerce, in their present flourishing state, or long retain her immense foreign possessions, or anything like her present population. . . .

A *country* can only continue long prosperous and be truly independent when it is sustained by agricultural intelligence, agricultural industry, and agricultural wealth. Though its commerce may be swept from the ocean—and its manufactures perish—yet, if its soil is tilled, and well tilled, by an independent yeomanry, it can still be made to yield all the absolute necessaries of life; it can sustain its population and its independence; and when its misfortunes abate, it can, like the trunkless roots of a recently cut down tree, firmly braced in, and deriving nourishment from the soil, send forth a new trunk, new branches, new foliage, and new fruits; it can rear again the edifice of its manufacturer, and spread again the sails of its commerce.

But agriculture is beneficial to a state in proportion as

its labors are encouraged, enlightened, and honored—for in
that proportion does it add to national and individual
wealth and happiness.

Agriculture feeds all. Were agriculture to be neglected,
population would diminish, because the necessaries of life
would be wanting. Did it not supply more than is necessary for its own wants, not only would every other art be
at a stand, but every science and every kind of mental improvement would be neglected. Manufactures and commerce originally owed their existence to agriculture. Agriculture furnishes, in a great measure, raw materials and
subsistence for the one and commodities for barter and
exchange for the other. In proportion as these raw materials and commodities are multiplied, by the intelligence
and industry of the farmer and the consequent improvement of the soil, in the same proportion are manufactures
and commerce benefited—not only in being furnished with
more abundant supplies, but in the increased demand for
their fabrics and merchandise. The more agriculture produces, the more she sells—the more she buys; and the business and comfort of society are mainly influenced and
controlled by the results of her labors.

*Agriculture, directly or indirectly, pays the burdens of
our taxes and our tolls,* which support the government,
and sustain our internal improvements; and the more
abundant her means, the greater will be her contributions. The farmer who manages his business ignorantly
and slothfully, and who produces from it only just enough
for the subsistence of his family, pays no tolls on the
transit of his produce and but a small tax upon the nomi-
nal value of his lands. Instruct his mind and awaken him
to industry, by the hope of distinction and reward, so that
he triples the products of his labor, the value of his lands
is increased in a corresponding ratio, his comforts are
multiplied, his mind disenthralled, and two thirds of his
products go to augment the business and tolls of our
canals and roads. If such a change in the situation of one
farm would add one hundred dollars to the wealth and

one dollar to the tolls of the state, what an astonishing aggregate would be produced, both in capital and in revenue, by a similar improvement upon 250,000 farms, the assumed number in the State of New York. The capital would be augmented 25 millions, and the revenue two hundred and fifty thousand dollars per annum.

Agriculture is the principal source of our wealth. It furnishes more productive labor, the legitimate source of wealth, than all the other employments in society combined. The more it is enlightened by science, the more abundant will be its products; the more elevated its character, the stronger the incitements to pursue it. Whatever, therefore, tends to enlighten the agriculturist tends to increase the wealth of the state and the means for the successful prosecution of the other arts and the sciences, now indispensable to their profitable management.

Agriculturists are the guardians of our freedom. They are the fountains of political power. If the fountains become impure, the stream will be defiled. If the agriculturist is slothful, and ignorant, and poor, he will be spiritless and servile. If he is enlightened, industrious, and in prosperous circumstances, he will be independent in mind, jealous of his rights, and watchful for the public good. His welfare is identified with the welfare of the state. He is virtually fixed to the soil; and has, therefore, a paramount interest, as well as a giant power, to defend it from the encroachment of foreign or domestic foes. If his country suffers, he must suffer; if she prospers, he too may expect to prosper. Hence, whatever tends to improve the intellectual condition of the farmer, and to elevate him above venal temptation, essentially contributes to the good order of society at large and to the perpetuity of our country's freedom.

Agriculture is the parent of physical and moral health to the state, it is the salt which preserves from moral corruption. Not only are her labors useful in administering to our wants, and in dispensing the blessing of abundance to others, but she is constantly exercising a salutary influence upon the moral and physical health of the state and in perpetuating the republican habits and good order of society. While rural labor is the great source of physical health and constitutional vigor to our population, it interposes the most formidable barrier to the demoralizing influence of luxury and vice. We seldom hear of civil commotions, of crimes, or of hereditary disease, among those who are steadily engaged in the business of agriculture. Men who are satisfied with the abundant and certain resources of their own labor, and their own farms, are not willing to jeopard these enjoyments by promoting popular tumult, or tolerating crime. The more we promote the interest of the agriculturist, by developing the powers of his mind, and elevating his moral views, the more we shall promote the virtue and happiness of society.

The facts which are here submitted must afford ample proof that agriculture is all-important to us as a nation; and that our prosperity in manufactures, in commerce, and in the other pursuits of life, will depend, in a great measure, upon the returns which the soil makes to agricultural labor. It therefore becomes the interest of every class to cherish, to encourage, to enlighten, to honor, and to reward those who engage in agricultural pursuits. Our independence was won by our yeomanry, and it can only be preserved by them.

Agriculture Considered as an Employment

Every provident parent is anxious to see his children settled for life in some business that promises to confer wealth and respectability; and every young man who aims to arrive at future and honorable distinction is anxious to select that employment which is most likely to realize his wishes. It is with a view to enable both parent and son to act wisely in this matter that we propose to point out some of the advantages which agriculture holds out to those who embark in it as a pursuit. . . .

1. AS A MEANS OF OBTAINING WEALTH

Adequate to our wants, and to all the beneficial purposes of life, agriculture certainly holds a preeminent rank. With that industry and prudence which Providence seems to have made essential to human happiness, and that knowledge which we all have the means of acquiring, its gains are certain, substantial, and sufficient—sufficient for ourselves, for the good of our children, and the healthful tone of society. It does not, we admit, afford that prospect of rapid gain which some other employments hold out to cupidity, and which too often distract and bewilder the mind and unsettle for life the steady business habits of early manhood; yet neither does it, on the other hand, involve the risks to fortune and to morals, to health and to happiness, with which the schemers and speculators of the day, who would live by the labor of others, seem ever to be environed. Great wealth begets great care and anxiety, and is too apt to engender habits unfriendly alike to the possessor and to society. Wealth that comes without labor is often wasted without thought; but that which is acquired by toil and industry is preserved with care, and expended with judgment. The farmer, therefore, who secures an annual and increasing income by his industry, though it be small in the outset, is much more likely to become ultimately rich, not only in dollars and cents but in all the substantial elements of happiness, than the man of almost any other profession in life.

We have shown that farm lands have been made to produce an annual income of thirty dollars an acre; and have said that by good husbandry they may certainly be made to produce a net income of fourteen dollars an acre. Now, if a farmer, upon a hundred acres of land, can save fourteen hundred dollars a year to buy superfluities for his family, educate his children, and to add to his capital, he must, at the end of twenty years, be either a rich man or an improvident one; and if improvident, he will probably remain poor, be his employment what it may. But

suppose the net income of a farm should be but half, or a
quarter, of the sum we have assumed—that is, $7, or $3.50,
an acre—even this income, prudently managed, will in
a few years place the possessor in independent circumstances.

2. AS PROMOTIVE OF HEALTH AND THE
DEVELOPMENT OF THE MIND

The grand requisites to health, or rather for the pre-
vention of diseases, are declared by Dr. Johnson, one of
the highest medical authorities of the age, to be *exercise
in the open air, temperance in our living, moderation in
our pleasures and enjoyments, restraint on our passions,
limitation to our desires, and limitation to our ambition.*

What employment is there in life so highly favorable
to all the benign influences of exercise, so conducive to
repose and tranquillity of mind, and which has so few
temptations to intemperate enjoyments, as that of agriculture. And the only ambition which is likely to obtrude
upon the farmer, and this is in no wise, we believe, prejudicial to the health either of his body or his mind, is the
ambition of increasing the prolific properties of the soil
whereby he may benefit himself and society. Political
ambition, which, like a cancer, is apt to prey upon and
corrupt the mortal upon whom it fixes its fangs, abides
not upon the farm; at least it should not abide there, for
that farmer must be either weak or unfortunate who is
willing to give up the certain and tranquil pleasures of a
rural home for the vexing, precarious, and corrupting cares
and responsibilities of political eminence, otherwise than
as duty may require it at his hands. "Horticulture and
agriculture are better fitted for the promotion of health
and of sound morals," says an eminent medical author,
"than any other human occupation." The business of agriculture is one of exercise in its most approved forms. It
brings into healthful action the entire muscular system;
and when exercised with prudence, as all employments
should be, it insures appetite, digestion, sleep, a sound

constitution, and a contented mind. "The declaration is as trite as it is true, that exercise promotes virtue, and subdues the storms of passion."

Although the garden and the farm may be made to furnish a great many delicacies and luxuries for the table, yet these delicacies and luxuries are such as conduce alike to health and to rational pleasure. It is a remark of St. Pierre, that every country and every clime furnishes, within itself, the food which is best fitted for the wants of the animals which dwell in it. The same remark, with a trifling modification, will apply to the farm. The products of the farm and garden *do* constitute the best food for the farmer; and there is no class who can indulge in a greater variety of native products, or enjoy them in a higher state of freshness and perfection, than those who raise them. And upon the farm, and among an intelligent rural population, the pleasures of social intercourse are not curtailed by the cold formalities, nor taxed by the extravagant folly, of the town and city. The agriculturist relies upon his own resources, upon his industry and the blessing of Providence, for the enjoyments of life. His farm and his family are the special objects of his care, and his ambition is to obtain good crops, a good name and reputation in society, and to deserve them, by a liberal and kind deportment to all around him. He is exempt from a crowd of evils, of rivalships and jealousies, of corroding cares and feverish anxieties, which not unfrequently hang around other professions, mar the pleasures of life, and undermine health. He should hate no one; for he should dread no rivals. If his neighbor's field is more productive than his own, he borrows a useful lesson. If his own field is the most productive, it affords him pleasure to benefit his neighbor by his example. He learns to identify his own, with the prosperity of his neighborhood and of his country. . . .

The elements are subservient to his use; the vegetable and animal kingdoms are subject to his control! And the natural laws which govern them all, and which exert a controlling influence upon his prosperity and happiness, are constantly developing to his mind new harmonies, new beauties, perfect order, and profound wisdom, in the works of Nature which surround him. Nor need he, in these studies of usefulness, be restricted to his own personal observation. He may call to his aid, both in the prosecution of his business and the improvement of his intellectual faculties, the counsels of eminent men of every age and every country, who have left for our use the record of their experience and their wisdom. And we say it without qualification, that there are few professions in the community which give more leisure for general reading, or whose employments embrace a greater scope of *useful* reading, than the business of agriculture. The artisan is generally obliged to employ his winter evenings in labor; and those engaged in the liberal professions, and in mercantile business, are not only accustomed to do the like, but their study is in a measure restricted to their particular calling. The agriculturist, on the contrary, may devote his evenings, or most of them, to study—to the improvement of his mind—to the acquisition of useful knowledge. He may devote three hours out of the twenty-four to study without infringing upon his necessary business, or fatiguing his mind, or impairing his health. This is allowing eight hours for sleep, ten for labor, and three for contingencies. What profession is there, which, if well conducted, gives a larger portion of time to the acquisition of general knowledge? And what a scope of usefulness may be embraced by these studies! The properties of the soils which give him bread and meat—their adaptation to particular crops, the cause of their deterioration, the modes of renovating or increasing their fertility by farm manures, by lime, gypsum, marl, and by admixture of earths, by draining, irrigation, and alternating crops; the animals which are consigned to his care—their form, internal structure, appropriate management, the nature, cause, and cure of their diseases, the various foods most profitably raised for the nourishment of the different kinds, and the best modes of preparing and feeding it; the crops which he cultivates—their relative value, their habits, proper succession, exhausting influence upon the soil, and the best modes of their management; the agency of air, heat, light, and moisture in preparing vegetable food, in the processes of vegetable nutrition and development, and the means of accelerating or retarding their agency: all these are matters which come specially within the province of the agriculturist.

The Drovers

The very title, *Songs of Labor,* which John Green-leaf Whittier (1807–92) gave to the volume of his verse published in 1850 has a democratic, American sound. He felt that work, handwork, was a proper subject for poetry and he sang about it with warmth. The workman was glorified; his work was viewed through a sentimental haze. Whittier hymned the activities of shoemakers, fishermen, lumbermen, shipbuilders, huskers, and drovers. His stanzas on the drovers first appeared in the *National Era* and, after revision, in the pages of *Songs of Labor.* The diction he uses in "The Drovers" is often either soft or conventionally poetic. For instance, the dust the oxen raise is seen as the smoke of battle. The horns of the oxen are said to glisten like the plumes and crests of, no doubt, knighthood. But Whittier's aim is by no means to sentimentalize. He wants his stanzas to be read, for one thing, by workmen in order to increase their self-respect. When he grouped together his poems on the drovers, the shoemakers, and the rest, he expressed this hope about his "simple lays":

Haply from them the toiler, bent
   Above his forge or plough, may gain
A manlier spirit of content,
   And feel that life is wisest spent
Where the strong working hand makes strong the working brain.

SOURCE: J. G. W(hittier), *National Era*, November 11, 1847.

The Drovers

A freer, manlier life than ours,
    No son of toil is living—
Through heat and cold, and sun and showers
    Still onward cheerly driving.
But, see, the day is closing cool,
    The woods are dim before us,
The white fog of the wayside pool
    Is creeping slowly o'er us.

The night is falling, comrades mine,
    Our foot-sore beasts are weary,
And through yon elms the tavern sign
    Invites us all to tarry.
The landlord beckons from his door,
    His beechen fire is glowing;
These ample barns with feed in store
    Are filled to overflowing.

From many a valley frowned across
    By brows of rugged mountains;
From hill-sides where through spongy moss
    Gush out the river fountains;
From quiet farm-fields, green and low,
    And bright with blooming clover;
From vales of corn the wandering crow
    No richer hovers over;

Day after day our way has been
    O'er many a hill and hollow;
By lake and stream, by wood and glen,
    Our stately drove we follow.
Through dust-clouds rising thick and dun,
    As smoke of battle o'er us,
Their white horns glisten in the sun,
    Like plumes and crests before us.

We see them slowly climb the hill,
    As slow behind it sinking;
Or, thronging close, from roadside rill
    Or sunny lakelet drinking.
Now, crowding in the narrow road,
    In thick and struggling masses,
They glare upon the teamster's load
    Or rattling coach which passes.

Anon, with toss of horn and tail,
    And paw of hoof and bellow,
They leap some farmer's broken pale,
    O'er meadow-close or fallow.
Forth comes the startled good man; forth
    Wife, children, house-dog, sally,
Till once more on their dusty path
    The baffled truants rally.

We drive no starvelings, scraggy grown,
    Loose-legged, and ribb'd and bony,
Like those who grind their noses down
    On pastures bare and stony—
Lean oxen, rough as Indian dogs,
    And cows with dust-dry udders,
Disputing feebly with the frogs
    The crop of saw-grass meadows!

In our good drove, so sleek and fair,
    No bones of leanness rattle;
No tottering, hide-bound ghosts are there,
    Of Pharaoh's evil cattle.
Each stately beeve bespeaks the hand
    That fed him unrepining;
The fatness of a goodly land
    In each dun hide is shining.

We've sought them where in warmest nooks
    The sweetest feed is growing,
And priced them by the clearest brooks
    Through honeysuckle flowing;

Wherever hill-sides, sloping south,
    Are bright with early grasses,
Or, tracking green the lowland's drouth
    The mountain streamlet passes.

But now the day is closing cool,
    The woods are dim before us,
The white fog of the wayside pool
    Is creeping slowly o'er us,
The cricket to the frog's bassoon
    His shrillest time is keeping,
The sickle of yon setting moon
    The meadow mist is reaping.

The night is falling, comrades mine,
    Our foot-sore beasts are weary
And through yon elms the tavern sign
    Invites us all to tarry.
To-morrow, eastward, with our charge
    We'll go to meet the dawning,
Ere yet the pines of Kearsarge
    Have seen the sun of morning.

When snow-flakes o'er the frozen earth
    Instead of birds are flitting;
When children throng the glowing hearth,
    And quiet wives are knitting,
While in the fire-light strong and clear
    Young eyes of pleasure glisten,
To tales of all we see and hear
    The ears of home shall listen.

From many a Northern lake and hill,
    To Ocean's far-off water,
Shall Fancy play the Drover still,
    And make the long night shorter.
Then let us still through sun and showers
    And heat and cold be driving;
A freer, manlier life than ours,
    No son of toil is living!

The Butcher, the Baker, the Candle-Stick Maker

After agriculture came the trades and professions. In *Popular Technology*, first published in 1836 and re-printed seven times in the 1840s, Edward Hazen surveyed them all—or nearly all. In his two compact volumes he found eighty-seven to describe. They range from something as everyday as carpentering to something as esoteric as gilding. Hazen's pages, originally intended as a guide for boys in school, tell us a good deal. The most obvious thing they say, so obvious that it might be overlooked, is that here is a society marked by a great freedom of choice, a society infused with the belief in free will. The unquestioned assumption is that a boy can become whatever he wants to become. Eighty-seven occupations are spread out before him; given the necessary energy, he can enter any one of them. Furthermore, we can see in Hazen's book a strong sense of the democracy of that time. He devotes almost as much space to a typical trade as to a typical profession. Even the lawyer, most respected of professional men, does not receive much more attention than the butcher or baker. Hazen takes each occupation seriously and without snobbishness: work is important to America regardless of its technical or social level. Also, though this is less striking, Hazen's work reminds us that some Americans had a sense of the past and were by no means immersed only in the present. For Hazen is care-ful to sketch the historical background of each occupa-tion, often going as far back as Greece and Rome. Lastly, by his detailed, step-by-step descriptions of the workings of each craft, Hazen gives us a feeling for the economic texture of the time. He weaves a rich and sometimes surprising tapestry. He reminds us that more things have changed than we realize. To us today the butcher, for instance, is merely a pair of eyes peering out through a supermarket peephole. To Hazen he was a substantial human being, vigorous, corpulent, and in some danger of dying early of too much meat. And the baker is seen by Hazen not only in terms of his product but as a person who must work a daily schedule different from his fellows. He is a man who labors through the night so that we can have fresh bread in the morning.

We begin our selections from Hazen with his chapter on the butcher. The first half-dozen points are mainly preliminary so we may start with Point 7.

SOURCE: Edward Hazen, *Popular Technology; or, Professions and Trades,* (New York, 1842), I, 57–58, 40, 42–43, 129–33, 215, 219–20.

The Butcher

7. The butchers obtain their animals from the farmers, or from drovers, who make it a business to purchase them in the country, and drive them to market. The farmers near large cities, who have good grazing farms, are accustomed to buy lean cattle, brought from a distance, with a view to fatten them for sale. There are also persons in the cities, who might, with propriety, be called cattle brokers; since they supply the butchers of small capital with a single animal at a time, on a credit of a few days.

8. Every butcher who carries on the business, has a house in which he kills his animals, and prepares them for sale. When it is intended to slaughter an ox, a rope is thrown about his horns or neck, with which he is forced into the *slaughter-house*, and brought to the floor by the aid of a ring. The butcher than knocks him on the head, cuts his throat, deprives him of his hide, takes out his entrails, washes the inside of his body with water, and cuts him up into quarters. The beef is now ready to be conveyed to the market-house. The process of dressing other

quadrupeds varies but little from this in its general details. The cellular substance of mutton, lamb, and veal, is often inflated with air, that the meat may appear fat and plump.

9. In large cities and towns, the meat is chiefly sold in the market-house, where each butcher has a stall rented from the corporation. It is carried there in a cart, and cut into suitable pieces with a saw, knife, and a broad iron cleaver.

10. In some of the large cities, it is a practice among the butchers, to employ *runners* to carry the meat to the houses of those customers who may desire this accommodation. In villages, where there is no market-house, the butcher carries his meats from door to door in some kind of vehicle.

11. Those who follow this occupation usually enjoy good health, and, as they advance in years, in most cases, become corpulent. Their good health arises from exercise in the open air; and their corpulency, from subsisting principally on fresh meats. It is thought, however, that their longevity is not so great as that of men in many other employments.

The Baker

1. The business of the Baker consists in making bread, rolls, biscuits, and crackers, and in baking various kinds of provisions. . . .

15. In many of the large cities of Europe, the price and weight of bread sold by bakers, are regulated by law. The weight of the loaves of different sizes must be always the same; but the price may vary, according to the current cost of the chief materials. The law was such in the city of London, a few years ago, that if a loaf fell short in weight a single ounce, the baker was liable to be put in the pillory; but now, he is subject only to a fine, varying from one to five shillings, according to the will of the magistrate before whom he may be indicted.

16. In this country, laws of a character somewhat similar have been enacted by the legislatures of several states, and by city authorities, with a view to protect the community against impositions; but whether there is a law or not, the bakers regulate the weight, price, and quality of their loaves by the general principles of trade.

17. There is, perhaps, no business more laborious than that of the baker of loaf bread, who has a regular set of customers to be supplied every morning. The twenty-four hours of the day are systematically appropriated to the performance of certain labours, and to rest.

18. After breakfast, the yeast is prepared, and the oven-wood provided: at two or three o'clock, the *sponge is set:* the hours from three to eight or nine o'clock, are appropriated to rest. The baking commences at nine or ten o'clock at night; and, in large bakeries, continues until five o'clock in the morning. From that time until the breakfast hour, the hands are engaged in distributing the bread to customers. For seven months in the year, and, in some cases, during the whole of it, part of the hands are employed, from eleven to one o'clock, in baking pies, puddings, and different kinds of meats, sent to them from neighboring families.

19. In large cities, the bakers usually confine their attention to particular branches of the business. Some bake light loaf bread only; others bake unleavened bread, such as crackers, sea-biscuit, and cakes for people of the Jewish faith. Some, again, unite several branches together; and this is especially the case in small cities and towns, where the demand for different kinds of bread is more limited.

The Candle-maker

1. The subject of the candle-maker's labors may be defined to be a wick, covered with tallow, wax, or sperma-ceti, in a cylindrical form, which serves, when lighted, for the illumination of objects in the absence of the sun. The business of candle-making is divided into two branches;

the one is confined to the manufacturing of tallow candles, and the other, to making those composed of wax or spermaceti.

2. The process of making candles from tallow, as conducted by the tallow-chandler, needs only a brief description, since it differs but little from the method pursued by families in the country, with which most persons are familiar. The difference lies chiefly in the employment of a few conveniences, by which the candles are more rapidly multiplied.

3. The first part of the process consists in preparing a wick, to serve as a foundation. The coarse and slightly twisted yarn used for this purpose, is spun in the cotton-factories; and, being wound into balls, is, in that form, sold to the tallow-chandlers, as well as to individuals who make candles for their own consumption.

4. A sufficient number of threads is combined, to form a wick of a proper size; and, as they are wound from the balls, they are measured off, and cut to the proper length, by a simple contrivance, which consists of a narrow board, a wooden pin, and the blade of a razor. The pin and razor are placed perpendicular to the board, at a distance determined by the length of the proposed wick. The wicks are next put upon cylindrical rods, about three feet long; and a great number of these are arranged on a long frame.

5. To obtain the tallow in a proper state for use, it is separated from the membranous part of the suet, by boiling the latter in an iron or copper kettle, and then subjecting the *cracklings* to the action of a press. The substance that remains, after the tallow has been expressed, is called *greaves*, which are sometimes applied to fattening ducks for market. This is especially the case in the city of London.

6. The *tried* tallow is prepared for application to the wicks, by heating it to a proper temperature. It is then poured into a suitable receptacle, where it is kept in *order* either by a moderate fire underneath, or by the occasional addition of hot tallow.

7. The *broaches*, as the sticks with their wicks are called, are taken up, several at a time, either between the fingers or by means of a simple instrument denominated a *rake*, and dipped into the tallow. They are then returned to the frame, and suffered to cool, while successive broaches are treated in the same way. The dipping is repeated, until the candles have been thickened to the proper size.

8. In the preceding plate [here omitted], is represented a workman in the act of dipping several broaches of candles, suspended on a rake, which he holds in his hands. The mode of making dipped candles just described, is more generally practised than any other, and in this manner five or six hundred pounds can be made by one hand, in a single day. In some establishments, however, a more complicated apparatus is used, by which every part of the process is greatly expedited.

9. Mould candles are made very differently. The moulds consist of a frame of wood, in which are arranged several hollow cylinders, generally made of pewter. At the lower extremity of each cylinder, is a small hole, for the passage of the wick, which is introduced by means of a hook on the end of a wire. The cotton is fastened at the other end, and placed in a perpendicular situation in the centre of the shafts, by means of a wire, which passes through the loops of the wicks. The melted tallow, having been poured on the top of the wooden frame, descends into each mould. After the candles have become sufficiently cold, they are extracted from the cylinders with a bodkin, which is inserted into the loop of the wick. One person can thus mould two or three hundred pounds in a day.

10. Candles are also made of bees-wax and spermaceti; but the mode of their manufacture differs in no particular from that of common mould candles. The wicks for wax-candles are usually made of a peculiar kind of cotton, which grows in Asiatic Turkey.

11. Before the wax is applied to this purpose, the coloring matter is discharged. This is effected by bleaching

the wax, in the following manner. It is first divided into
flakes, or thin laminæ, by pouring it, in a melted state,
through a colander upon a cylindrical wheel, which, at the
same time, is kept revolving, while partly immersed in
cold water. The wax, having been removed from the water,
is placed upon a table or floor covered with some kind of
cloth. Here it is occasionally sprinkled with water, until
the bleaching has been completed. The process occupies
several weeks, or even months, according to the state of
the weather, that being best which is most favorable to a
rapid evaporation.

12. Spermaceti is a substance separated from sperm oil,
which is obtained from a species of whale, called *physeter
macrocephalus*, or *spermaceti cachalot*. This oil is obtained from both the head and body of the animal, but
that procured from the former contains twice the quantity
of spermaceti.

13. To separate the spermaceti from the oil yielded by
the body, it is first heated, then put into casks, and suffered to stand two or three weeks, in order to *granulate*.
The oily part is now filtrated through strainers; and the
remainder, which is called *foots*, is again heated, and put
into casks. After having stood several weeks, these are put
into bags, and submitted to the action of a powerful press.
The spermaceti thus obtained, is melted and moulded
into cakes. The oil thus separated from the spermaceti, is
called spring or fall strained; because it is filtered and
expressed only during those seasons of the year.

14. The oil from the head of the whale is treated like
that from the body, in almost every particular. The difference consists, principally, in omitting the use of the
strainer, and in the employment of stronger bags and a
more powerful press. The oil obtained from the *head-matter*, is called *pressed*, since it is separated by the action of
the press only. It is also denominated *winter-strained*, because the operation is performed in the cold weather.

15. The spermaceti, having been melted and moulded
into cakes, is reserved until the succeeding summer, when

it is cut into thin shavings, by means of a large shave, similar to the *spoke-shave* of the wheelwrights, and again pressed as before. The oil of this last pressing is called *taut pressed*, and is the least valuable kind, since a slight degree of cold causes it to become thick. The spermaceti obtained from the oil of the body, and that from the head-matter, are melted together, and purified by means of potash-ley.

16. The sperm-oil, thus freed from the spermaceti, is extensively used in lamps as a means of illumination; and, for many purposes, it is far more convenient than tallow. In the country, lard is frequently employed instead of oil, especially by the German population. In some European and Asiatic countries, vegetable oils supply the place of animal fats, in this application. . . .

Attorney at Law

1. A lawyer is one who, by profession, transacts legal business for others, who, in this relation, are called *clients*. A lawyer is either an attorney or councillor, or both. The part of legal business, belonging peculiarly to the attorney, consists in preparing the details of the *pleadings* and the *briefs* for the use of the councillor, whose especial province it is to make the argument before the court. When the lawyer prepares his own case and makes the argument, as he generally does, he acts in the capacity of both attorney and councillor. In the court of chancery the lawyer is denominated *solicitor*, and in the admiralty court, *proctor*. Before a person is permitted to practise law in our courts, he is required to pass through a regular course of study, and afterwards undergo an examination before persons learned in the law. . . .

15. When a client has stated his case in detail to his attorney, it is the province of the latter to decide upon the course most proper to be pursued in regard to it. If the client is the plaintiff, and litigation is determined upon, the attorney decides upon the court in which the

case should be brought forward, and also upon the manner in which it should be conducted.

16. The suit having been brought, say into the County Court, it is tried according to law. If it involves facts or damages, it is canvassed before a jury of twelve men, who are bound by oath or affirmation to bring in their verdict according to the evidence presented by both parties. It is the business of the lawyers, each for his own client, to sum up the evidence which may have been adduced, and to present the whole in a light as favorable to his own side of the question as possible.

17. When the case involves points of law which must needs be understood by the jury, to enable them to make a correct decision, the advocates of the parties present their views with regard to them; but, if these happen to be wrong, the judge, in his charge to the jury, rectifies the mistake or misrepresentation. The case having been decided, each party is bound to submit to the decision, or appeal, if permitted by law, to a higher tribunal.

18. Causes to be determined on legal principles only, are brought before the judge or judges for adjudication. In such cases, the advocates present the statute or common law supposed to be applicable, and then reports of similar cases, which may have been formerly decided in the same or similar courts. These reports are the exponents of the common law of the case, and are supposed, in most instances, to furnish data for correct decisions.

19. Besides the management of causes in public courts, the lawyer has a great mass of business of a private nature; such as drawing wills, indentures, deeds, and mortgages. He is consulted in a great variety of cases of a legal nature, where litigation is not immediately concerned, and especially in regard to the validity of titles to real estate; and the many impositions to which the community is liable from defective titles, render the information which he is able to afford on this subject, extremely valuable.

20. In the preceding account of this profession, it is easy to perceive that it is one of great utility and respon-

sibility. It is to the attorney, that the oppressed repair for redress against the oppressor; and to him, the orphan and friendless look, to aid them in obtaining or maintaining their rights. To this profession, also, as much as to any other, the American people may confidently look for the maintenance of correct political principles.

The Working Woman

Women also worked, it is worth remembering. Most earned their keep as housewives and received their reward in more than money. A modest but always increasing number of others held domestic and factory jobs. Though a few women were to be found in many different occupations, the great majority were either "hired girls" or mill hands. Factory work was the best paid and most widely heralded. A girl who earned $3 a week in a New England cotton mill could get only half of that in other jobs. But the American woman was still a second-class citizen in the 1840s and there were powerful feelings that she should remain so. She was regularly paid less than any man who would do the same work. She was the first to be laid off, the first to have her wages cut in times of need. In fact she was the first to lose under any conditions. Even in good times the New England textile mills of antebellum days sometimes lowered—not raised but lowered—the wages of the female operatives. The wage cuts caused by the panic of 1837 were long in being restored in spite of the fact that the country's economy had recovered by the early 1840s.

But these inequities were generally taken for granted. Things were, many women workers doubtless felt, not too bad. In fact in some places they were considered positively good—and nowhere more so than in Lowell, Massachusetts. The textile mills in Lowell were famous as one of the showplaces of Yankee capitalism. They were cited as impressive evidence that in this country the factory owner was not concerned with money alone. He was concerned about the welfare and morals of his workers, especially if most were women. In this respect-

able atmosphere the *Lowell Offering* was born. It added
literature to the other assets of the mills, for it was
"written, edited, and published by female operatives employed in the mills." So the pink cover testified. The
pages of this monthly magazine were crowded with po-
lite literature, all from the pens of the girls. The air is
utopian, a little unreal. And yet the best testimony to
the fact that conditions in Lowell actually were good
is that the *Offering* could print material which was not
uncritical of the mills and mill work. The candor displayed by one "Susan" in some letters to her friend Mary
is exemplary. As she describes the life of a "female
operative" she sees much to applaud but also notices
some blemishes. Susan's first letter, printed in the May
1844 number but not reprinted here, tells about her
reception in Lowell and her impressions of the boarding
house where she went to live. The second letter, from
the June number, deals directly with her work; her
third, from the August number, deals with her work
and the people she meets in connection with it. These
two letters are given below.

SOURCE: "Susan," "Letter Second," *Lowell Offering*, IV (June
1844), 169–72, and "Letter Third" (August 1844), 237–40.

Letter Second

LOWELL, April –, ——.

Dear Mary: In my last I told you I would write again,
and say more of my life here; and this I will now attempt
to do.

I went into the mill to work a few days after I wrote to
you. It looked very pleasant at first, the rooms were so
light, spacious, and clean, the girls so pretty and neatly
dressed, and the machinery so brightly polished or nicely
painted. The plants in the windows, or on the overseer's
bench or desk, gave a pleasant aspect to things. You will
wish to know what work I am doing. I will tell you of the
different kinds of work.

There is first, the carding-room, where the cotton flies most, and the girls get the dirtiest. But this is easy, and the females are allowed time to go out at night before the bell rings—on Saturday night at least, if not on all other nights. Then there is the spinning room which is very neat and pretty. In this room are the spinners and doffers. The spinners watch the frames; keep them clean, and the threads mended if they break. The doffers take off the full bobbins, and put on the empty ones. They have nothing to do in the long intervals when the frames are in motion, and can go out to their boarding-houses, or do any thing else that they like. In some of the factories the spinners do their own doffing, and when this is the case they work no harder than the weavers. These last have the hardest time of all—or can have, if they choose to take charge of three or four looms, instead of the one pair which is the allotment. And they are the most constantly confined. The spinners and dressers have but the weavers to keep supplied, and then their work can stop. The dressers never work before breakfast, and they stay out a great deal in the afternoons. The drawers-in, or girls who draw the threads through the harnesses, also work in the dressing-room, and they all have very good wages—better than the weavers who have but the usual work. The dressing-rooms are very neat, and the frames move with a gentle undulating motion which is really graceful. But these rooms are kept very warm, and are disagreeably scented with the "sizing," or starch, which stiffens the "beams," or unwoven webs. There are many plants in these rooms and it is really a good green-house for them. The dressers are generally quite tall girls, and must have pretty tall minds too, as their work requires much care and attention.

I could have had work in the dressing-room, but chose to be a weaver; and I will tell you why. I disliked the closer air of the dressing-room, though I might have become accustomed to that. I could not learn to dress so quickly as I could to weave, nor have work of my own so soon, and should have had to stay with Mrs. C. two or three weeks before I could go in at all, and I did not like to be "lying upon my oars" so long. And, more than this, when I get well learned I can have extra work, and make double wages, which you know is quite an inducement with some.

Well, I went into the mill, and was put to learn with a very patient girl—a clever old maid. I should be willing to be one myself if I could be as good as she is. You cannot think how odd every thing seemed to me. I wanted to laugh at every thing, but did not know what to make sport of first. They set me to threading shuttles, and tying weaver's knots, and such things, and now I have improved so that I can take care of one loom. I could take care of two if I only had eyes in the back part of my head, but I have not got used to "looking two ways of a Sunday" yet.

At first the hours seemed very long, but I was so interested in learning that I endured it very well; and when I went out at night the sound of the mill was in my ears, as of crickets, frogs, and jewsharps, all mingled together in strange discord. After that it seemed as though cotton-wool was in my ears, but now I do not mind it at all. You know that people learn to sleep with the thunder of Niagara in their ears, and a cotton mill is no worse, though you wonder that we do not have to hold our breath in such a noise.

It makes my feet ache and swell to stand so much but I suppose I shall get accustomed to that too. The girls generally wear old shoes about their work, and you know nothing is easier; but they almost all say that when they have worked here a year or two they have to procure shoes a size or two larger than before they came. The right hand, which is the one used in stopping and starting the loom, becomes larger than the left; but in other respects the factory is not detrimental to a young girl's appearance. Here they look delicate, but not sickly; they laugh at those who are much exposed, and get pretty brown; but I, for one, had rather be brown than pure white. I never saw so many pretty looking girls as there are here. Though the number of men is small in proportion there are many marriages here, and a great deal of courting. I will tell you of this last sometime.

You wish to know minutely of our hours of labor. We go in at five o'clock; at seven we come out to breakfast; at half-past seven we return to our work, and stay until half-past twelve. At one, or quarter-past one four months in the year, we return to our work, and stay until seven at night. Then the evening is all our own, which is more than some laboring girls can say, who think nothing is more tedious than a factory life.

When I first came here, which was the last of February, the girls ate their breakfast before they went to their work. The first of March they came out at the present breakfast hour, and the twentieth of March they ceased to "light up" the rooms, and come out between six and seven o'clock.

You ask if the girls are contented here: I ask you if you know of *any one* who is perfectly contented. Do you remember the old story of the philosopher, who offered a field to the person who was contented with his lot; and, when one claimed it, he asked him why, if he was so perfectly satisfied, he wanted his field. The girls here are not contented: and there is no disadvantage in their situation which they do not perceive as quickly, and lament as loudly, as the sternest opponents of the factory system do. They would scorn to say they were contented, if asked the question; for it would compromise their Yankee spirit—their pride, penetration, independence, and love of "freedom and equality" to say that they were *contented* with such a life as this. Yet, withal, they are cheerful. I never saw a happier set of beings. They appear blithe in the mill, and out of it. If you see one of them, with a very long face, you may be sure that it is because she has heard bad news from home, or because her beau has vexed her. But, if it is a Lowell trouble, it is because she has failed in getting off as many "sets" or "pieces" as she intended to have done; or because she had a sad "break-out," or "break-down," in her work, or something of that sort.

You ask if the work is not disagreeable. Not when one is accustomed to it. It tried my patience sadly at first, and does now when it does not run well; but, in general, I like it very much. It is easy to do, and does not require very violent exertion, as much of our farm work does.

You also ask how I get along with the girls here. Very well indeed; only we came near having a little flurry once. You know I told you I lodged in the "long attic." Well, a little while ago, there was a place vacated in a pleasant lower chamber. Mrs. C. said that it was my "chum's" turn to go down stairs to lodge, unless she would waive her claim in favor of me. You must know that here they get up in the world by getting down, which is what the boys in our debating society used to call a paradox. Clara, that is the girl's name, was not at all disposed to give up her rights, but maintained them staunchly. I had nothing to do about it—the girls in the lower room liked me, and disliked Clara, and were determined that it should not be at all pleasant weather there if she did come. Mrs. C. was in a dilemma. Clara's turn came first. The other two girls in the chamber were sisters, and would not separate, so they were out of the question. I wanted to go, and knew Clara would not be happy with them. But I thought what was my duty to do. She was not happy now, and would not be if deprived of her privilege. She had looked black at me for several days, and slept with her face to the wall as many nights. I went up to her and said, "Clara, take your things down into the lower chamber, and tell the girls that I *will not come*. It is your turn now, and mine will come in good time."

Clara was mollified in an instant. "No," said she; "I will not go now. They do not wish me to come, and I had rather stay here." After this we had quite a contest—I trying to persuade Clara to go, and she trying to persuade me, and I *"got beat."* So now I have a pleasanter room, and am quite a favorite with all the girls. They have given me some pretty plants, and they go out with me whenever I wish it, so that I feel quite happy.

You think we must live very nice here to have plum-cake, &c. The plum-cake, and crackers, and such things as the bakers bring upon the corporations, are not as nice as we have in the country, and I presume are much cheaper. I seldom eat any thing that is not cooked in the family. I should not like to tell you the stories they circulate here about the bakers, unless I *knew* that they were true. Their brown bread is the best thing that I have tasted of their baking.

You see that I have been quite *minute* in this letter, though I hardly liked your showing the former to old Deacon Gale, and 'Squire Smith, and those old men. It makes me feel afraid to write you all I should like to, when I think so many eyes are to pore over my humble sheet. But if their motives are good, and they can excuse all defects, why I will not forbid.

'Squire Smith wishes to know what sort of men our superintendents are. I know very well what he thinks of them, and what their reputation is up our way. I am not personally acquainted with any of them; but, from what I hear, I have a good opinion of them. I suppose they are not faultless, neither are those whom they superintend; but they are not the overbearing tyrants which many suppose them to be. The abuse of them, which I hear, is so very low that I think it must be unjust and untrue; and I do frequently hear them spoken of as *men*—whole-hearted full-souled men. Tell 'Squire Smith they are not what he would be in their places—that they treat their operatives better than he does his "hired girls," and associate with them on terms of as much equality. But I will tell you who are almost universally unpopular: the "runners," as they are called, or counting-room boys. I suppose they are little whipper-snappers who will grow better as they grow older.

My paper is filling up, and I must close by begging your pardon for speaking of the Methodists as having lost their simplicity of attire. It was true, nevertheless, for I have not seen one of the old "Simon Pure" Methodist bonnets since I have been here. But they may be as consistent as

other denominations. How few of us follow in the steps
of the primitive Christians.

Yours as ever.

Letter Third

LOWELL, July –, ——.

Dear Mary: You complain that I do not keep my promise
of being a good correspondent, but if you could know
how sultry it is here, and how fatigued I am by my work
this warm weather, you would not blame me. It is now
that I begin to dislike these hot brick pavements, and glaring buildings. I want to be at home—to go down to the
brook over which the wild grapes have made a natural arbor,
and to sit by the cool spring around which the fresh soft
brakes cluster so lovingly. I think of the time when, with
my little bare feet, I used to follow in aunt Nabby's footsteps through the fields of corn—stepping high and long
till we came to the bleaching ground; and I remember—
but I must stop, for I know you wish me to write of what
I am now doing, as you already know of what I have done.

Well; I go to work every day—not earlier than I should
at home, nor do I work later, but I mind the confinement
more than I should in a more unpleasant season of the year.
I have extra work now—I take care of three looms: and
when I wrote you before I could not well take care of
two. But help is very scarce now, and they let us do as
much work as we please; and I am highly complimented
upon my "powers of execution." Many of the girls go to
their country homes in the summer. The majority of the
operatives are country girls. These have always the prefer-
ence, because, in the fluctuations to which manufactures
are liable, there would be much less distress among a population who could resort to other homes, than if their entire
interest was in the city. And in the summer these girls go
to rest, and recruit themselves for another "yearly cam-
paign"—not a bad idea in them either. I shall come home

next summer; I have been here too short a time to make
it worth while now. I wish they would have a *vacation* in
"dog days"—stop the mills, and *make* all the girls rest; and
let their "men-folks" do up their "ditching," or whatever
else it is they now do Sundays.

But these mills are not such dreadful places as you imagine them to be. You think them dark damp holes; as close
and black as—as the Black Hole at Calcutta. Now, dear M.,
it is no such thing. They are high spacious well-built edifices, with neat paths around them, and beautiful plots of
greensward. These are kept fresh by the "force-pumps" belonging to every corporation. And some of the corporations have beautiful flower gardens connected with the
factories. One of the overseers, with whom I am acquainted,
gave me a beautiful boquet the other morning, which was
radiant with all the colors of the rainbow, and fragrant
with the sweet perfume of many kinds of mints and roses.
He has a succession of beautiful blossoms from spring till
"cold weather." He told me that he could raise enough
to bring him fifty dollars if he chose to sell them; and
this from a little bit of sand not larger than our front
yard, which you know is small for a country house. But it
is so full—here a few dollars have brought on a fresh soil,
and "patience has done its perfect work." What might not
be accomplished in the country with a little industry and
taste.

But I have said enough of the outside of our mills—
now for the inside. The rooms are high, very light, kept
nicely whitewashed, and extremely neat; with many plants
in the window seats, and white cotton curtains to the windows. The machinery is very handsomely made and painted,
and is placed in regular rows; thus, in a large mill, presenting a beautiful and uniform appearance. I have sometimes
stood at one end of a row of green looms, when the girls
were gone from between them, and seen the lathes moving
back and forth, the harnesses up and down, the white cloth
winding over the rollers, through the long perspective;
and I have thought it beautiful.

Then the girls dress so neatly, and are so pretty. The mill girls are the prettiest in the city. You wonder how they can keep neat. Why not? There are no restrictions as to the number of pieces to be washed in the boarding-house. And, as there is plenty of water in the mill, the girls can wash their laces and muslins and other nice things themselves, and no boarding woman ever refuses the conveniences for starching and ironing. You say too that you do not see how we can have so many conveniences and comforts at the price we pay for board. You must remember that the boarding-houses belong to the companies, and are let to the tenants far below the usual city rent—sometimes the rent is remitted. Then there are large families, so that there are the profits of many individuals. The country farmers are quite in the habit of bringing their produce to the boarding-houses for sale, thus reducing the price by the omission of the market-man's profit. So you see there are many ways by which we get along so well.

You ask me how the girls behave in the mill, and what are the punishments. They behave very well while about their work, and I have never heard of punishments, or scoldings, or anything of that sort. Sometimes an overseer finds fault, and sometimes offends a girl by refusing to let her stay out of the mill, or some deprivation like that; and then, perhaps, there are tears and pouts on her part, but, in general, the tone of intercourse between the girls and overseers is very good—pleasant, yet respectful. When the latter are fatherly sort of men the girls frequently resort to them for advice and assistance about other affairs than their work. Very seldom is this confidence abused; but, among the thousands of overseers who have lived in Lowell, and the tens of thousands of girls who have in time been here, there are legends still told of wrong suffered and committed. "To err is human," and when the frailties of humanity are exhibited by a factory girl it is thought of for worse than are the errors of any other persons.

The only punishment among the girls is dismission from their places. They do not, as many think, withhold their wages; and as for corporal punishment—mercy on me! To strike a female would cost any overseer his place. If the superintendents did not take the affair into consideration the girls would turn out, as they did at the Temperance celebration, "Independent day;" and if they didn't look as pretty, I am sure they would produce as deep an impression.

By the way, I almost forgot to tell you that we had a "Fourth of July" in Lowell, and a nice one it was too. The Temperance celebration was the chief dish in the entertainment. The chief, did I say? It was almost the whole. It was the great turkey that Scroggs sent for Bob Cratchet's Christmas dinner. But, perhaps you don't read Dickens, so I will make no more "classical allusions." In the evening we had the Hutchinsons, from our own Granite State, who discoursed sweet music *so sweetly*. They have become great favorites with the public. It is not on account of their fine voices only, but their pleasant modest manners—the perfect sense of propriety which they exhibit in all their demeanor; and I think they are not less popular *here* because they sing the wrongs of the slave, and the praises of cold water.

But, dear Mary, I fear I have tired you with this long letter, and yet I have not answered half your questions. Do you wish to hear anything more about the overseers? Once for all, then, there are many very likely intelligent public-spirited men among them. They are interested in the good movements of the day; teachers in the Sabbath schools; and some have represented the city in the State Legislature. They usually marry among the factory girls, and do not connect themselves with their inferiors either. Indeed, in almost all the matches here the female is superior in education and manner, if not in intellect, to her partner.

The overseers have good salaries, and their families live very prettily. I observe that in almost all cases the mill girls make excellent wives. They are good managers, orderly in their households, and "neat as wax-work." It seems as though they were so delighted to have houses of their own to take care of, that they would never weary of the labor and the care.

The boarding women you ask about. They are usually widows or single women from the country; and many questions are always asked, and references required before a house is given to a new applicant. It is true that mistakes are sometimes made, and *the wrong person gets into the pew*, but

> Things like this you know must be,
> Where'er there is a factory.

I see I have given you rhyme; it is not all quotation, nor *entirely original*.

I think it requires quite a complication of good qualities to make up a good boarding woman. "She looks well to the ways of her household," and must be even more than all that King Solomon describes in the last chapter of Proverbs. She not only in winter "riseth while it is yet night, and giveth meat to her household, a portion to her maidens," but she sitteth up far into the night, and seeth that her maidens are asleep, and that their lamps are gone out. Perhaps she doth not "consider a field to buy it," but she considereth every piece of meat, and bushel of potatoes, and barrel of flour, and load of wood, and box of soap, and every little thing, whether its quantity, quality, and price are what discretion would recommend her to purchase. "She is not afraid of the snow for her household," for she maketh them wear rubber overshoes, and thick cloaks and hoods, and seeth that the paths are broken out. "Her clothing is silk and purple," and she looketh neat and comely. It may be that her husband sitteth *not* "in the gates," for it is too often the case that he hath abandoned her, or loafeth in the streets. "She openeth her mouth with wisdom, and in her tongue is the law of kindness." Her maidens go to her for counsel and sympathy, if a decayed tooth begins to jump, or a lover proves faithless;

and to keep twoscore young maidens in peace with themselves, each other and her own self, is no slight task. The price of such a woman is, indeed, *above rubies.* "Give her of the fruit of her hands, and let her own works praise her."

I have now told you of mill girls, overseers and their wives, and boarding-housekeepers, and I feel that I have won forgiveness for neglecting you so long. You think that I have too high an opinion of our superintendents. I hope not. I do think that many of them are chosen as combining, in their characters, many excellent qualities. Some of them may be as selfish as you suppose. But we must remember that they owe a duty to their employers, as well as to those they employ. They are agents of the companies, as well as superintendents of us. Where those duties conflict I hope the sympathies of the man will always be with the more dependent party.

Country people are very suspicious. I do not think them perfect. A poet will look at a wood-cutter, and say "there is an honest man;" and as likely as not the middle of his load is rotten punk, and crooked sticks make many interstices, while all looks well without. A rustic butcher slays an animal that is dying of disease, and carries his meat to the market. The butcher and the woodman meet, and say all manner of harsh things against the *"grandees"* of the city, and quote such poetry as,

> GOD made the country—
> Man made the town, &c.

It is true that with the same disposition for villany the man of influence must do the most harm. But, where there is most light, may there not be most true knowledge? And, even if there is no more principle, may there not be, with more cultivation of mind, a feeling of honor and of self-respect which may be of some benefit in its stead.

But I have written till I am fairly wearied. Good by.

Yours always.

The Transportation Revolution

It is some distance from the cotton mills and their ladylike operatives to road making and the rough gangs of road laborers. However, any impressions of economic America ought to include a notice of the transportation revolution which was beginning. It was important that farms were cultivated and articles manufactured, but a country's economy also needed ways for getting people and things from place to place. Roads, canals, ships, and even railways were already involved; here roads may represent them all. Easing travel was perhaps more desirable in the United States than in any other country. There were at least two reasons, of different kinds. One was the fact that the country was already large and growing larger. The other was that Americans, notoriously restless, liked to move about. The great movement was out west to the frontier but there was also movement in every other direction, partly for economic reasons and partly, it should be added, for pleasure. Even as early as the 1840s Americans were beginning to tour. The first gazeteers and travel books were being produced, and they found an increasing number of buyers.

A Manual of the Principles and Practice of Road-Making by W. M. Gillespie (1816–68) was entered for copyright in 1847 and soon was reprinted. It was a straightforward book based on a good deal of research and observation. Its author was a professor of civil engineering at Union College in Schenectady. He had observed road-building in Europe and supervised it in the United States. He looked around him with a cold eye and announced in the preface of his book, "The common roads of the United States are inferior to those of any other civilized country." With that forthright start he went on to describe "What Roads Ought to be" in his first chapter and in succeeding chapters how they should be located, built, and improved. Thereafter he wrote a chapter on railroads and, lastly, one on the proper management of town roads. The portions reprinted below, from the third edition, are in Chapter IV, "Improvement of the Surface."

Here we have the detailed description of process, as we did earlier in the pages of Hazen's *Popular Technology*. There is no drama in the procedures but that does not mean an absence of social interest. We receive a picture of America trying to cope with the transportation revolution just as today we are trying to cope with the automobile. "A common but very inferior pavement, which disgraces the streets of nearly all our cities, is constructed of rounded water-worn *pebbles*," says Gillespie at one point in the irritated tones of a modern town planner complaining about traffic congestion. In general Gillespie is trying to tell us how to modify our environment to make it more to our liking, and his instructions are detailed because they are intended for the men who will actually do the work.

SOURCE: W. M. Gillespie, *A Manual of the Principles and Practice of Road-Making*, 3d edition (New York, 1850), pp. 216–25.

Paved Roads

A good pavement should offer little resistance to wheels, but give a firm foothold to horses; it should be so durable as to seldom require taking up; it should be as free as possible from noise and dust; and when it is laid in the streets of a city, it should be susceptible of easy removal and replacement to give access to gas and water pipes.

A common but very inferior pavement, which disgraces the streets of nearly all our cities, is constructed of rounded water-worn *pebbles*, or "cobble-stones." The best are of an egg-like shape, from 5 to 10 inches deep, and of a diameter equal to half their depth. They are set with their greatest length upright, and their broadest end uppermost. Under them is a bed of sand or gravel a foot or two deep. They are rammed over three times, and a layer of fine gravel spread over them to fill their interstices.

The glaring faults of this pavement are that the stones, being supported only by the friction of the very narrow space at which they are in contact, are easily pressed down by heavy loads into the loose bottom, thus forming holes and depressions; and at best offer great resistance to draught, cause great noise, cannot be easily cleaned, and need very frequent repairs and renewals.

The pavement which combines most perfectly all desirable requisites, is formed of squared blocks of stone, resting on a stable foundation, and laid diagonally.

We will examine successively the merits of different foundations; the quality of stone preferable; their most advantageous size and shape; their arrangement; the manner of laying them; their borders and curbs; their advantages; and their comparison with McAdam roads.

Foundations

The want of a proper foundation is one of the most frequent causes of the failures of pavements. A foundation should be composed of a sufficient thickness of some incompressible material, which will effectually cut off all connection between the subsoil and the bottom of the paving-stones, and should rest upon a well-drained bottom, for which in cities a perfect system of sewerage is indispensable. The principal foundations are those of *sand*, of *broken stone*, of *pebbles*, and of *concrete*.

Foundations of sand.—This material, when it fills an excavation, possesses the valuable properties of incompressibility, and of assuming a new position of equilibrium and stability when any portion of it is disturbed. To secure these qualities in their highest degree, the sand should be very carefully freed from the least admixture of earth

or clay, and the largest grains should not exceed one-sixth
of an inch in diameter, nor the smallest be less than one-
twenty-fifth of an inch. The bed of the road should be
excavated to the desired width and depth, and be shaped
with a slope each way from the centre, corresponding with
that which is to be given to the pavement. This earth bottom should be well rammed, and a layer of sand, four
inches thick, be put on, be thoroughly wetted, and be
beaten with a rammer weighing forty pounds. Two other
layers are to be in like manner added, and the compres-
sion will reduce the thickness of twelve inches to eight. The
number of layers should be regulated by the character of
the subsoil. Two inches of loose sand are to be then added
to fill the joints of the stones, which may be now laid.
The pressure of loads upon these stones is spread by the
incompressible sand over a large surface of the earth beneath. This is the favorite system in France.

Foundations of broken stone.—A bed is to be excavated,
deep enough to allow twelve inches of broken stone to be
placed under the pavement. A layer of four inches is first
put on, and the street then opened for carriages to pass
through it. When it has become firm and consolidated,
another layer of four inches is added and worked in as
before; and finally a third layer; making in fact a complete
McAdam road. Upon it the dressed paving-stones are set.
This method, though efficient, is very inconvenient, from
the length of time which it occupies, and the difficulty of
draught while it is in progress.

Foundations of pebbles.—Such a pebble pavement as is
described on pages 41–42, resting itself on sand, gravel, or
broken stones, has been recommended to be adopted as
the foundation of the dressed block pavement, for streets
in which there is a great deal of travel.

Foundations of Concrete.—Concrete is a mortar of finely
pulverized quicklime, sand, and gravel, which are mixed
dry, and to which water is added to bring the mass
to the proper consistence. It must be used immediately.
Béton (to which the name of Concrete is often im-

properly given) is a mixture of *hydraulic* mortar with gravel or broken stone; the mortar being first prepared, fine gravel incorporated with it, the layer of broken stones subsequently added to a layer of it 5 or 6 inches thick, and the whole mass rapidly brought by the hoe and shovel to a homogeneous state. Three parts of sand, one of hydraulic lime, and three of broken stone is a good proportion. A mixture of one part of Roman cement, one of sand, and eight of stone, has also been employed very successfully. *Béton* is much superior to Concrete for moist localities.

The excavation should be made fourteen inches lower than the *bottom* of the proposed pavement, and filled with that depth of the concrete or *béton*, which sets very rapidly, and becomes a hard, solid mass, on which a pavement may then be laid. This is, perhaps, the most efficient of all the foundations, but also the most costly at first, though this would be balanced by its permanence and saving of repairs. It admits of access to subterraneous pipes with less injury to the neighboring pavement than any other, for the concrete may be broken through at any point without unsettling the foundation for a considerable distance around it, as is the case with foundations of sand or broken stones; and when the concrete is replaced, the pavement can be at once reset at its proper level, without the uncertain allowance for settling which is necessary in other cases. The blocks set on the concrete are usually laid in mortar. . . .

DOCUMENT 6

(PLATES 1–5)

Town and Country

A good way to visualize the economic side of our civilization in the 1840s is in terms of town and country —and the kinds of roads connecting the two. Town and country are symbols as well as actualities. They stand for more than making a living; they stand for a manner of life. The roads between them also are figurative as well as literal. They carried ideas and attitudes along with passengers and cargo. The pictures to follow, which go together as a group, are useful to us not only for the images they contain but also for their psychological and social implications. They have something to say implicitly as well as explicitly.

They range in subject from the farm to the factory, from our English past to the American present of the 1840s, from scenes of quiet to those of bustle, from the mildly melancholy to the comic. They vividly illustrate the separation of rural from urban, yet they also show how America even then was moving toward uniformity. One of the major causes was the improvement, the salient improvement, in the means of transportation. To-day we are still not all alike but transportation continues irresistibly to make us more and more nearly so. In this group of pictures from the 1840s, transportation therefore has a place. The railroad train, the cart, the canal, the bridge: all these drew town and country closer together in the 1840s; and all these are depicted.

PLATE 1. A *View of the Nursery on the Farm of the Late Judge Buel*. Engraved by G. L. Brown.

SOURCE: *American Magazine*, I (November 1841), frontispiece. Library of Congress.

Agriculture was being altered in the 1840s. More mind was being applied to it and less folklore. One of the pioneers in scientific farming was Jesse Buel, once a county magistrate (hence the title "Judge") and the well-known author of *The Farmer's Companion*. Through precept and example Judge Buel showed that farming could be made to flourish. The *American Magazine* paid a tribute to his influence when it published this line-cut. The orderly acres of shrubs and young trees which are spread out before us, the extensive greenhouses and outbuildings in the background, and the handsome home in the center of the picture all indicate the vigor of Buel's effort. There is also a train, which will perhaps carry his farm products to their market.

Two things in the picture have implications that should be pointed out. One is the train. So prominently displayed that it nearly dwarfs the nursery, it suggests the coming industrial age for which Buel was trying to prepare American agriculture. The other is the large amount of landscape in the picture. American art was focusing on landscape by the 1840s; here over a third of the composition is devoted to it. The discovery of nature was a prominent part of the Romantic movement, here as abroad, and artist after artist painted or drew the gentle, rich beauties of the Romanticized countryside. "A View of the Nursery" contains many of the customary components including the water, the twisted tree, and the almost inevitable cows.

PLATE 2. *Rural Life*. Painted by G. Morland and engraved by J. Bannister.

SOURCE: *Graham's Magazine*, XXXI (November 1847), 241. Library of Congress.

The importance of agriculture as well as its gradually changing condition had cultural as well as economic implications. Now that farming was less of a struggle with frontier land and more of a settled way of life, it began to be sentimentalized to a degree it had not been before. Having on the whole won his battle with nature, the farmer could look around him complacently and enjoy the rural scene. The city dweller, forgetting the routine hardships of the farmer, could go further still and idealize country life almost beyond recognition. This is why *Graham's Magazine* could in the late 1840s print the idyllic English scene "Rural Life" without risking any derisive comments from its American readers.

"Rural Life" deserves a careful look because there are several significant things about it. The most apparent is that it prettifies farming life. But an examination of the picture can disclose others. It should be noticed that the atmosphere is quiet, the movement slow. Nature and all living things are heavy with calm. The lady stands still as she holds the goat by the horns; it looks contemplatively at the feeding kid. The farm boy in his peasant smock looks up and does nothing. The trees and grass in the background crowd the canvas, shutting in the human and animal figures, making them remote from our own brisk busyness. At the far left, a meaningful touch, we see some gravestones. They remind us of the futility of our antlike dartings. The cumulative effect of these various elements is profound. They satisfy the half-conscious resistance to the demands for activity and change that Jesse Buel, for example, stood for. They represent a hidden asperity against the way American economic life was going, against its fretful and increasing movement. They represent the longing for peace and quiet; the urge for immobility and death that, in Freudian theory, always wars against the active, aggressive principle.

PLATE 3. *Rock Manufacturing Co's Woolen Mills, Rockville, Ct.* Lithograph issued by Kellogg & Bulkeley, n.d.

SOURCE: The Harry T. Peters "America on Stone" Lithography Collection, the Smithsonian Institution.

In spite of the eminence of agriculture the development of America into an industrial nation was under way. The start was modest but by the opening of the 1840s New England's industry, at least, was a fact to be reckoned with. New factories were built as the decade went along and old ones continued to operate. The Rock Manufacturing Co., whose mills are shown here, dated back to 1821. Its plant was one of the pioneers in drawing workers off the farm.

The very size of the establishment is imposing. The main building is six stories high, and the plant and grounds cover almost a city block. The relation of industry to transportation is clearly indicated. The train is puffing along near the top of the lithograph and there is a canal leading right into the grounds. The scene and its treatment are both far removed, in general, from the pastoralism of "Rural Life." In "Rural Life" everything is curved, close, and soft. In the Rock Manufacturing Co. lithograph, on the other hand, we see straight lines and geometrical precision, balance and clarity, and a sense of space. And yet the contrast is not absolute. The two pictures have a quiet in common. The tiny human figures move little if at all; only the train is in travel. In its primness the lithograph reminds us of a Grant Wood painting.

It is worth noting that Kellogg & Bulkeley, the enterprising Hartford lithographers, found the mills worth reproducing and also included a diagram of the establishment.

They hoped no doubt that their lithograph would hang on a good many office and factory walls.

PLATE 4. *The Custom House, Wall Street*. Lithograph by Robert Kerr, 1845.

SOURCE: Library of Congress.

The outstanding omen of the new order was the burgeoning of the business city, with New York as the most colorful example. It was a long way from the New England village or the Southern county seat. It was even further from the quiet of the farm. During the decade the urban population nearly doubled; the rural population increased by about one-fourth. Here, packed with people, is one of the sights of New York, glimpsed in a lighter moment. The architect Robert Kerr drew this lithograph as the first in a series of views in New York. The Custom House stands in Attic dignity in the center of the picture and the perspective is so arranged that we have to look up at it. In powerful contrast to its whiteness and lightness Kerr has put the teeming human and animal life below. The life seems almost Hogarthian in its richness and humor but it lacks Hogarth's bitterness. Everything is good-natured on Wall Street. In the lower left-hand corner a trio of cronies jest in open, low-comedy attitudes while to their right two others carry on a serious conversation. Next to them three bad little boys chomp on the cheroots they certainly should not be seen with. In the lower right-hand corner a poleman stands with his placard advertising a concert by the violin virtuoso Ole Bull. Carts and carriages move in the middle foreground, along the dirty street. At the intersection a pitchman is apparently selling something, or trying to, as he harangues the motley crowd before him.

This is "City Life" indeed, the opposite in almost every way to the "Rural Life" reproduced above. Furthermore, it is American city life, no London slum, no Paris pigsty.

Everything is alive—and noisy. Robert Kerr maintained that he drew his picture from nature and there is no reason to doubt it.

PLATE 5. *New Suspension Bridge at Fairmount.* Drawn by W. Croome and engraved by Rawdon, Wright, Hatch & Smillie.

SOURCE: *Graham's Magazine*, XX (June 1842), frontispiece. Library of Congress.

Here, with city smokestacks in the background, is the transportation revolution exemplified. Bridges and waterways, city streets and country roads, all complement one another. The new bridge at Fairmount is necessary to ease the life of Philadelphia; its traffic, both vehicular and human, uses it more and more. The bridge, however, satisfies more than a practical need. It satisfies the desire for beauty. Its long, clean lines are both elegant and functional. The artist has caught their grace in his composition and focuses on it. On the left side of the drawing the building is mainly straight lines and angles except for the curves above the doors and windows. But even these are tight and so serve as a contrast to the graceful, extended span of the bridge. Its smooth line becomes the most attractive one in the entire composition.

The human beings are unimportant, put in the picture for the sake of a little color. Even the two fishermen in their dory serve mostly to accent the role of the bridge; for the bow of the dory and the hatted head of the one fisherman both point to the center of the span of the bridge, as if they were road signs giving directions. People could be proud of the Fairmount bridge, esthetically as well as economically. The alert editors of *Graham's Magazine* realized this when they commissioned Croome to depict the subject. They reported complacently in the text to accompany the picture, that the structure was widely acknowledged to be the "most graceful bridge in the country."

PART II

Making a Home

DOCUMENT 7

Sweet Home

To the rather aggressive, restless, individualistic American of the 1840s thoughts of home and mother offered the greatest sentimental relief. Nothing in our culture could call forth the rhetoric of feeling so well. Home at any time in his life could be counted on to bring a sentimental response, but the home of his childhood was closest to his heart. Not any kind of home, however. For American culture it had best be either middle-class or else lower-class rural. Going back to the 1840s, we can recover very few apostrophes to home if it happens to be in a city slum or, at the other extreme, in a manufacturer's mansion. Over all, the favorite childhood home was the country cottage. When the child was grown and married, home for him still had a slightly rustic air. It was still most often pictured as a single-family dwelling surrounded with grass and trees, and bordered with a picket fence. Within, preferably in the parlor according to the American dream, sat the father while he read a good book, the mother while she sewed and gazed at her spouse, and the doll-like children while they looked at a lesson or primly held a toy.

The sentimental celebration of home could be found in various aspects of the culture of the time. It was found in music, most tellingly in the songs of Stephen Foster; in art, most often in the popular lithographs sold by Currier & Ives and their competitors; in poetry most often in the ballads by the tender female poets. And in prose it fostered a whole school of fiction, as embodied in the so-called domestic novel.

Here, however, in a brief editorial essay from the *Farmer and Mechanic* is as thoroughgoing a eulogy as any. It lavishes praise on home in general as well as on the American home in particular. Yet, significantly, it is not home as a place to live in but as a place to leave. It is assumed that the American, characteristically mobile, will go somewhere else and return home only in his thoughts.

SOURCE: Anonymous, "Home," *Farmer and Mechanic*, New York, October 21, 1847.

Home

There is something in the word home that wakes the kindest feelings of the heart. It is not merely friends and kindred that render the places so dear, but the very hills and rocks and rivulets throw a charm around the place of one's nativity. It is no wonder that the loftiest harps have been tuned to sing of home, "sweet home." The rose that bloomed in the garden where one has wandered in early years careless in innocence, is lovely in its bloom, and lovelier in its decay. No songs are sweet like those we heard among the boughs that shade a parent's dwelling, gay as the birds that warble over us. No waters are bright like the clear silver stream that winds among the flower-decked knolls, where in childhood we have often strayed to pluck the violet or the lily, or twine a garland for some loving school-mate. We may wander away and mingle in the "world's fierce strife," and form new associations and friendships, and fancy that we have almost forgotten the land of our birth; but at some evening hour, as we listen perchance to the autumn winds, the remembrance of other days comes over the soul, and fancy bears us back to childhood's scenes, and we roam again amid the familiar haunts, and press the hands of the companions long since cold in their graves—and listen to voices we shall hear on earth no more. It is then a feeling of melancholy steals over us, which like Ossian's music, is pleasant, though mournful to the soul.

The Swiss general who leads his soldiers into a foreign

land must not suffer the sweet airs of Switzerland to be sung within the hearing of his soldiers, for at the thrilling sound they would leave the camp, and fly away to their own green hills. The African, torn from his willow braided hut, and borne away to the land of charters and of chains, weeps as he thinks of home, and sighs and pines for the cocoa land beyond the waters of the sea. Years may have passed over him, and strifes and toils may have crushed his spirits—all his kindred may have found graves upon the corals of the ocean; yet were he free how soon he would seek the shores and skies of his boyhood dreams! The New England mariner, amid the icebergs of the northern seas, or breathing the spicy gales of the evergreen isles, or coasting along the shores of the Pacific, though the hand of time may have blanched his raven locks, and care have ploughed deep furrows on his brow, and his heart may have been chilled by the storms of the ocean, till the fountains of his love had almost ceased to gush with their heavenly current—yet, upon some summer's evening, as he looks upon the sun sinking behind the western wave, he will think of home and his heart will yearn for the loved days, and his tears will flow like the summer's rain. How does the heart of the wanderer, after long years of absence beat, and his eyes fill, as he catches a glance of the hills of his nativity: and when he has pressed the lips of a mother or a sister, how soon does he hasten to see if the garden, and the orchard and the stream look as in days gone by? We may find climes as beautiful, and skies as bright, and friends as devoted, but that will not usurp the place of home.

DOCUMENT 8

The Domestic Circle

There was no shortage of advice. Today's marriage counselor, today's expert on child rearing, today's newspaper columnist (that self-taught seer on domestic affairs), all were unknown in the 1840s. But no one missed them, for there was always the minister. His advice was asked the more eagerly because he spoke both out of human wisdom and out of a close study of Scripture. The Bible was the guide and he knew the Bible best. This meant not only the application of the Ten Commandments to domestic life but also the constant use of the entire Bible as a source for examples and precepts. All the answers lay in its pages. Consequently, the Christian cleric cited Scripture, chapter and verse, as consistently as the modern scholar footnotes his sources. A typical instance is the Reverend Matthew Sorin, a minister in Philadelphia. His book of advice, *The Domestic Circle,* is sprinkled with citations. The practice seems odd to us; in Sorin's day it gave his ideas extra authority.

The book is valuable not only because it gives characteristic advice but also because it describes American home life at the middle-class level. Sorin was foreign-born and so he observes us more closely, takes us less for granted, than would a native of our country. He apologizes for the inadequacies of the book, saying that it might better have been written "by one specially adapted to the principles and habits of society in this country" but he is too modest. His objectivity is buttressed by considerable insight. As he goes along in the book his pace is somewhat heavy-footed but his tread is sure. The selection given below is from the first discourse, "Nature and Obligations of the Marriage Compact," and deals specifically with the many duties involved in the marriage relation.

Besides the basing of the book on the Christian religion there are two more qualities in *The Domestic Circle* that strike the observer. The first is the emphasis on rigid propriety; the second, the total absence of any concern about sex. Otherwise much of the book is still current. The advice has a familiar ring: don't let one parent pamper the child after the other has punished it; don't let relatives interfere with the management of the family; don't gossip about your domestic problems; and so on.

SOURCE: Matthew Sorin, *The Domestic Circle; or, Moral and Social Duties Explained and Enforced* (Philadelphia, 1840), pp. 38–61, abridged.

Nature and Obligations of the Marriage Compact

II. The duties arising out of [the marriage] relation. To enter into particulars, so as to embrace all that might be said, would be hardly expedient. We shall, therefore, confine ourselves chiefly to general principles, embracing as much as possible, those leading points of duty in the domestic circle, which are reciprocally binding between man and wife. Of these the

1st. *Is mutual affection.* According to the order and constitution of the divine government, man is appointed to rule in the affairs of this life. It is his prerogative to hold the reins of domestic government, and to direct the family interest, so as to bring them to a happy and honorable termination. This appointment of God is intimated in the order of the creation; and its propriety is manifested in the order of the fall. But still, as it is the right of the husband to rule, so it is his duty to rule with moderation and love—to love his wife "even as Christ loved the Church." Eph. v. 25. And so, also, the obedience of the wife is not to be the reluctant offering of an ungracious spirit, but the cheerful service of a delighted mind; "that

if any obey not the word, they also may, without the word,
be won by the conversation of the wives." 1 Pet. iii. 1–5.
This affection is a most tender, sincere, and kind-hearted
regard for each other, manifesting itself in all their words,
spirit, and behavior. It assumes all the varied forms of forbearance, gentleness, meekness, and active sympathy, in
times of bodily affliction, or mental distress; it is the spirit

> To be resigned, when ills betide,
> Patient, when favors are denied,
> And pleased with favors given.

If it is religiously binding on every man to love his neighbor as himself, then certainly, it is one of the plainest cases
imaginable, that man and wife should love with an inde-
finable fervor and fixedness of affection, strengthened by
all that is manly, and softened by all that is tender in human nature. Here, indeed, charity may hope all things,
believe and endure all things, and even cover a multitude
of sins, and violate no one's rights, nor endanger the
public good. And this exercise of charity is of the very
greatest importance, because that such are the duties and
afflictions of domestic life, that the one cannot be discharged, nor can the other be endured, without it. Separated, in heart, either, or even both the parties, are feeble
even as a bruised reed, and are unable to endure the
slightest blast of adversity. But if firmly united in the
bonds of a rational and fervent affection, they can endure,
with sublimest fortitude, the angry shaking of the fiercest
storm. The marriage compact, when formed under the influence of proper motives, principles, and affections, is like
a splendid edifice rearing its majestic dome, alike amidst
the clouds and sunshine of heaven, and bearing both the
vicissitudes of youth, and the infirmities of age, with fortitude and cheerfulness. . . .

2. *Mutual confidence*. Nothing is, or can be of more
importance than this, in maintaining, in active and ener-
getic exercise, conjugal affection. To destroy confidence, is
to remove the foundations of all that is excellent or valu-

able in the family circle. Where this is wanting conjugal sympathy and tenderness die, and an infusion of bitterness is tasted in every thing, and the whole round of family duties becomes a heartless, hollow, and insipid thing. And hence, any thing tending, even remotely, to unhinge the faith of either party, is to be deprecated, even more than death itself. If they have secrets to keep, let them keep them to themselves; if they have wounds, let those wounds bleed inwardly—a family wound should never be exposed to the air. They should repulse as an angel of darkness and death, any one who would officiously pry into the peculiarities of their domestic history, or insinuate any thing to either, disreputable of the other. By the manifest appointment of heaven, and by the very nature of the relation they sustain, they are constituted sentinels over each other's reputation, and they should die rather than relinquish their charge.

Let it be deeply engraven on their minds, that as there are none on earth to whom they can be so nearly allied, as in the relationship existing between wife and husband, so there is none in whom it ought to be their privilege to trust with more implicit confidence; and if it is otherwise, it is unfortunate, indeed;—a heavier curse one could scarcely wish upon his greatest foe. And hence neither should indulge any vague suspicions, nor fill their minds with dark and dissocial reasonings, for these are the very bane of personal as well as of domestic peace; the poison of human kindness, the very mildew of the soul, they eat into the moral constitution like rust, and canker all that is good or generous in the nature of man. Therefore, they should cultivate mutual confidence, they should honor each other's word, defend each other's reputation, nor ever relinquish their confidence, until circumstances compel the surrender. . . .

3. *Mutual attention and respect.* Not the empty round of ceremonious attentions, that are ostentatiously crowded into the family circle, on certain occasions, seemingly more to please beholders, than to express the genuine sentiments

of the soul. We speak of that simple, artless, and unpremeditated respect and attention, which genuine love inspires. There are, however, persons who are industrious and careful in business, skilful in the management of their affairs, high and influential in their professions; and some who are reputed persons of piety, who appear never to feel the obligation of rendering to wife or husband, as the case may be, more attention than to their domestics or their children.

There is an apparently premeditated abruptness and repulsiveness in their manners, which, like every other thorny substance, is most keenly felt by those who, unfortunately, are nearest to it. It is said, in extenuation of this fault, that it is their way, and that they mean no harm; but, even admitting this to be true, it certainly is an evil way, which they ought to abandon; a way that does no honor to themselves, and is a great inconvenience to others. That even persons of the most rugged temperament, can act a better part, is scarcely to be disputed. To prove this point, place them in a selection of society appropriate to your purpose, and few are more yielding or complaisant than they. We have, therefore, cause to fear that the course we now reprehend, instead of possessing what is usually claimed for it, the excellency of blunt and unvarnished simplicity and frankness, is rather an exhibition of ignorant rudeness and uncultivated pride. Respect is due to all, and especially to wife and husband, and the more so, because, whatever may be said to the contrary, much of the happiness of the present life depends on little things. . . .

Mutual respect and attention between man and wife, are essential to render them respectable in the eyes of their domestics and children; and also to maintain that healthy flow of soul, that cheerfulness and buoyancy of spirit so necessary in bearing the ills, and performing the duties of life. As kindness and respectful treatment are due to all persons, so they are specially due to ourselves as wife and husband; for we cannot love those whom we do not treat respectfully, nor can they love us in return. Let it then be a principle of established authority, like the laws of the Medes and Persians, that changeth not, to extend to each other that affectionate attention which is mutually due between equals. Let every thing be studiously avoided that goes to lessen either party in their own estimation, or in that of other persons; and let it never be forgotten, that even a smile or frown, may gild with brightness, or overcast with clouds, that most sacred spot on earth, which you call home.

4. *Mutual assistance.* The first woman was given to man, not to live upon his labor, nor yet to labor for his living; she was designed to be one with himself, an equal sharer in his sorrows and joys, she was to be a help-meet for him. The relation in which man and wife are placed, relative to all that is either pleasurable or painful in the domestic circle, renders it not less a dictate of nature, than a precept of religion. They should bear each other's burdens, and give their united efforts in sustaining the cares, and performing the duties of life. It is true, that they both have not the same class of duties to perform; they have their different and appropriate spheres of action. But these, however, are not at variance with each other; but, like the different parts of a wisely constructed and well regulated machine, are designed and calculated to act together in perfect harmony; a harmony always heightened by the cheerful concurrence of the parties, and tending to manifest the glory of God, and swell to overflowing, the tide of their mutual happiness. There is a threefold assistance that married persons owe to each other, in giving interest and enjoyment to the family circle.

1. There is an assistance in promoting the temporal interests of the family. I now take it for granted, that neither of the parties has any separate interests, because that they ought not to have any; and hence neither the wife nor husband can say, in strict propriety, that either has, separately, an exclusive right in any thing. The husband lives for his wife, and she for her husband, and both

live for their children. And, therefore, in advancing every thing which tends to ensure family comfort or respectability, that may afford the means of education to their children, or of benevolence to other persons; that may provide a defence against reverse of fortune, sickness, and premature age, both are equally concerned. Neither, therefore, should ever, for a moment, suppose that he or she is at liberty to rest or riot on the industry and good management of the other. Such a course is not only disreputable, but also criminal. And wherever it is indulged, it will inevitably render the party so offending, despicable, if not in their own eyes, yet in those of more discriminating and impartial judges.

And yet it is indisputably certain that there are many instances of this inexcusable neglect and inattention to business and domestic order; this want of manifested concern in the enlargement and stability of the family interests. It may be in one or even in both the parties—the husband and wife—in either case, it is deeply to be deplored. Peradventure the one is inattentive to his business abroad, the other to her pantry, her wardrobe, or her person, at home; or, it may be, that the one does not afford the requisite supplies, or the other makes a careless and wasteful distribution of them; and thus the industry and good management of the one is perfectly neutralised, by the negligence or prodigality of the other. And in some instances, the kindness and good offices of their friends are rendered of little or no value, by the want of spirit and enterprise common to them both; and hence poverty and want, as the inevitable consequences, ensue,—these are soon followed by the loss of confidence, coldness, indifference, and unkind allusions to the past, and mutual recriminations; and thus all the sacred and tender familiarities of home, perish away into a cold and heartless round of chilling ceremonies.

In order to carry out this principle of mutual assistance, persons must be contented to live within their income. No man should go feasting and dashing through the country, or from city to city, as a person of fashion and show, while his wife is pining away at home; it may be, nursing his sick or afflicted children, or bending beneath the burden of her cares—working and weeping in solitude over the painful contrast between her married and single condition; and on the other hand, let no woman, urged on by a silly ambition to be ranked among the more fashionable circles of life, plunge her husband into the expense of unnecessary finery and sumptuous entertainments, which he cannot afford; and thus keep him early and late at the anvil or the counter, dispirited and embarrassed in his business, until engulfed in the sorrow and confusion of a dishonorable and irremediable bankruptcy.

And here it may be proper to remark, that the power of female influence over the domestic circle and family destiny, is immense. What does it avail, if a man be ever so industrious—rise early and retire late, and eat the bread of carefulness, though he be all activity, enterprise, and management, if he have an improvident or negligent wife, if she is not a keeper at, and of home, and does not watch over the fruits of his industry; but leaves this duty to be performed by her children or domestics: in nine cases out of ten that man spends his strength for nought, and his labor in vain. Let a woman be but true to her trust, understand and manage her domestic affairs with discretion, and if she have a husband worthy of her affections, they have a strong and sufficient guarantee of prosperity and competency in the world.

There is, perhaps, more generally than is supposed, a strict propriety in a frequent comparison of views and reorganization of measures for the promotion of the family interests. In order to this, it is not necessary to interrupt or displace the innocent mirthfulness of the family hearth, and to suspend the sacred charities of domestic life, by crowding into the family circle the confusion and litigious excitement of the great business world. The end here proposed, can be secured without this inconvenience; and that it ought to be, is implied in the nature of the marriage compact. The wife, most certainly, has a right to know something of the state of her husband's affairs, unless some reason of affection for her, arising out of the state of her health, or the character of her mind, dictate an opposite course as the more tender and respectful. But waiving these exceptions, such consultation is perfectly reasonable. No man would cross the ocean, or undertake a tedious and perilous journey, without first consulting with his family; and yet many do engage in business speculations not less hazardous, venture and lose their all, without consulting their families, when, if they had been consulted, the prudence, peradventure, even the timidity of the wife, might have restrained the precipitancy of the husband, and thus have averted the ruin. But this was not done; the family walked on securely, until in an evil hour, when worldly fancy fed on golden dreams, the rains descended, and the floods came; misfortune rushed upon them like an avalanche from some Alpine height, cold and pitiless as death, and overwhelmed them all in deep and heart-rending sorrow.

The policy here recommended, would in all probability, more generally ensure success in business; because that it would more certainly engage the hearty co-operation of all the parties; and in the event of any failure, the disappointment would be borne with greater fortitude and cheerfulness, because it would be more readily and more equally divided.

2. Again, *there is a mutual assistance in the maintenance of order—in the education and government of children.* It is difficult to say which of the parents should be the more prominent in the instruction of their offspring. If practicable, it would seem that their efforts should be conjoined, for the simple reason that both are equally interested, and the children ought to be made to regard their parents as equally concerned for their welfare.—In some cases a father, and in others the mother, will find it more convenient to impart or superintend the instruction of the children. And there may be some unaccountable

partiality on the part of the child, or peculiar aptness to teach in the parent, or some other cause may serve to indicate the will of God in relation to this question. There have been many instances of great intellectual and moral worth, apparently the result of maternal instructions, and others again not less illustrious, who have been more immediately indebted to a father's care. But the ordinary and high way of heaven's appointment to the development of the mind, and proper formation of the moral powers, calls for the combined efforts of both the parents. In this department of their duty, two evils are to be carefully avoided; first, the conflicting views and feelings between the parents themselves; and secondly, the interference of domestic relations.

The rights of parents in their children, are equal. If those children are honorable and prosperous in the world, it is the happiness of both. If they are prodigal and vicious, it is not more the misfortune of the one than of the other.

It is, therefore, a self-evident duty, and one most solemnly binding on parents, to contribute their united skill, influence, and authority, to "train up their children in the way they should go."

But most unfortunately, it occasionally happens that one of those parents, perhaps not intentionally, but yet most effectually, neutralises the instruction and salutary discipline exercised by the other, by a very unseasonable and ill-judged expression of affection. It may be that the child is negligent or disobedient, or by some irregularity of life, has rendered it highly proper, if not strictly necessary, to visit its transgression with stripes; and the parent privy to the offence, proceeds to discharge the duty, however painful, of correcting the delinquent child. When to his or her infinite regret, and the permanent injury of the youthful offender, the chastisement of the one is worse than destroyed by the caresses of the other, and the correction administered as a wholesome medicine, is changed into a deadly poison—a savor of death unto death, by a declaration on the part of the opposing parent, that it was

unjust and cruel, and ought not to have been inflicted.
And it may be that the child is even petted and soothed
with sweetmeats, and assurances of protection in time to
come. . . .

Reprehensible as is the practice here referred to, we
now turn to one still more so; it is the officious and un-
called for interference of domestic relations—relations living in the family, actuated by a class of feelings peculiar
to themselves, and it may be arising out of the relation
they sustain to the domestic circle. They appear to think
to render themselves more acceptable to the parents, by
the manner in which they demean themselves towards the
children. And hence they not unfrequently conceal or ex-
tenuate their faults, and with equal violence to truth, commend and exalt their virtues; and in those seasons of
retribution inseparable from a well-ordered family government, rush in between the offended parent and the guilty
child, as the self-constituted protectors of the little culprit.
Peradventure, the child is seized as in a paroxysm of com-
passion, and is torn away from the hand of the correcting
parent, and is thus taught to regard even a distant relation
as their guardian angel, and their own parents as unpitying
and cruel persecutors.

In what particular class of crime, to give such conduct
its appropriate location, is difficult to say—it is almost a
nameless wickedness against the domestic circle. It is a sin
against the parents and the child, the Church and the
State, against heaven and earth. Parents are specially concerned in preventing any such invasion of their rights, and
of the established order of heaven, they should never consent to such a surrender of their authority under any
pretence whatever, seeing they can never make a corresponding transfer of their responsibilities.

3. *There is also a mutual assistance in promoting each
other's spiritual welfare.* It is manifestly a divine appointment, that human beings should be instrumental in the
advancement of each other's happiness, generally, and certainly it is not less a suggestion of nature, than a duty of

religion, that the more nearly persons are related, the more
deeply they should sympathise in each other's pleasures
or pains; and the more ardently they should labor for each
other's felicity, and most of all should husband and wife,
"who are no more twain, but one flesh," exemplify this
principle before their family, and before the world.

If that man be justly regarded as a domestic despot—a
man without a heart, who should tyrannise over the weakness and dependent condition of his wife—who through
a mean and niggardly capriciousness, should deny her the
ordinary comforts and enjoyments of life, then most certainly the vocabulary of earth does not contain an epithet
sufficiently expressive of scorn, appropriately to describe
the man, who binds the conscience of his wife, as it were,
in chains of affliction and iron, and thus keeps her in
continual dread of losing her soul, merely to gratify his
graceless bigotry.

And yet there are instances in which persons plight their
solemn vows of fidelity and affection to others of religious
opinions adverse to their own, secretly intending to compel a reception of their own distinctive sentiments, by
argument if they can, but by coercive measures if need
be. But who can give utterance to the detestation, which
every upright mind must feel, against a person of this
description, who, while he is smiling with all the apparent
cheerfulness of a bridegroom's heart, is secretly meditat-
ing with cold creeping hypocrisy, the unpitying persecution
of a heartless bigot; or who, after the irrevocable amen of
the marriage ceremony, tears his new made wife from all
her well tried friends, and dearly loved religious associations? Surely such a one knows but little of the sympathy, that should bind even man to man, and that
constitutes the great active principle of terrestrial happiness; and still less does he know of the principles and
affections, which give confidence, comfort, and sanctity to
the marriage union, and, least of all, of the spirit and
power of the religion of Christ Jesus. . . .

In addition to these general views, we may here, with

propriety, notice some other special duties, which are mutually due between man and wife. Thus it is required of woman to show a spirit of subordination, and to obey her husband." Eph. v, 22. But it is also required of the husband that he love and protect his wife—that he cultivate for her the most tender affection—that he protect her according to his power, in person—health—property—and reputation. Every thing pertaining to her comfort, should be granted, as far as in his power, with a ready and cheerful mind. "He is to love his wife as Christ loved the Church." Eph. v, 25. "As it is required of the wife, that she reverence her husband, not as a superior being, but as her superior in the domestic economy; and that, therefore, she should not usurp authority over the man, because Adam was first formed, then Eve." 1 Tim. ii, 11, 14. So it is also binding on the husband not to render himself ridiculous and contemptible in the eyes of his wife, by any indecencies of speech, or vile and trifling associations. He is to maintain his place, not so much by physical power or brute force, as by the excellency of his example, and those developments of mental and moral superiority, and greater tact in the management of affairs, which it is reasonable to expect from his relation, and which will, in most cases, insure a ready and cheerful submission to rule. 1 Pet. iii, 3, 7. Again, as it is the duty of the woman to be a keeper at home, and not to be wandering from her place, like an unhappy spirit seeking rest and finding none, Titus, ii, 5, so most unquestionably, it is the duty of the husband to render that home as interesting and cheerful as possible. Let him throw around it, all the attractions he can—let him render it cheerful with the music of his own voice, and instructive with the fruit of his own reading and experience. Let him share in the little details of domestic toil, nor think it unworthy a man to assist in nursing his young, or ministering to his afflicted children. Thus "let every one, in particular, love his wife even as himself; and the wife see that she reverence her husband." Eph. v. 33.

A marriage union thus enlightened by reason, cemented by affection, and sanctified by religion, sustained by its appropriate sympathies, and an undeviating fidelity, by a cheerful co-operation in carrying forward the interests, and establishing the reputation of the domestic circle on a pure and Scriptural basis, is one of the sweetest scenes of earthly felicity, and holiest associations of human nature; over which the monarchy of heaven presides. Such the marriage union was at its first institution, and such it is designed to be even now, and so to continue until time shall be no more; and its high and sacred typical allusions shall be consummated at the marriage supper of the Lamb.

DOCUMENT 9

The Workman's Household

Most material about the American family was written by middle-class authors for middle-class readers. Typically, it was prepared by the minister and designed for the merchant and his wife. Only at intervals was there an attempt to address either the upper or the lower class. Here and there we come across an antebellum homily against great wealth and the corruption it can bring to the home. This is still, however, before the Gilded Age and the corruptions are not yet considered flagrant. Here and there we see printed sermons or lectures intended to lead the workingman to a more rewarding family life. These are a little more frequent. One attempt is embodied in a small book called *The American Mechanic,* published in 1838 and republished more than once during the 1840s. Its author was James W. Alexander (1804–59), who wrote under the name of Charles Quill. He was a Princeton professor and Presbyterian minister.

The book discusses more than the domestic side of the mechanic's life; it goes into his recreations and studies at considerable length. The counsel is sane, the style informal and direct. Quill said in his preface that he would be amply rewarded "if this volume find its way into the shop and manufactory, or be read aloud from the workman's bench." His brisk, anecdotal approach is exemplified in the three brief chapters on the mechanic's family printed here.

Writing for a simpler audience than Sorin does in *The Domestic Circle,* Quill describes the ideal wife in more vivid terms. She should be "gentle as the antelope, untiring as the bee, joyous as the linnet; neat, punctual, modest, confiding." Her place is "eminently at the fireside." The ideal children, according to Quill, are the result of their parents' love and discipline. They will be lively, diligent, and honest, provided their parents have on the one hand constantly demonstrated their love and on the other have kept them in order. For "implicit obedience . . . is perfectly consistent with the utmost affection, and should be enforced from the beginning, and absolutely."

SOURCE: Charles Quill (James W. Alexander), *The American Mechanic* (Philadelphia, 1838), pp. 44–49, 69–79.

The Mechanic's Wife

In America, every mechanic is supposed to have, or to be about to have, a wife. The many thousands of these spouses are divided into sorts. Thus we have good and bad; very good and very bad; unspeakably good and insufferably bad; and—as a sort of *par* expression—*tolerable*. It is not every good woman who is a good wife; nor is it every good wife who is a good wife for the mechanic. A working man needs a working wife; but as to qualities of mind, manners, and morals, she cannot run too high in the scale. There is an error prevalent concerning this.

GILES says, "I do not want a wife with too much sense." Why not? Perhaps Giles will not answer; but the shrug of his shoulders answers, "Because I am afraid she will be an overmatch for me." Giles talks like a simpleton. The unfortunate men who have their tyrants at home are never married to women of sense. Genuine elevation of mind cannot prompt any one, male or female, to go out of his or her proper sphere. No man ever suffered from an overplus of intelligence, whether in his own head or his wife's.

HODGE says, "I will not marry a girl who has too much manners." Very well, Hodge: you are right; *too much* of any thing is bad. But consider what you say. Perhaps you mean that a fine lady would not suit you. Very true; I should not desire to see you joined for life to what is

called a "fine lady," to wit, to a woman who treats you as
beneath her level, sneers at your friends, and is above her
business. But this is not good manners. Real good manners and true politeness are equally at home in courts and
farm houses. This quality springs from nature, and is the
expression of unaffected good will. Even in high life, the
higher you go the simpler do manners become. Parade and
"fuss" of manners are the marks of half-bred people. True
simplicity and native good will, and kind regard for the
convenience and feelings of others, will ensure good manners, even in a kitchen: and I have seen many a vulgar
dame in an assembly, and many a gentlewoman in an
humble shed. Nay, your wife *must* have good manners.

RALPH declares, "I hope I may never have a wife who is
too strict and moral." Now, my good Ralph, you talk nonsense. Who taught you that cant? I perceive you do not
know what you mean. Are you afraid your wife will be too
virtuous?

"Bless me! no."

Then you rather prefer a moral wife to an immoral
one?

"Surely."

Are you afraid, then, of a religious wife?

"Why something like that *was* in my head; for there is
neighbour Smith's wife, who gives him no peace of his
life, she is so religious."

Let me hear how she behaves herself.

"Why, she is forever teaching the children out of the
Bible."

Indeed! And you, Ralph, are an enemy of the Bible?

"O, no! But then—ahem—there is reason in all things."

Yes, and the reason you have just given is that of a
child, and, like the child's *because*, is made to do hard
service. But let me understand you. Does Mrs. Smith
teach the children any thing wrong?

"O, no! But plague it all! if one of them hears Smith
let fly an oath, it begins to preach at him."

Then you wish, when you have children, to have liberty

to teach them all the usual oaths and curses, and obscene jokes that are common.

"Dear me, Mr. Quill, you won't understand me."

Yes, I understand you fully: it is you, Ralph, who do not understand yourself. Look here. Mrs. Smith is so religious that if she proceeds as she has begun, her children will break their father of his low blasphemies. I hope you may get just such a wife.

"But then, Smith can't spend a couple of hours at the tavern for fear of his wife!"

Ah! what does he go to the tavern for?

"Just to sit and chat, and drink a little."

And how does his wife interfere? Does she fetch him home?

"No."

Does she chastise him on his return?

"O, no!"

Does she scold him then?

"No."

What is it then that disturbs him?

"Why, she looks so solemn and mournful, and shuts herself up so and cries, whenever he is a little disguised, that the man has no satisfaction."

Good! And I pray he may have none until he alters his course of life.

A proper self-respect would teach every noble-hearted American, of whatever class, that he cannot set too high a value on the conjugal relation. We may judge of the welfare and honour of a community by its wives and mothers. Opportunities for acquiring knowledge, and even accomplishments, are happily open to every class above the very lowest; and the wise mechanic will not fail to choose such a companion as may not shame his sons and daughters in that coming age, when an ignorant American shall be as obsolete as a fossil fish.

Away with flaunting, giggling, dancing, squandering, peevish, fashion-hunting wives! The woman of this stamp is a poor comforter when the poor husband is sick or bankrupt. Give me the *house-wife*, who can be a "help-meet" to her Adam:

> ———— For nothing lovelier can be found
> In woman, than to study household good,
> And good works in her husband to promote.

I have such a mechanic's wife in my mind's eye: gentle as the antelope, untiring as the bee, joyous as the linnet; neat, punctual, modest, confiding. She is patient, but resolute; aiding in counsel, reviving in troubles, ever pointing out the brightest side, and concealing nothing but her own sorrows. She loves her home, believing with Milton, that

> The wife, where danger and dishonour lurks,
> Safest and seemliest by her husband stays,
> Who guards her, or *with her the worst endures*.

The place of woman is eminently at the fireside. It is at home that you must see her, to know who she is. It is less material what she is abroad; but what she is in the family circle is all-important. It is bad merchandise, in any department of trade, to pay a premium for other men's opinions. In matrimony, he who selects a wife for the applause or wonder of his neighbours, is in a fair way towards domestic bankruptcy. Having got a wife, there is but one rule—*honour and love her*. Seek to improve her understanding and her heart. Strive to make her more and more such an one as you can cordially respect. Shame on the brute in man's shape, who can affront or vex, not to say neglect, the woman who has embarked with him for life, "for better, for worse," and whose happiness, if severed from his smiles, must be unnatural and monstrous. In fine, I am proud of nothing in America so much as of our American wives.

The Mechanic's Children

Let a group of children be gathered at a school or playground, and whether they be rich or poor, gentle or simple, they will coalesce so as to realize the most complete levelling theory. If this is true of the very poor, how much more apparent is it, when the comparison takes in the offspring of the well-doing mechanic. Children, take them one with another, are beautiful creatures—at least in America,—nay all the world over. Sir Joshua Reynolds has observed that children, until mistaught, always throw their limbs into graceful attitudes. I trouble myself very little, when I meet a rosy, ingenuous, clean, and happy child, with the inquiry, whether it be aristocratic or plebeian in its origin. John Randolph, of Roanoke, was often in the habit of alluding to certain families, as having no ancestral portraits. Now I question whether the great orator would not have given Bushy Forest, or even Roanoke, for a pair of boys. It is better to have fruit on the limbs, than ever so many dead roots under ground. A cluster of merry, healthy boys and girls, is better than a family crest, or old plate, or faded pictures, or a genealogical tree, or the pitiful pride of penniless grandeur. These olive branches around one's table afford good presumption of a certain degree of health and virtue; and are just what the effete patricians of lordly Britain often sigh for in vain. Every now and then some great family goes out, like a dying lamp, with an impotent conclusion. Blessed are those poor men who are rich in children such as I mean!

I plead guilty to the charge of living at the corner of a very narrow alley with a somewhat ignoble name. My window looks upon this humble avenue, which is properly a *cul-de-sac*. At a certain hour of every day it is filled with boys and girls; for at the further end of it there is a "madam's school." My writing is ever and anon interrupted by the joyous laugh or the scream of ecstasy from these romping creatures: I seldom fail to look out, and am generally as long nibbing my pen at the window, as they are in making their irregular procession through the lane. True, they have pulled a board off my garden fence, and foraged most naughtily among my gooseberries; but what of that?

I have many a time paid a heavier tax for a less pretty sight. They are happy: and so am I, while I look at them.

Surely nothing can be more graceful or attractive than the fawn-like girl, not yet in her teens, not yet practising any factitious steps, and not yet seduced into the bold coquetry and flirting display of the "young miss." Whose children are these? The children of mechanics; almost without exception. Call it not pride in the anxious mother, that she decks these little ones in the cleanliest, fairest product of her needle, and shows off with innocent complacency the chubby face or the slender ankle; call it not *pride*, but *love*. The mechanic's wife has a heart; and over the cradle, which she keeps in motion while she plies her task, she sometimes wanders in musing which needs the aid of poesy to represent it. She feels that she is an *American* mother; she knows her boy not only *may* but *must* have opportunities of advancement far superior to those of his parents. She blushes in forethought to imagine him illiterate and unpolished when he shall have come to wealth: and therefore she denies herself that she may send him to school.

What a security Providence has given us for the next race of men, in the gushing fulness of that perpetual spring—a mother's heart! I said I was proud of our American wives: I am ready to kneel in tears of thankfulness for our American mothers.

But let me get back from the mothers to the children. Our future electors and jurymen, and legislators, and judges, and magistrates, are the urchins who are now shouting and leaping around a thousand shops and schoolhouses. Shall their parents live in disregard of the duty they owe these budding minds? I am half disposed to undertake a sort of lectureship, from house to house, in order to persuade these fathers and mothers that, with all their affection, they are not sufficiently in earnest in making the most of their children. I would talk somehow in this way. "My good sir, or madam, how old is that boy? Very well; he is well grown for his age, and I hope you

are keeping in mind that he will live in a different world
from that in which you and I live. Bring him up accord-
ingly. Lay upon him very early the gentle yoke of discipline. Guard him from evil companions. Save him from
idleness, which is the muck-heap in which every rank,
noisome weed of vice grows up. Put work into his hands,
and make it his pleasure. Make him love home; and by all
means encourage him to love his parents better than all
other human beings. Allow me to beg that you will not
fall into the absurd cant which some people, parrot-like,
catch and echo, against book learning. Determine that this
fellow shall know more than ever you have known; then he
will be an honour to your declining years. Keep him at a
good school; reward him with good books; and he will one
day bless you for it. I know men in our legislature, who
were brought up to hard work, and are now very rich; but
they cannot utter a single sentence without disgracing
themselves by some vulgar expression or some blunder in
grammar. They know this, but have found it out too late.
They feel that their influence is only half what it might
have been, if their parents had only taken pains to have
them well taught. Now look ahead, and give your child
that sort of fortune which no reverse in trade can take
away."

It is a great and prevalent error, that children may be
left to run wild in every sort of street-temptation for several
years, and that it will then be time enough to break them
in. This horrid mistake makes half our spendthrifts, gam-
blers, thieves, and drunkards. No man would deal so with
his garden or lot; no man would raise a colt or a puppy on
such a principle. Take notice, parents, unless you till the
new soil, and throw in good seed, the devil will have a
crop of poison-weeds before you know what is taking place.
Look at your dear child, and think whether you will leave
his safety or ruin at hazard.

What! more about the children? Yes; for they are to be
the *men* of the coming age; and he has looked but drowsily

at the signs of the times, who has not discerned that these
little ones are to act in a world very different from our own.
The question is, shall we prepare them for it?

These pauses in business, these cloudy days of distress,
are given us for some end; perhaps as intervals of *consideration*. Let us then consider the ways and means of
making something out of these beloved representatives of
our very selves. Let us build something of the spars that
float from our wreck; this will be our best speculation.

> Let us know,
> Our indiscretion sometimes serves us well,
> When our deep plots do fail; and that should teach us
> There's a divinity that shapes our ends,
> Rough-hew them how we will.

Sit down among your little children, and let me say a
word to you about family-government. We good people of
America, in our race for self-government, are in danger of
not governing ourselves. Our lads grow up insubordinate—
finding out to our and their cost, that "it is a free country." An English traveller could find no *boys* in the United
States; all being either children or men. The evil is un-
deniably on the increase. Parents are abandoning the reins;
and when once this shall have become universal, all sorts
of government but despotism will be impracticable.

Take that froward child in hand at once, or you will
soon have to be his suppliant rather than his guide. The
old way was perhaps too rugged, where every thing was
accomplished by mere dint of authority; but the new way
is as bad on the other side: no man is reduced to the
necessity of choosing an extreme.

We often visit houses where the parents seem to be
mere advisory attendants, with a painful sinecure. Let
such hear the words of a wise Congressman of New Jersey,
and a signer of the Declaration: "There is not a more dis-
gusting sight than the impotent rage of a parent who has
no authority. Among the lower ranks of people, who are
under no restraints from decency, you may sometimes see

a father or mother running out into the street after a child who has fled from them, with looks of fury and words of execration; and they are often stupid enough to imagine that neighbours or passengers will approve them in their conduct, though in fact it fills every beholder with horror." I am afraid none of us need go many rods from home to witness the like. What is commonly administered as reproof is often worse than nothing. Scolding rebukes are like scalding potions—they injure the patient. And angry chastisement is little better than oil on the fire. Not long since, I was passing by the railroad from Newark to New York. The train of cars pursued its furious way immediately by the door of a low "shanty," from which a small child innocently issued, and crossed the track before us just in time to escape being crushed by the locomotive. We all looked out with shuddering, when lo! the sturdy mother, more full of anger than alarm, strode forth, and seizing the poor infant, which had strayed only in consequence of her own negligence, gave it a summary and violent correction in the old-fashioned, inverse method. Inference: parents often deserve the strokes they give.

Implicit obedience—and that without question, expostulation, or delay—is the keystone of the family arch. This is perfectly consistent with the utmost affection, and should be enforced from the beginning, and absolutely. The philosopher whom I cited above says of parental authority: "I would have it *early* that it may be *absolute*, and absolute that it may not be *severe*. It holds universally in families and schools, and even the greater bodies of men, the army and navy, that those who keep the strictest discipline give the fewest strokes." Some parents seem to imagine that their failures in this kind arise from the want of a certain mysterious *knack*, of which they conceive themselves to be destitute. There is such a knack; but it is as much within reach as the knack of driving a horse and chaise, or handling a knife and fork, and will never be got by yawning over it.

Not only love your children, but show that you love

them; not by merely fondling and kissing them, but by being always open to their approaches. Here is a man who drives his children out of his shop, because they pester him; here is another who is always too busy to give them a good word. Now I would gladly learn of these penny-wise and pound-foolish fathers, what work they expect ever to turn out, which shall equal in importance the children who are now taking their mould for life. Hapless is that child which is forced to seek for companions more accessible and winning than its father or its mother.

You may observe that when a working man spends his leisure hours *abroad*, it is at the expense of his family. While he is at the club or the tavern, his boy or girl is seeking out-of-door connexions. The great school of juvenile vice is the STREET. Here the urchin, while he "knuckles down at taw," learns the vulgar oath, or the putrid obscenity. For one lesson at the fireside, he has a dozen in the kennel. Here are scattered the seeds of falsehood, gambling, theft and violence. I pray you, as you love your own flesh and blood, make your children cling to the hearthstone. Love home yourself; sink your roots deeply among your domestic treasures; set an example in this as in all things, which your offspring may follow. The garden-plant seems to have accomplished its great work, and is content to wither, when it has matured the fruit for the next race: learn a lesson from the plant.

DOCUMENT 10

Mother

All that was matriarchal in the American home could be summed up in the lyric by the Reverend George Washington Bethune (1805–62), "To My Mother." It was printed among his *Lays of Love and Faith* (1848). His father, a vague figure, appears briefly in the poem; but the poet's mother is now a widow and so, to an almost morbid extent, he focuses all his filial love on her. The lyric is a classic example of the cliché, though it can be argued in Bethune's defense that even as early as 1848 nothing new could be said about the child-bearing American female. It may be interesting to note the differences between the "Mother" of Bethune's poem and today's "Mom."

SOURCE: George W. Bethune, *Lays of Love and Faith, with Other Fugitive Poems* (Philadelphia, 1848), pp. 16–19.

To My Mother

My mother! Manhood's anxious brow
    And sterner cares have long been mine;
Yet turn I fondly to thee now,
    As when upon thy bosom's shrine
My infant griefs were gently hushed to rest,
And thy low-whispered prayers my slumbers blest.

I never call that gentle name,
    My mother! but I am again
E'en as a child; the very same
    That prattled at thy knee; and fain

Would I forget, in momentary joy,
That I no more can be thy happy boy;

Thine artless boy, to whom thy smile
    Was sunshine, and thy frown sad night;
(Though rare that frown, and brief the while
    It veiled from me thy loving light;)
For well-conned task, ambition's highest bliss
To win from thy approving lips a kiss.

I've lived through foreign lands to roam,
    And gazed on many a classic scene;
But oft the thought of that dear home,
    Which once was ours, would intervene,
And bid me close again my languid eye,
To think of thee, and those sweet days gone by.

That pleasant home of fruits and flowers,
    Where by the Hudson's verdant side,
My sisters wove their jasmine bowers,
    And *he* we loved, at eventide
Would hastening come, from distant toil to bless
Thine and his children's radiant happiness!

Those scenes are fled; the rattling car
    O'er flint-paved streets profanes the spot,
Where in the sod we sowed the "Star
    Of Bethlehem" and "Forget-me-not;"
Oh! Wo to Mammon's desolating reign,
We ne'er shall find on earth a home again!

I've pored o'er many a yellow page
    Of ancient wisdom, and have won,
Perchance, a scholar's name; yet sage
    Or poet ne'er have taught thy son
Lessons so pure, so fraught with holy truth,
As those his mother's faith shed o'er his youth.

If e'er through grace my God shall own
    The offerings of my life and love,

Methinks, when bending close before his throne,
 Amid the ransomed hosts above,
Thy name on my rejoicing lips shall be,
And I will bless that grace for heaven and thee!

For thee and heaven; for thou didst tread
 The way that leads to that blest land;
My often wayward footsteps led,
 By thy kind words and patient hand;
And when I wandered far, thy faithful call
Restored my soul from sin's deceitful thrall.

I have been blest with other ties,
 Fond ties and true, yet never deem
That I the less thy fondness prize.
 No, mother! in the warmest dream
Of answered passion, through this heart of mine,
One chord will vibrate to no name but thine!

Mother! thy name is widow; well
 I know no love of mine can fill
The waste place of thy heart, nor dwell
 Within one sacred recess; still,
Lean on the faithful bosom of thy son,
My parent! thou art more—my *only* one!

DOCUMENT 11

(PLATES 6–10)

House and Home

The American home was so important—it was the central social institution of the 1840s—that it needs to be seen from a variety of points of view. We can see it, above all, as the relation between husband and wife and between parents and children; this is the main thing we have done in the printed selections. We can shift the focus a little, as we do in our first two pictures, "Married" and "The Bridal Prayer," and see something more about domestic mores. We can see marriage and the family idealized and prettified, and we can also see it in terms of female apprehensions. Shifting again, we can see in the next picture, "Maternal Instruction," home as the educator. Shifting once more, we can see the home in its physical setting and representation: home as the house. The house we live in is almost as much a manifestation of our taste as the clothing we wear. Consequently, by looking at the setting of the American domestic drama we can better understand its characters.

The first two pictures, mentioned before, allow us to infer the taste of the time but the fourth picture, "View of a Common Country House," is brilliantly explicit. There is no better index to the changes in taste than its "before and after" rendition of an American residence. It shows a once simple house now thoroughly befrilled. To us today the change is for the worse, yet we too can imagine a future time when a fancy front for a house will look better to us than a plain one. The fifth picture, a drawing of a light fixture, represents the furthest flight of American taste in the 1840s. A bird, a snake, and a trio of bare-breasted nymphs combine to make up a work of high "camp." Only an expanding society could sanction such a florid design. As a matter of fact, it points ahead to the lushness of the Gilded Age.

PLATE 6. *Married*. Signed by Sarony; lithographed and issued by Sarony & Major, about 1848.

SOURCE: The Smithsonian Institution.

Here we have both house and home, the family and its setting. "Married" gives us a vivid picture of middle-class domestic ideals and taste. The ideals were of course changing much less rapidly than the taste. The conception of the ideal family remained the same for most of the nineteenth century, while the conception of the ideal house went through a minor revolution. To take the house first, we see in it the results of considerable change. It is now, if we can judge the whole by the part, adorned throughout. But this was not always true. In the earlier, less affluent days of the Republic a house was much more nearly a machine for living. It stood relatively bare. It appeared plain and functional. By the 1840s, however, the American house was becoming elaborately decorated, inside and out. The interior we glimpse in "Married" is a good example. Keeping in mind that lithographs and magazine illustrations are apt to show the ideal rather than the real, we can nevertheless notice the new taste everywhere. The sofa is richly upholstered, intricately carved, and embellished with fringe as is the footstool. The wallpaper, the picture frames, and the carpet are all ornate. The setting is appropriate for the stylishly dressed family we see.

The family is presented in its most appealing form. Of all domestic pictures the most popular was that of the attractive young parents with their little children. In "Married" the idealized couple has lost nothing of the smooth look of youth. Both adult faces are flawless, finely featured. The children are pretty, except for the baby, which looks like a badly made doll. Only in one respect does "Married" fail to represent the pattern. Here the husband is looking at the wife. Usually she gazes in veneration at him.

PLATE 7. *The Bridal Prayer*. Designed by T. H. Mateson and engraved by T. Doney.

SOURCE: *Columbian Magazine*, VI (July 1846), frontispiece. Library of Congress.

The setting for the tableau of "The Bridal Prayer" is typically elaborate. We see more of the heavily furnished American home. But the main interest naturally lies in the figures and what they say to us. In the previous picture "Married" we have seen the official, the ideal, view of the marital relation. All is serenity and fulfillment. The implications of "The Bridal Prayer" go deeper. The bride is solemn, as would be expected; for marriage in the 1840s was emphatically a sacrament. However, it is the anxious mother who is the revealing figure here. She represents the apprehensions about marriage, the feminine helplessness in it, the many burdens sure to fall on the wife. Her face, as she regards the daughter about to leave her, is a troubled testimony to all those things in matrimony that go unsaid in "Married."

Though the foundations of marriage were firmer a century ago, the ties more binding for both sexes, the man still had an advantage. It was much greater than it is now. Law and custom combined to keep his wife a subordinate. A woman had few if any satisfactory alternatives to marriage. She could seldom have a career, as she can now. If her marriage turned out badly she had little help from the courts; the proportion of divorces granted to women in the 1840s compared to the proportion today is minute. The social and religious sanctions for marriage were as strong as the legal ones. Like the prohibitions against divorce and female rebellion, their effect could be seen everywhere. The sanctions can best be epitomized in the church wedding. It is often pictured in the prints and periodicals of this time.

Certainly we should not exaggerate the low status of women. The sanctions and prohibitions applied to husband as well as wife. And the wife often had resources which gave her some advantage in daily life. Yet the fact of the "double standard" remained. It was a man's world and in the American home the husband stood first. No wonder the mother in "The Bridal Prayer" looks anxious.

PLATE 8. *Maternal Instruction.* Painted by J. C. Timbrell and engraved by J. Bannister.

SOURCE: *Godey's Lady's Book,* XXX (March 1845), opposite p. 108. Library of Congress.

One of the family's prime functions in the 1840s, far more than it is now, was to educate the young. The public schools were primitive, despite some imposing exceptions, compared to the schools of today. Especially in the country and on the frontier they stayed open only a few months of the year; their facilities were scant; and their teachers ill-prepared. The great gap was filled by the fact that the home too was a schoolhouse. Everywhere it supplemented the efforts of the classroom. Nowadays we expect the school to do more and more of the work of the home; in those days the reverse was true. The mother in the frontier cabin taught her children the rudiments of reading, writing, and arithmetic; the mother in the merchant's house went beyond that and perhaps brought in a tutor or two as well. The point was that a good deal of the education of the 1840s began at home.

In "Maternal Instruction" the mother is helping her little girl learn the alphabet. The page of the primer is open apparently to D for dog, and the mother holds her ivory crochet hook over the letter while the little girl tries to recognize it. Her sister watches with a look of mild interest. The setting once again is heavily Victorian, with the hangings and carving we associate with the time. The composition itself shows the hand of the experienced artist. The triangular arrangement of the figures is attractive. The alternation of light and shade complements the figure arrangement. The light tones of the mother contrast with the darker tones of the furniture and wall, while the darker figures of the two children are set against the lightness of the window and the window casing. The result is a rhythm for the eye that is regular, self-contained, and satisfying.

PLATE 9. *View of a Common Country House* and *View of the Same, Improved*. Artist and engraver unknown.

SOURCE: *Horticulturist*, I (July 1846), opposite p. 13. Smithsonian Institution.

The family was related to the house it lived in. In an important sense "making a home" meant building and furnishing one. Doing that gave a clue, often, to the major shift in American taste, the shift from plain to fancy. Two things were required to affect the change: the inclination to bring it about and the ability to do it. By the 1840s the ability was there. The American economy was booming. The boom would not end till the Panic of 1857 and would start again promptly after the Civil War. Consequently, so far as houses were concerned, those who wanted them with frills could have them. The reasons why they wanted them are hard to define but the chief one seems to have been the example of British taste. America still looked across the ocean for advice and example, and British culture remained the model. A combination of Romantic and Gothic modes of fashion, which we generally for convenience call "Victorian," dominated the British Isles. For the 1840s the strongest evidences of this influence could be detected in the great popularity of Sir Walter Scott's novels; in the magazine art, which often showed knights, castles, and much arras, as well as more modern and lavish English interiors; and in the rich elaboration of female clothing. Different from one another though these manifestations were, they all revealed the fashionable and fancy as opposed to the old-fashioned and plain.

The most striking single example of the change can be seen in a pair of pictures from a magazine called the *Horticulturist*, whose editor was a leading tastemaker of his time, Andrew Jackson Downing. In "View of a Common Country House" we see a simple, pleasantly symmetrical dwelling. In "View of the Same, Improved" the difference is dramatic. The small porch, with its unpretentious classical pediment, has been replaced by a complicated construction which runs across the whole front of the house. Labels and diamond lights have been added to the previously plain windows. And the roof has been transformed by adding fancy chimney stacks, scrollwork bargeboards, and an entire front gable.

PLATE 10. *Design for a Candelabra.* Drawn by J. A. Dallas.

SOURCE: *Illustrated Monthly Courier,* I (December 1848), 92. Library of Congress.

Within as well as without the house, the shift in taste showed itself. Furniture, furnishings, and decorations all grew rather flamboyant. The extremes of domestic taste are best seen, for that time as for this, in the pages of certain of the magazines. These were not the most noted ones, such as *Godey's*, nor those with the most sophisticated editors, such as the *Horticulturist* with its Andrew Jackson Downing. They were the fugitive periodicals, for example the *Illustrated Monthly Courier*. During its brief life it printed several designs almost as extreme as the one we have for the candelabra. But the candelabra is the most noteworthy. Except where it abuts against the wall it has nothing but rich curves and curlicues. The eagle, the orb, the serpent, and the shell all serve to support three Nilotic nymphs who in turn uphold the beaded lamps. This design, though drawn in the 1840s, points to the future, to the lusher and more garish period after the Civil War. Some of the artifacts we are interested in remind us of the past, that is of a period prior to the 1840s; here is one that speaks for the time to come.

PLATES 1 THROUGH 19

PLATE 1. *A View of the Nursery on the Farm of the Late Judge Buel.* Engraved by G. L. Brown. From *American Magazine,* I (November 1841), frontispiece. Courtesy of the Library of Congress.

PLATE 2. *Rural Life.* Painted by G. Morland and engraved by J. Bannister. From *Graham's Magazine*, XXXI (November 1847), 241. Courtesy of the Library of Congress.

ROCK MANUFACTURING CO'S WOOLEN MILLS, ROCKVILLE, C
Established 1821.

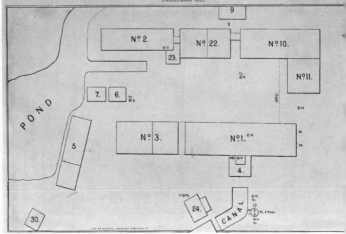

PLATE 3. *Rock Manufacturing Co's Woolen Mills, Rockville, Ct. Lith*ograph issued by Kellogg & Bulkeley, n.d. Courtesy of the Harry T Peters "America on Stone" Lithography Collection, the Smithsonia Institution.

PLATE 4. The Custom House, Wall Street. Lithograph by Robert Kerr, 1845. Courtesy of the Library of Congress.

PLATE 5. *New Suspension Bridge at Fairmount.* Drawn by W. Croome and engraved by Rawdon, Wright, Hatch & Smillie. From *Graham's Magazine*, XX (June 1842), frontispiece. Courtesy of the Library of Congress.

PLATE 6. *Married*. Signed by Sarony; lithographed and issued by Sarony & Major, about 1848. Courtesy of the Smithsonian Institution.

PLATE 7. *The Bridal Prayer.* Designed by T. H. Mateson and engraved by T. Doney. From *Columbian Magazine*, VI (July 1846), frontispiece. Courtesy of the Library of Congress.

PLATE 8. *Maternal Instruction*. Painted by J. C. Timbrell and engraved by J. Bannister. From *Godey's Lady's Book*, XXX (March 1845), opposite p. 108. Courtesy of the Library of Congress.

PLATE 9. *View of a Common Country House and View of the Same, Improved.* Artist and engraver unknown. From *Horticulturist*, I (July 1846), opposite p. 13. Courtesy of the Smithsonian Institution.

PLATE 10. *Design for a Candelabra*. Drawn by J. A. Dallas. From *Illustrated Monthly Courier*, I (December 1848), 92. Courtesy of the Library of Congress.

PLATE 11. Poughkeepsie Female Academy. Engraving by Dossing(?). From *American Magazine*, II (February 1842), 56. Courtesy of the Library of Congress.

PLATE 12. *The Philosopher & His Kite*. Designed by J. L. Morton and engraved by H. S. Sadd. From *Columbian Magazine*, III (February 1845), frontispiece. Courtesy of the Library of Congress.

SCIENTIFIC AMERICAN.

CYLINDER PRINTING PRESS.

The above engraving represents one of R. Hoe & Co.'s double cylinder printing presses. They are capable of throwing off from four to five thousand impressions per hour. The types are placed on a solid, cast iron plate, or bed, of which the motion is horizontal and reciprocating. The sheets of paper belonging in the proper position, are caught by means of small cast iron fingers which are attached to and revolve with the cylinder, and are thus drawn around just as the types move past, whereby an impression is given. At the instant the paper receives the impression the fountain the paper; receives the impression the fun-

CHEMISTRY.

Continued from No. 10.

AIR AND WATER.

Air.—By the examinations of modern chemists, it has been shown that air is not an element, but is a compound body, consisting chiefly of two gases, oxygen and nitrogen. Strong

doing has combined with an equivalent proportion of that substance, the quantity of which is thus indicated. The presence of watery vapor in the air may be demonstrated by exposing chloride of calcium, or caustic potash. It absorbs the moisture, melts, and is found to have increased in weight.

in chemical, distillation and other processes are requisite to produce a pure liquid. In nature water is never altogether pure. When it contains a chemical compound of lime, it is said to be hard, and in this condition it decomposes the soap which is employed with it.

(To be continued.)

striking, flies out at the ends of the press, and is laid upon a table. Printing by steam is an operation of much curiosity, and should be seen by all visiting the city.

Importance of Ventilation.

It is estimated that an assembly of five hundred people give off, in the course of two hours, fifteen gallons of water into the air. In a close hall or church, much of this moisture is breathed over and over, and the raiment of the congregation, as well as the walls and ceil

---

PLATE 13. Cylinder Printing Press. Artist and engraver unknown. From *Scientific American*, II (December 1846), 86. Courtesy of the Smithsonian Institution.

PLATE 14. *Faust and Margaret.* Drawn (?) by Abraham Woodside. From *Illustrated Monthly Courier*, I (October 1848), 61. Courtesy of the Library of Congress.

PLATE 15. *Spring-Time.* Designed by T. H. Matteson and engraved by M. Osborne. From *Union Magazine,* II (May 1848), opposite p. 229. Courtesy of the Library of Congress.

PLATE 16. *Search the Scriptures*. Issued by N. Currier, n.d. Courtesy of the Library of Congress.

PLATE 17. *Our Father*. Designed and executed by Rice & Pratt. Issued by Sarony & Major, 1847. Courtesy of the Library of Congress.

PLATE 18. *The Floating Chapel of the Holy Comforter.* Drawn by J. F. Badeau and engraved by J.H.G. From *Holden's Dollar Magazine*, IV (October 1849), frontispiece. Courtesy of the Library of Congress.

PLATE 19. *Indiana Yearly Meeting of Friends* 1844. Drawn by Mote. Issued by John Pease and Jer. Hubbard. Courtesy of the Harry T. Peters "America on Stone" Lithography Collection, the Smithsonian

PART III

The World of Knowledge

The School Bell

For most Americans, learning meant school; and the emblem of the school in the mind of the 1840s was the one-room schoolhouse and its versatile teacher. This little village school actually existed during the 1840s in greater numbers than did any other kind. Its fabric ranged from rickety to firm; its teacher could be anything from an incompetent to an inspiration. In the towns and cities the typical school was larger and generally better. The school bell also rang in the home: for very young children everywhere and for children of all ages on the frontier, the home was an educator. The picture we saw in the previous section of the mother teaching her child reflected a frequent reality. However, the public school whether large or small was the major means for education. The private academy and the church school were by no means negligible, particularly when they helped to educate an elite, but they were not the mainstream. The census figures for 1840 show this dramatically: there were 3248 academies and grammar schools and 47,207 primary schools.

It was already a staple of the American creed that the public schools were vital to the working of the Republic. The platform pronouncements, the lyceum lectures, and the orations to this effect were innumerable. Some of them were mere gesture but there were so many in all that they indicate an American attitude. Democratic education was improving, and thoughtful foreign visitors were impressed. Yet it had a long way to go. Not only was education in the country as a whole less good than it should have been; it was much worse in some parts of the country than others. The variation was in fact formidable. New England's proportion of children in

school was nearly twice that of the Middle Atlantic
states and six times that of the states in the South. Even
in the affluent states improvement came slowly. In 1830
a Pennsylvania society for better schools reported bitterly
that out of 400,000 children in the state, less than
150,000 were being schooled; by 1840 the situation was
not greatly improved.

To obtain one of the best insights into what conditions
were and how they could be improved we can go to a
book by Thomas H. Palmer (1782–1861). It appeared,
it happened, as the result of a contest. The American
Institute of Instruction, one of the most notable educational societies of the time, offered a prize in 1838 for
the outstanding essay on good schools. The prize was
won by Palmer, who was a Scottish-born reformer and
educationalist. His ample essay appeared in book form
as *The Teacher's Manual* in 1840. The ideal he advo-
cated was democratic education, the best schooling for
all the people. To achieve it some housecleaning, he
thought, was in order. The most important thing was
to get and keep better teachers. He found many a teacher
to be a careless, clumsy amateur. The ultimate fault was
not the school's, however, but the community's. It made
education a stepchild. Better salaries—and better treatment—would mean better teachers; and better teaching
was the key. If we had it, then the basic subjects, now
indifferently taught, would come alive. Learning to
read, now so often merely a mechanical process, would
grow interesting. And reading was vital to education,
Palmer emphasized: Johnny had to be able to read.

Palmer's manual attracted wide attention; it clearly
helped the schools. The portions of the manual reprinted
here come from the chapters headed "Intellectual Education" (as distinguished from physical and moral education). They deal first with the professionalization of
teachers and then, in more detail, with the improvement
of instruction in the basic subjects.

SOURCE: Thomas H. Palmer, *The Teacher's Manual; Being an Exposition of an Efficient and Economical System of Education* (Boston, 1840), pp. 25–36.

Intellectual Education

Under the head of *Intellectual Education*, the most prominent object, the one, indeed, on which all the others depend, is that of the *qualification of teachers*. Without good teachers, it is vain to look for good schools. And how can we have good teachers, unless they have encouragement, properly to prepare themselves for their arduous and responsible task. In every profession, but that of teacher, employment can be had during the whole year; or, if there be a season when business is regularly at a stand, the emoluments are proportionally greater; or, matters are so arranged, that one kind of occupation can be pursued at one season, and another for the rest of the year, as in the case of the tanner and shoemaker. In this profession, alone, except in the cities and large villages, no one can gain even a scanty subsistence. For the plan universally practised, of alternating male schools, in Winter, and female, in Summer, renders it impossible for a teacher to gain a living, unless the wages should, at the very least, be doubled. With respect to male teachers, this is comparatively of less importance; as the college vacations are purposely arranged, so as to allow the students to attend to the Winter schools. But the female teachers are thrown out of employment precisely at that season, when it is most difficult to procure any other. The unavoidable consequence, then, of this alternating system, is, that there is literally no such profession as that of a female teacher. The whole business is conducted by raw apprentices, in place of experienced workmen,—young girls, just grown up, who adopt it, not with any view of obtaining thereby a subsistence, but merely for some temporary purpose. One, for example, wishes to complete her education at a distant boarding-school; a second wants some article of dress, too costly for her parents to furnish; a third is anxious to procure some musical instrument; a fourth wishes to avoid the necessity of attending to her father's dairy. For objects such as these, school-keeping, *for a few months*, is the universal resource. And this is almost the sole dependence of the whole country, for female teachers. But what can be expected from inexperienced, young girls, who engage in teaching with views like these? Is it not rather surprising, that they effect so much as they do?

Nor is this the sole evil attending the alternating system. It does not merely exclude from the profession all who have not *other* means of maintaining themselves; but, independently of this, it is a ruinous system. For, when a teacher opens a school, she is, of course, totally ignorant of the habits, manners, and capacity, of her pupils; and they understand as little of her methods of tuition and discipline. Some time will elapse, before the school *can* work smoothly, before both parties thoroughly understand each other. Should she prove unequal to the task, her engagement will still generally be completed; for, as her incompetency, probably, is not discovered, before the expiration of half her term, most parents will rather submit to the inconvenience a little longer, than give rise to contention in the district, by insisting on a change. It is a common saying, "Her engagement will soon be over. We shall soon have a better teacher." Vain expectation! How can we expect a better, when we have only raw, inexperienced, young girls to choose from?

But, even supposing the school to be satisfactory, a considerable part of each term must be lost in organizing, and getting to understand each other; and, before much progress can be made, the term is at an end, and the good teacher must give way to another, differing, probably, in habits, disposition, and methods of tuition, and, of course, as before, profoundly ignorant of the pupils. Would it be possible, for the best trained teachers, with the best system of tuition, to effect much good, under such an arrangement?

It appears evident, then, if we really intend our children to receive a good education, that this alternating system must be abandoned, and that *female* teachers, at least, must have permanent schools. Seminaries for teachers, alone, can never effect the object. We must be able to show, that a *maintenance can* certainly be derived from the profession, before we can expect any properly to prepare for it, and before females in middle life, however well prepared, *can* look towards it as a means of support. When we have done this, many years will not elapse, before we shall have a large body of competent teachers.

Let the office be established, and a sufficiency of incumbents will not long be wanting. A substitute for this alternating system, more economical, as well as more efficient, will be found in its proper place.

Seminaries for teachers have been established in various parts of the country, sometimes as independent schools, at others, as branches of academies or colleges; but, as yet, the beneficial results have been trifling. The proper object of these institutions, it is to be feared, has been too frequently lost sight of. The plan has commonly been, to *extend* the knowledge of the students to the *higher* branches of learning, rather than to instruct them in the *art of teaching*, more especially the *art of teaching the elements* of school learning,—reading and arithmetic. To render a seminary for teachers really useful, the instructer must go back to numeration and the A, B, C, for it is *here* that the great deficiency lies.

The practical part, also, is wanted in these seminaries. Theory, alone, is not sufficient. A school of children, of from five to ten years of age, attached to such institutions, is altogether indispensable. Here, also, the capacity of children of different ages must be studied, and the teachers must make themselves familiarly acquainted with the extent of their vocabularies. For want of this knowledge, the most serious yet ridiculous blunders are committed.

In a late visit to Philadelphia, I was invited to attend a lecture from a teacher of some eminence in that city, before the pupils of the public schools. At the appointed hour, I found the directors of the schools assembled, and two or three hundred children of both sexes, apparently between the ages of six and ten. The speaker, shortly after, took his place, and, to my great surprise and disappointment, delivered a well-written lecture, which lasted about three quarters of an hour, on the *extent and importance* of the *exact sciences!!* At the commencement of the discourse, the eyes of the little auditors were fastened on the speaker with an expression of eager expectation and delight. But alas! it would not do. To them, the language and subject were alike "heathen Greek;" and soon, very soon, the attempt to follow the lecturer had to be abandoned in despair. Eager expectation was succeeded by listlessness and fatigue, and a most wearisome sitting had the poor little souls to endure.

The effect of such misplaced lectures, as these, cannot fail to be highly injurious to their auditors. They blunt the intellectual perceptions, give rise to habits of dreamy wandering of mind, and are destructive of the valuable faculties of observation and attention, without which, all attempts to confer a good education are futile. It may be said, that this is an extreme case; and it is to be hoped that it is so; but still, there can be no doubt, that there exists among teachers, a deplorable ignorance, (or, which amounts to the same thing, carelessness,) as to the extent of the vocabulary and capacity of their auditors: a remark, by the way, applicable to others, besides *school* teachers. This is a subject well worthy the attention of visiters and superintendents of Teacher's Seminaries.

Discipline is a subject of the first importance in schools. Without subordination and good government, no school can make any considerable progress. The principal errors, on this head, may be thus enumerated:

1. Discipline may be too lax, and the efficiency of the school destroyed by noise and confusion. Efforts are oc-

casionally made to restrain disorder, but these are momentary only, and affairs quickly relapse into their usual state.

2. Discipline may be so strict, as, without intervals of relief at regular short intervals, may prove alike hurtful to the physical and mental powers of the pupil. The necessity for relaxation and exercise has been so fully shown, as to make it unnecessary, here, to add another word. But, although unreasonable confinement defeats its object, that is no objection to good discipline. Let it be brief in its period, and it cannot be too strict in degree.

3. A still more grievous error, and by far the most common, is a want of firmness. The rules are strict, but they are seldom carried into effect; and, when they are, relaxation immediately follows. We have been told of a teacher, who frequently relaxed discipline to such a degree, that the whole school was in an uproar. Awakened thus from his stupor, he would seize his cane, and belabor all round, till order was completely restored. This state of quiet, however, would last but a short time. The universal silence would soon be broken by a low whispering, which, remaining unnoticed, gradually increased in intensity, ending, finally, in loud talk, laughter, and jumping across the benches, which, of course, brought about the same round of general whipping, universal silence, &c. This picture is probably highly exaggerated; but there are few, who have not seen schools managed, more or less, on the same principles.

4. Some teachers resort to the rod, even on the most trifling occasion. It is always in their hands, and seldom long unemployed. Thus, both master and scholar are brutified and debased, the law of love becomes extinct in their bosoms, and nothing can produce the slightest effect on the pupil, but pure force.

5. Others have so little command of their temper, as to indulge in habitual scolding. They speak harshly to the pupils for the merest trifle, the natural consequence of which is, that their reproofs lose all their effect. Such a

course operates injuriously on the temper, both of teacher and pupil. Fretfulness and irritability pervade the whole school.

6. The moral sense of the pupil is seldom, if ever, appealed to. Every regulation is grounded on mere authority; no attempt being made to show, that nearly all the benefits, flowing from good discipline, result to the individual advantage of the pupil. So far is this occasionally lost sight of, that, sometimes, the children will learn to regard themselves and teacher as opposites to each other; as having two distinct interests; it being their master's object to lay on restrictions, and abridge their liberty, while it is their business, by all sorts of means, combination among themselves, concealment, trick, falsehood, or open disobedience, to baffle his watchfulness, and evade his severity.

7. Finally, there are some teachers, whose manners and habits are essentially vulgar. These will pinch the ears, and pull the hair of their pupils; or, still worse, beat them about the head with a book, a cane, or whatever happens to be in the hand. Such punishments as these are altogether wrong. They are dangerous; and seldom fail to excite resentment in place of contrition, the main legitimate object of punishment.

Is there, then, nothing good in our system of public instruction? Is it, throughout, a mass of blunders? By no means. It contains much that is good, though, as has been seen, there is mingled with it much that is evil. But, as the present question is, how shall it be *purified* of its errors, and rendered as efficient as possible, it would be altogether out of place to speak, here, of its advantages, or its beauties. Let us continue, then, our searching inquiry into its errors and deficiencies, so that, when we come to prepare our improved system, we may know how to avoid every thing that may have the slightest tendency to impede our progress, or, in any manner, lessen its efficiency.

Although many of the remarks, which follow, will be applicable to the higher branches of learning, yet our chief attention will be devoted, at present, to the initiatory steps. The proper management of these is of the very first importance, and, unfortunately, this is the very part of education that has attracted least attention. The teaching of reading, spelling, and the alphabet, has been considered a task that any one might execute. We forget, that to this point can be traced nearly all our bad habits, habits which exert so prejudicial an effect on the whole future course of study, and which no after discipline can completely remove. Let us, then, in future, avoid this serious error. Let us no longer consider it as unworthy of our attention; nor turn, with an eye of indifference, from the basis of knowledge, fully convinced, that on the solidity of the foundation, depends all the beauty and usefulness of the structure.

The first branch of knowledge, to which the attention of the child is directed on entering school, is *Reading*. Hitherto his studies have been altogether delightful. His progress has been constant and rapid; for, as yet, he has dealt with nothing but real knowledge. No barren sounds, no unintelligible words have occurred, to embarrass and impede him. But now, very different becomes his situation. A *book* is placed in his hands, which he is told he must learn to *read*, that he may know how to become wise and good, and he is delighted with the prospect. But, alas! how grievous the disappointment! For months, nay, sometimes for years, his studies consist of nothing but mere *sounds*, to which it is impossible he can annex any idea whatever. His school-hours are solely occupied with As and Bs, abs, ebs, and ibs. Now, what must be the effect of all this, upon an intelligent child? Surely, it is sufficiently evident, that his active mind cannot be exclusively employed in such tiresome drudgery. For this is nothing but a mere affair of memory, in which the reason and judgment of the child is never called into action. The natural, the unavoidable, result of such a process is, that he acquires a habit of mechanically repeating those sounds, while his mind is occupied with objects of a totally different nature. He can repeat his A, B, C, his ab, eb, ib, &c.; and, all the while, his mind can be far distant, at play with his schoolmates, or at the family fireside. And thus, at the very outset, the child lays the foundation of the grand impediment to the easy attainment of knowledge, the impassable barrier to self-education,—the habit of mental wandering.

This plan of education is the synthetic method, which, commencing with elements, joins them to form compounds, and, again compounding those, forms them into the substances with which we are acquainted. Thus, should we be taught mineralogy according to this system, we should first have to learn the names of all the elements of which stones were composed, and then, by joining them in the proper proportions, we should form stones. But such is not the method in which we are instructed by Nature. It is, in fact, doubtful, whether we are acquainted with any elementary substance. It is true, our chemical works give us a list of some fifty or more substances, which are *called* elements; but it is doubtful, whether any one of them really is so. They should be considered only as *elements, according to the present state of knowledge*. Future discoveries will probably reduce the number, or totally change the whole list. But to return. Nature's mode of teaching is altogether *analytic*. She first presents us with a group, forming a perfect whole, and then instructs us how to *analyse* it, or divide it into its component parts. For instance: a child knows a *tree*, and can name it, long before he has ever heard or thought of leaves, twigs, branches, trunk, or root; a *house*, before he has become acquainted with shingles, boards, brick, stone, or lime; a *man*, before head, limbs, neck, or body. At a more advanced period of his education, he extends his knowledge by new analyses. For instance: he examines into the nature of leaves &c., of trees; of stones and lime, which enter into the formation of a house; of flesh and bones, which form the man. Were he to wait till he knew the A, B, C of Nature, before he made himself acquainted with the objects around him, he would never know them at all. Let not the above remarks be understood as objecting to the inductive method of philosophizing. Science can have no sure foundation, save on observation, experiment, and induction. But it by no means follows, that the *knowledge of reading* must be acquired by the same method, especially by young children, whose reasoning faculties are as yet undeveloped. Besides, it will be found, that even the sciences are *taught*, chiefly, by analysis. It is in the *cultivation* of science by the philosopher, not in its *communication* by the teacher, that induction is indispensable.

Having thus pointed out the serious evil, arising from the synthetic mode of teaching reading, namely, the habit of mental wandering, or thinking of one thing while reading another; having shown, also, that Nature, in *her* teachings, follows the opposite course, that of analysis; it would appear, that all that is necessary, to induce every reasonable mind to approve of the change, is, to show its practicability in the present case. This, however, can be correctly ascertained by experiment, only. And, although every teacher can make the experiment for himself, (and it is one which will require but a short time sufficiently to test,) yet it may be satisfactory to know, that every trial, hitherto made, which has come to the knowledge of the writer,—and those are by no means few in number,—have proved eminently successful. He would also state, that he has tested the plan on the younger members of his own family, with similar success. The first subject of these last experiments was a boy between four and five years old, who, in the space of three months, without previous knowledge of either letters or words, simply by receiving a lesson for about five minutes a day, the rest of his time spent in amusement, learnt to read all the lessons in Worcester's Primer in a beautiful style, and, what was still better, intelligently. He would, therefore, urge a similar trial on every parent anxious for the improvement of education, and particularly for the removal of that barrier to self-instruction, the pernicious habit above referred to. A minute description of this method of tuition will appear in its proper place. All that is necessary further to observe here is, that the chief difference between the two methods is in the *order* of the steps. Letters and syllables must be learned in the new as well as in the old method; but, by a change in the time of teaching them, they are acquired with less than half the difficulty, and without any danger of acquiring bad habits, which are so difficult to eradicate.

The reading course, which we have seen commence so inauspiciously, does not generally improve much in its progress. A great deal of time, it must be acknowledged, and much labor, are expended in the endeavor to remedy what should never have been allowed to be formed, viz., bad habits in reading. But all such efforts are commonly vain. The teacher himself rarely reads well; and, when the pupil has acquired the stiff mechanical habits which the synthetic course never fails to generate, the remedy is altogether beyond his reach. Had the child read intelligently, from the first; had none of his time been misspent in reading words without connexion, and consequently, to him, without meaning; it might have been possible, even for a teacher who did not read well himself, to have trained up a school of good readers. For, whatever may be the opinion of those who have bestowed little attention on this subject, good reading is *the natural gift*, bad reading, entirely an artificial acquirement. For almost every child *speaks* naturally and fluently; and, when he knows the words, why should he not *read* in the same style? Simply, because, in the course of learning these words, he has acquired bad habits, habits arising entirely from the practice of attending to sound, unconnected with sense. We all know how completely man is the creature of habits, and how difficult it is to change them, when once formed. How, then, can it be expected of a child, especially when under the charge of a teacher who is ignorant of the cause of the evil, as well as of the means of cure?

But reading well aloud, though a desirable accomplishment for all, and indispensable for a public teacher, who seeks for extensive usefulness, is not so valuable to the whole community, as the power of reading silently with intelligence; and, if the latter had generally been achieved in our schools, we might, perhaps, have been content to spare the former. Unfortunately, however, this is by no means the case. The great improvements in schoolbooks, of late years, have doubtless been productive of much benefit in this respect; and, where the method of questioning, which has been introduced into nearly all, has been thoroughly and steadily followed, the evils arising from the faulty commencement may, with much labor to both teacher and pupils, have finally been overcome. Truly happy would it have been for the community, had this generally been the case; but, unfortunately, too many teachers have not, or rather *fancy* they have not, the *time* necessary for the questioning process: as if it were possible there should not be time for the most important part of education, *reading understandingly*. Surely no other study can compete with it, as to utility. Surely every thing else should give way to this. But it is to be feared, that this neglect does *not* arise from want of time, but rather from an indisposition in the teacher properly to task his own mind. For this is a matter that cannot be attended to mechanically, like most of the other operations of the school. It requires equal attention in teacher and pupil. Had answers been given to the questions, probably the want of time would never have been urged as a reason for their neglect. But answers would have completely nullified the process; the object being, to cause the pupil to exert his thinking powers.

There is one mode of using these questions, however, which is little better than their total neglect. The children are allowed the time, nay, even directed, to *study out* the answers. Where this mode is adopted, we shall never find intelligent reading. The answers are picked out and committed to memory; and then the reading is performed mechanically, without an effort to combine sense with sound. The sole dependence for the recitation is on the memory. It is evident, that, where this method has been adopted, the children, in after life, will not be readers; or that, at all events, their reading will not extend beyond novels or tales.

DOCUMENT 13

Greece and Rome

At the beginning of the educational road stood the village school. At the end stood the college (there were yet no true universities). The village school represented popular, useful education, education for everybody. The college represented education for the few. But the few were an elite and their education was important. Part of it was professional: the training of ministers, doctors, lawyers. Part of it was purely humane and in its essence consisted of an appreciation of the classics of Greece and Rome. Its proponents were chiefly responsible for keeping the oldest traditions of Western culture alive in America. Though these advocates were not many they were often fervent. They felt sure that they occupied the highest ground.

Among those standing bravely on Parnassus were a college president and two professors who spoke out for the classics in *Essays on Ancient Literature and Art* (1843). They were Barnas Sears (1802–80) of the Newton Theological Institution, B. B. Edwards (1802–52) of Andover Theological Seminary, and C. C. Felton (1807–62) of Harvard College. In the languages and literatures of Greece and Rome they saw the greatest wealth of learning man had yet discovered. The danger was, they felt, that its worth might now be underestimated. They did not take the rivalry of science, still struggling under the guise of natural philosophy, very seriously but they realized that they had in American practicality a deadly foe. What good were the classics? What did they profit a profit-seeking man? These were major American questions, the authors knew, and they answered them in part with reasoned arguments, in part with vigorous rhetoric. The introduction to the book, taken here from the 1849 edition, is their manifesto.

It begins by announcing change and progress in the study of the classics in America. This country is paying more attention to the great, timeless teachers of the Western world. Homer remains first in their number, and Sears and his colleagues rise to genuine eloquence in apostrophizing him. The benefits of classical study are both direct and indirect. The direct accrue most to the minister, the doctor, and the lawyer. The indirect accrue to all who strive for them, not the least benefit being the attainment of "completeness of character, both intellectual and moral." Modern foreign languages and literatures have their virtues too, the manifesto concedes. But it is the classics of Greece and Rome that "educate the soul."

SOURCE: Barnas Sears, B. B. Edwards, and C. C. Felton, *Essays on Ancient Literature and Art*, 2d thousand (Boston, 1849), pp. iii–xviii, abridged.

Introduction

In the United States, the question of classical education has often been discussed, and its utility sometimes vehemently denied. In the meantime, the study of the Greek and Roman authors, and the taste for ancient art, have been making constant progress, both in schools and colleges. Many of the choicest works of the classical writers have been carefully and learnedly edited by American scholars. Professor Woolsey's selection of the Attic Trage-dies has been welcomed with applause, both at home and abroad; and his recent edition of the Gorgias of Plato is the best edition of that admirable dialogue, for practical use, that has ever yet appeared. Other works, prepared on similar principles, have been published from time to time; and, at present, the classical course, in several of our colleges, instead of being limited to a volume or two of extracts, embraces a series of entire works in all the leading departments of ancient literature. The mode of studying antiquity has also been materially changed and improved within a few years. History, the arts, the domestic life, the private and public usages, the mythology, and the education of the ancients, have been carefully investigated, and their scattered lights concentrated upon the literary remains of antiquity. Thus classical scholarship in America is beginning to breathe the same spirit which animates it in the old world; it is beginning to be something higher and better than the dry study of words and grammatical forms; it is becoming a liberal and elegant pursuit; a comprehensive appreciation of the greatest works in history, poetry, and the arts, that the genius of man has ever produced.

Amidst the din of practical interests, the rivalries of commerce, and the great enterprises of the age, classical studies are gaining ground in public estimation. It must always be so with the advance of civilization. We must, however, confess with shame, that in American legislative assemblies, where we naturally look to find the highest courtesy of manners and the graces of literature, little proof of advancing culture, of any kind, is given. . . .

But the prospects of American education and refinement are more encouraging, if we turn from public to private life. It is a much more common thing for young men to continue their classical studies beyond the time of the college education, than it has been in former days. The orators and dramatists of Greece and Rome are frequently made the companions of the writers on law and divinity, though classical pursuits are sometimes represented as on the decline all over the world. . . .

But the Greek and Roman classics stand at the beginning and at the source of European culture. Nothing can displace them. Homer is the fountain-head of all European poetry and art. There he stands, venerable with nearly thirty centuries, touching his heroic harp to strains of unsurpassed, nay, unapproachable excellence and grandeur. All the features of a great heroic age,—the chivalry of the classical world,—from which European civilization

dates, and political and domestic order take their rise,—
stand forth in living reality, in his immortal pictures.
There he stands, radiant with the beams of the early Grecian morning, as "jocund day stands tiptoe on the misty
mountain top." Who is to drive him from his station
there? And how, then, is Homer to pass from the memory
and the hearts of men? Impossible. It is not a question to
be decided by a few petty and short-sighted utilitarian
views. Homer's reign is firmly established over the literary
world, and if any nation should ever become so barbarous
as to banish him from their schools, the penalty and dis-
grace would be their own. The language of Homer, as a
picturesque, melodious, and enchanting instrument of
thought, has never been surpassed.

Now these great ancients have been, time out of mind,
the teachers of the civilized world. They form a common
bond, which unites the cultivated minds of all nations and
ages together. He who cuts himself off from the classics,
excludes himself from a world of delightful associations
with the best minds. He fails to become a member of the
great society of scholars; he is an alien from the great community of letters. He may be a learned man; he may have
all the treasures of science at his command; he may speak
the modern languages with facility; but if he have not
imbued his mind with at least a tincture of classical taste,
he will inevitably feel, that a great defect exists in his intellectual culture.

We have said, that the neglect of classical studies
among liberally educated men was less general now than
formerly. And yet these pursuits are too often thrown
aside. Why should they be so? Why is classical study
abandoned at all, at the close of the college course? Are
there good reasons for laying it aside when one leaves the
walls of the university? The apology is substantially this.
It has no immediate connection with practical life. Imperative duty is not to be neglected for an elegant pastime.
The lawyer and the physician must direct their energies
to the business on which their living depends. The client

does not inquire, whether an advocate is conversant with Greek metres, or can write beautiful Latin. A religious society seeks for a good theologian and pastor. They care little for the classical phrase of his discourses. In other words, the members of the learned professions must not diverge to the right hand or to the left. Even if classical learning should be, in some respects, connected with the practical business of life, it is not so regarded by the mass of the people. The lawyer, who is known to possess a fine classical taste, is less popular, other things being equal, than his neighbor, who is a lawyer, and nothing else. If he would be much sought after by clients, he must not read Homer, unless by stealth.

This method of reasoning, however, does not seem to accord with facts. Some of the most successful men in all the professions have been accomplished classical scholars, pursuing the study of the ancient languages in the midst of exhausting labors. . . .

Reliance, however, in a question of this kind, need not be placed exclusively on special cases. It may be supported by satisfactory arguments, at least in relation to the clerical profession. A book written in Hebrew and Greek is their Magna Charta, their authoritative commission. Resort to translations is as obviously improper, as it would be for a constitutional lawyer to gain his knowledge of the political institutions of the State at second hand. A mastery of the original languages of the Bible was, probably, never attained by any one, who was not familiar with classical Greek. The main element of the New Testament is the later Attic dialect, as modified by the intermingling of words from other languages. Even authors of the highest name, in regard to style, like Xenophon and Pindar, throw much valuable light on the Scriptures. Homer and Herodotus remind the reader, in a thousand places, of the sweet simplicity and childlike artlessness which delight us in the narratives of the Pentateuch. Philo and Josephus are among the best helps for the interpretation of parts of the Bible. A large portion of the standard commentaries on the Scriptures, from the time of Jerome down, have been written in Latin.

The direct benefits of classical study to the medical and legal student may not be so obvious. The arguments which the lawyer employs, and the observations which direct the physician's practice, are more or less of recent origin. Still, medical science first struck its roots into Grecian soil. The fathers of the healing art wrote in the Greek language. The distinguished physician, Boerhaave, who was well acquainted with Latin and Greek before he was eleven years old, was forcibly struck, in the course of his subsequent reading, with the correct method and sterling sense of Hippocrates. An eminent American physician has said, that the best descriptions of the symptoms of disease are found in the Greek language. Roman law is the parent and germ of every code which has been formed since. No sovereign, not even Napoleon himself, has done so much for the science of law, as the Greek emperor Justinian. No language contains so many of the sources of scientific legislation as the Latin. It is a treasury of facts and principles down to our day.

It may be urged, indeed, that there is no necessity for repairing to the original fountain. All that is valuable in the treatises of Hippocrates, or in the rescripts of Justinian, are readily accessible in the modern languages. Why compel the student to ascend to the little spring hidden under the moss of an old language, when he can drink of a river that flows fast by his own door, and which has been increased by a thousand fresh fountains? A sufficient answer is, that we cannot understand a subject with certainty, if we do not trace it to its source. By the radical study of any topic, we come to feel an assurance of belief, which is one of the best elements of success, because it imparts to the mind a firm confidence in its own powers. It is said, that there are, in the writings of Hippocrates, some of the finest descriptions of the natural course of disease, disturbed neither by medicine nor violent interference. Now these characteristic touches, which are the marks of genius, as well as of an accurate understanding, cannot be enjoyed through a translation. The more picturesque they are, the more need of seeing the very shape and coloring by which they are delineated. So of law and political science. Who has laid the best foundation for statesmanship, the man that has patiently studied Demosthenes, Thucydides, and Polybius, in the original; or he whose knowledge of ancient Greece is made up from Langhorne's Plutarch, and Mitford's jaundiced history? Mere information is not the only thing which is needed. There are now American senators, whose heads are crammed with encyclopedias, but whose great, ponderous speeches have no other effect than to thin the senate chamber. A statesman needs that close, vivid apprehension of a principle or theory, which he can get from Thucydides, but not from Rollin. In the sciences of law and medicine, much is depending on nice discrimination in language, or exact definition; who is so well prepared to make accurate distinctions as he who is versed in the literature of those languages, where the greater number of medical and political terms have their origin?

Still more important are the indirect benefits of classical study. Among these are its effects in securing completeness of character, both intellectual and moral. The powers of the soul are various in their structure, and are developed only by various nourishment. Being a bright image of the perfect Mind that formed it, the soul has susceptibilities for all things beautiful and sublime in nature and in art. The law graven on it is violated whenever its affections are hemmed in upon one dusty track. A man may be so absorbed with the cure of the maladies of the body, or of legislation, that a single faculty of his mind attains an enormous growth, while he has no ear for the music which comes from every part of the visible creation, or those finer strains uttered by every well-attuned human soul.

An illustration of this tendency may be drawn from the clerical profession. A clergyman may limit his studies to

Oriental literature. He may be inordinately fond of the literary treasures of the East. The poetry of the Hebrews is, undoubtedly, loftier than that of any other people. "The sweet singer of Israel" is the child of nature. He opens his imaginative soul to the full impression of the scenes around him. He is fettered by no passion for ideal beauty, by none of the devices of rhyme, metre, or fastidious criticism. His song breaks out in the stately rhythm of nature. All things tend towards the sublime. He looks off from Lebanon, and sees the sun setting on the level bosom of the "great sea, and wide on every hand," without an intervening object. The same luminary, rising on a boundless desert of sand, is one of the grandest objects in nature. The tempest has a terrible commission to execute there. In his ideas of the true God, also, the Hebrew has, immeasurably, the superiority over the Greek and the Roman. By universal consent, the passages which are sublimest in Greek poetry, are those which make the nearest approach to the Hebrew delineations of the Divine attributes.

Yet, on the other hand, in the quality of beauty, the Greek has greatly the advantage. His language is an exact copy of himself, easy, graceful, flexible, fashioned to express the subtlest conceptions, and to charm the most practised ear; cultivated, till, as it should seem, cultivation could proceed no further; copious in its forms, perfect music in its movement. The scenery, too, of Greece, and the natural treasures which it contained, conspired to the same end. "Five hours' walk from the plain of Marathon," says Dr. Wordsworth, "are the marble quarries of Pentelicus, inviting, by its perfect whiteness and splendor, the chisel of Phidias and Praxiteles. On another side of Athens, are the quarries of the snow-white Megarian, and the grey stone of Eleusis, to which Rome was indebted for some of her best buildings." All things tended to make the Greeks a nation of artists. They had the richest materials in overflowing abundance, the kindest sky for the preservation of their works, and an exquisite inward sense for fair proportion and beautiful forms.

Now, have not such things an influence in training the mind of the theological scholar? If he fails to cultivate his original susceptibilities for sweet sounds and delicate thoughts, or, in other words, if he does not repair to the primary sources and true models for instruction, so far will his soul continue unformed and unsightly. If he cannot refresh his weary spirit, or unfold some of his better faculties by classical culture, he should accept it as a severe misfortune.

Is the study of the modern tongues an equivalent? The French language has immense stores of science; the German, of literature. Paris is the centre of medical knowledge; Berlin and Heidelberg, of legal. Still, it may be doubted, whether the best works in any modern language are fitted, in the highest degree, to educate the soul. How different is the impression which is felt in the perusal of what are called the classical works in French and German, from that which is experienced while reading the Tusculan Questions, or the Phaedo? The difference, indeed, is partly owing to association. The latter have the ancient coloring upon them. There are a thousand time-hallowed reminiscences with old Hesiod and Homer. The modern languages remind us of copy-rights, and of the steam power-press. Yet it is not to be wholly ascribed to the mellowing effect of time. No languages ever were, none ever will be polished, like the Greek and Latin. There is no similar instance in the ancient world. No such phenomenon will exist hereafter, because all the modern languages are necessarily undergoing rapid changes. The art of printing is as fatal to the perfection of the outward form in English or in German, as it is to the faultless calligraphy of the Persian scribe. Innumerable causes are at work to modify the German, a language which has some close affinities to the Greek. Should it cease to be, in some of the strange accidents of time, a spoken language, stopped in its mid-career, like a stream from the Alps suddenly congealed by the frost, what motley forms would it reveal! How different from the two classical languages! About these, there is a repose, a sculpture-like finish, a serenity, to which no modern dialect approaches. What a perfect correspondence between the thought and the expression. The writer does not stumble on a synonym, or a word somewhere in the neighborhood of that which was needed, like most modern authors, but hits the very word. We feel that it would be sacrilege to try to change it for another. In the best Greek writers, the collocation of words is wonderfully felicitous, not resulting from the laws of prosody alone, but from the musical soul of the writer. The Italian is called a beautiful language, but how unlike is its monotony to the endless variety of the Homeric hexameter, or the lofty rhythm of the Platonic prose.

It is sometimes asked, in a skeptical tone, why this idolatrous attachment to the classics? Why do Latin and Greek hold such a supremacy over the thousand tongues of earth? It is enough to answer, that the fact is beyond contradiction. We do not know why the Egyptian language was not more perfect. Yet we hardly feel bound to sit down and study Coptic for the purpose of improving our taste. It is not known why there have not been more than one Shakspeare and one Milton. But, because our attachment to these masters may be called idolatrous, ought we to betake ourselves to Sir Richard Blackmore's Creation and Glover's Leonidas? Just so with Greek and Latin. They happen to be the only languages which are developed according to the rules of perfect art. Therefore it is the wisdom of all public men, who would mature their own faculties, and labor worthily in their respective spheres, to devote a little time every day to these ancient masters of wisdom and eloquence.

The members of the learned professions are necessarily involved in wearying cares. In the whirl of business, or in the collisions of interest, the feelings of the heart are apt to be blunted, and, though once delicate and gentle, to become harsh and violent. Something is needed to soothe

the chafed spirit. What better resort than to Cicero's Epistles, or Homer's Odyssey, in order to calm the troubled heart, and recall the pleasant days of early youth. The very sight of an ancient classic sometimes acts as a spell to lay the irritated temper. It speaks with the voice of an affectionate monitor, full of the words of wisdom. . . .

A happy influence is exerted by classical study in another way. It is well known, that our mental and moral habits are intimately connected with our style of thinking and of speaking. Thus our sense of rectitude is very much dependent on the accuracy of the language which we employ. Confusion in speech leads to confusion in morals. Perspicuity in diction is often the parent of clear mental and moral conceptions. Hence, scarcely any thing is more important in the culture of the young, than exact attention to the nicer shades of thought; than the ability to discriminate in respect to all terms, those relating to moral subjects particularly, which are, in general, regarded as synonymous. One of the chief benefits of classical study goes to this very point. It is itself a process of accurate comparison. It is taking the valuation, as it were, of the whole stock of two most copious languages. Some of the principal authors use words with wonderful precision. Plato, for instance, defines with microscopic acuteness. His power of analysis was, perhaps, never equalled. His ear seemed to be so trained as to detect the slightest differences both in the sense and in the sound of words. This is one reason why no translation can do justice either to his poetic cadences, or to his thoughts. No one can be familiar with such an author, and really perceive the fitness of his words, and the truth of the distinctions which they imply, without becoming himself a more exact reasoner and a nicer judge of moral truth. Language, when thus employed, is not a dead thing. It re-acts, with quickening power, on our minds and hearts. When we use words of definite import, our intellectual and moral judgments will become definite. A hazy dialect is the parent of a hazy style of thinking, if it is not of doubtful actions.

The dishonest man, or the dishonest State, often allow themselves to be imposed upon by a loose mode of reasoning, and a looser use of language. Here, then, may be drawn an argument not unimportant, in favor of continued attention to those finished models of style and of thought, which are found in the studies in question. They nourish a delicacy of perception, and the sentiments and feelings gradually gain that crystal clearness which belongs to the visible symbols.

Once more, it is to be feared, that a degenerating process has been long going on in our vernacular tongue. There is danger that it will become the dialect of conceits, of prettinesses, of dashing coxcombry, or of affected strength, and of extravagant metaphor. Preachers, as well as writers, appear to regard convulsive force as the only quality of a good style. They seem to imagine that the human heart is, in all its moods, to be carried by storm. Their aim is the production of immediate practical effect. Hence, there is a struggle for the boldest figures and the most passionate oratory. The same tendency is seen in the hall of legislation, and pre-eminently in much of our popular literature. Passion; over-statement; ridiculous conceits; the introduction of terms that have no citizenship in any language on earth; a disregard of grammar; an affected smartness, characterize, to a very melancholy degree, our recent literature. To be natural, is to be antiquated. To use correct and elegant English, is to plod. Hesitancy in respect to the adoption of some new-fangled word, is the sure sign of a purist. Such writers as Addison and Swift are not to be mentioned in the ears of our "enterprising" age. The man or the woman, who should be caught reading the Spectator, would be looked upon as smitten with lunacy. In short, there is reason to fear, that our noble old tongue is changing into a dialect for traffickers, magazine-writers, and bedlamites.

One way by which this acknowledged evil may be stayed, is a return to such books as Milton, Dryden and Cowper loved; to such as breathed their spirit into the best literature of England; to the old historians and poets, that were pondered over, from youth to hoary years, by her noblest divines, philosophers, and statesmen. Eloquence, both secular and sacred, such as the English world has never listened to elsewhere, has flowed from minds that were imbued with classical learning.

DOCUMENT 14

The Animal Kingdom

Science was still struggling to establish itself in the America of the 1840s but it would not be ignored. The kind of science that Professor Louis Agassiz (1807–73) preached and practiced was most compatible to the American mind. In his lectures especially—and they were his means of reaching the largest audience—he made the outlines of his thinking clear and his exposition factual. His respect for the feelings of his audience, moreover, was evident. The bitterest scientific issue of his time, the one most charged with emotion, was summed up in the catch phrase "Geology vs. Genesis"; on it he took a moderate position. He did not deny God nor, on the other hand, did he spend time in praising Him. He studied nature for its own sake and on its own terms, but having done that, he was ready to agree that the results of his studies showed the omnipresence and omnipotence of the Creator. He did notable work both in the physical and the biological sciences. A course of his lectures called *An Introduction to the Study of Natural History* was put in type by Horace Greeley's printing house in 1847. The selection given below is from the opening lecture, which took up the subject of "The Animal Kingdom." Its matter and manner are revealing.

Agassiz begins with a bow to American practicality by noting that scientific knowledge is essential for our economic well-being. But he goes on to elevate the discussion by announcing that the grand aim of scientific knowledge is to understand the world of nature. This means analysis as well as description; it means finding out the why as well as the what. This is the proper function of the scientist, or as Agassiz calls him in the nineteenth-century way, the "philosopher." To put it a little differently, it is not enough for the philosopher to know isolated facts; he must aim at a synthesis. Nor is it enough, says Agassiz, for the listeners sitting before him. They too should try to see the grand design. It can be done, he assures them. The greatest help is the human soul, for it allows us to understand the idea the Creator had in shaping the world. Allaying the religious anxieties of his audience, he propounds the long-established view that the scrutiny of the world of nature will lead us to a greater appreciation of the mind of the deity who made it. "By a constant study of these works of Creation, we may come to understand the views, the objects of the Creator."

Further than this Agassiz will not go, however. He refuses to accept the biblical version of creation, saying flatly that geology proves that the world and its living forms were not created "at one moment." The process was gradual. Simple species came first, to be replaced by more complex ones. The last and most complex to emerge was man. Many marks distinguish him and set him apart. Confining himself here to physical marks, Agassiz says that one of the most significant is that man, alone among all animal life, can stand erect. He alone can "raise his eye directly toward the heavens." After Agassiz has established his general position, he turns to the description of the forms of the animal kingdom. He takes them one by one and occasionally draws sketches of them for the audience. It is to this systematic exposition that the rest of the first lecture is devoted.

SOURCE: Louis Agassiz, An Introduction to the Study of Natural History, in a Series of Lectures Delivered in the Hall of the College of Physicians and Surgeons, New-York (New York, 1847), pp. 5–8.

The Animal Kingdom

Natural History may be studied in very different points of view. Some may consider it as a source of information for useful purposes. The wealth of States depends frequently on the knowledge acquired by individuals of the structure of the soil. The working of mines has become an actual business since Geology as a science has given us the key to the investigation of the deeper regions under the surface of the ground. Many trades depend on the knowledge of certain phenomena of Nature. Even Navigation is the result of scientific investigation and discovery; and, at this time particularly, the vastly increased facilities of frequent intercourse between nations have been the result of the recent progress of natural science—of physical science especially. Thus, though viewed in this strictly utilitarian aspect a sufficient inducement may be furnished for the study of Nature and of the objects of Natural History in particular, the subject is yet to be regarded from a more elevated point of view. It is not enough for a philosophical mind to know the natural phenomena. It may be enough to know some isolated phenomena in order to derive important aid in the arts, but to the philosopher such superficial acquaintance with Nature is not sufficient. He wants to understand Nature. He is not satisfied with the knowledge of isolated phenomena.

When I say that the philosopher desires to understand Nature, I will perhaps better explain my meaning by an example. When we enter on the study of an author we may begin at a very low stage. With one of the classic Poets of antiquity, for example, we may begin by translating sentence by sentence, with great difficulty, and in this way we may go through the most beautiful language of ancient poetry. But would it by any means follow because we have thus spelled over the pages of Homer, that we understand him? Another and a higher sort of mental process is requisite to enable us to know, to understand, that sublime author. It is only when we have become acquainted with the condition of human society in that age—the rivalry which existed between the nations of Asia and Greece—and the mythology of that remote time, that our sympathies approach the level of the poet's work and our hearts own the influence of the poet's spirit.

So it is with the study of Nature. We may know by their name a great many animals. We may be able to indicate with accuracy the characteristic differences between the various tribes of animals. We may be able to distinguish the trees in our forests and the plants cultivated in our gardens; nay, we may know any isolated plant that flourishes upon the surface of our globe, and yet we may after all know nothing of the plan of creation. There is a higher point of view from which we attain a deeper insight into that plan. We must understand the connection between the various parts of Creation, and, rising higher still, direct our contemplations to the Author of all, who has formed the whole and subjected it to all those modifications extending through long ages which Geology has revealed, from the remotest epoch up to the period when Man was created and introduced upon the surface of the globe with the animals and plants which we now behold.

Understand, then, that the study and knowledge of Nature consist in something more than the acquaintance with the isolated beings which exist upon the surface of our globe. We must understand the connections existing between these beings, and the relations which they sustain to the Creator of them all.

But the question may be asked, is it possible for man to acquire more than a superficial insight into natural phenomena? This question has been answered in many different ways. Some have maintained that all we can expect to come at is an artificial classification, agreeing in a greater or less degree with the natural phenomena; that a real insight into all the varied departments of Nature by man is unattainable. But if we view the progress of natural science, and observe the investigations made in every succeeding generation in the matter of isolated phenomena—if we bear in mind how many things which appear isolated have been combined into one and the same point of view, we are furnished with a strong ground of hope that it will be given unto Man to attain that insight into Nature.

There is another reason why Man may expect fully to

understand Nature. We feel in ourselves that we are not mere matter. We have a soul. We have an intelligence. We have feelings by which we are in connection with each other. These feelings—that intelligence—carry us beyond the limits of our globe. We thus rise to the notion of a God. We have that within ourselves which assures us of a participation in the Divine Nature; and it is a peculiar characteristic of Man to be able to rise in that way above material Nature, and to understand intellectual existences. The possibility of obtaining an insight into Nature is thus strengthened by the analogy between the Human and Divine Natures. On that principle, Man being made in the image of God, it is possible for his intelligence to comprehend the doings of God in Nature. Hence by a constant intercourse with these works—by a Natural Religion—by a constant study of these works of Creation, we may come to understand the views, the objects of the Creator in doing these works—in introducing these phenomena as realities into existence. We may, in one word, come to a full understanding of Nature from the very reason that we have an immortal soul.

Again, our body is so similar to the bodies of animals. The organization of our body discovers intimate relations with their physical condition. We pass from the lower type of animals so gradually to the higher, until we find Man, with his superior organization. Thus on one hand we see that owing to the intellectual nature of Man he has peculiar relations with the Author of all things, while on the other hand, from his physical nature he has a root in the soil—a material foundation, and hence both the intellectual and the material world is laid open to his contemplation, affording substantial grounds for the belief that he is competent to attain a full understanding of the works of creation and the plan of God when bringing the world into existence.

That all this creation has not been the result of one creative act, we know from geological observation. This globe—the animals which exist upon it now—have not been brought into existence at one moment. We have learned from geological observation that a long series of epochs have succeeded each other, and that during every epoch animals and plants, organic beings of various types, were successively living and died away to make room for others, till the surface of the globe was occupied by the animals and plants which now exist with Man as their head.

The most superficial knowledge of those phenomena soon gave rise to the notion that the introduction of Man has been the object of the creation of this globe, and the position which Man now occupies upon the surface of this globe is such that this notion appears to us quite natural. I think it may be shown by actual demonstration, as far as physical phenomena can be demonstrated, that the view of the Creator in forming the globe—in allowing it to undergo these successive changes which Geology has discovered, and in introducing gradually all these different types of animals which have passed away, was, after all, to introduce Man upon the surface of our globe, and to bring him into connection with the other organized beings and with the soil in connection with which he does now exist.

There is one reason to believe that this is so. That reason is this: We see from every point of view in which we may regard the Animal Kingdom—and I shall from this moment limit all my remarks to the Animal Kingdom, in order not to trespass beyond the bounds properly set to this discourse—we see that Man possesses the most complex and most perfect structure. Even his position is remarkable and significant. Man's erect position in standing or walking shows that he is placed at the head of creation. All the lower animals have a horizontal position. The fishes move horizontally. Gradually as we ascend in the scale of animated beings we behold them raising their heads a little. Snakes have no feet, but they are able to elevate the head; and if we proceed farther we find successive types in which the position becomes an oblique one, until the head is raised more perpendicularly. But to Man alone is given the most important position—the vertical position, which allows him to make use of his hand and fingers and to raise his eye directly toward the heavens. In this very position—in this material construction of his body, we have an evidence of the superiority of man. But in every respect, if we consider his structure, we see that Man stands at the summit of animal being—and that it is just so to regard Man as at the head of Creation, will be one object of these Lectures.

Again, if we consider the construction of animals upon the surface of our globe, we will find that the lower types have been first created—that they belong to the most ancient rocks—that the deepest rocks contain none of the higher animals, and that gradually some more perfect types were introduced till at last Man was created, and it may be shown geologically, by actual investigation and without the slightest reference to any historical or sacred tradition, that Man has been created the last.

Again, if it cannot be shown from this point of view that the introduction of man was actually the object of the Creator, it may be at least shown that Man was the last and most perfect work that proceeded from His almighty hand. But that it was actually the object of the Creator to introduce Man at the head of the Animal Kingdom can, I hope, be shown by combining the knowledge we have acquired with regard to his physical structure, and his relations with the different other classes of animals and with the surface of the globe at large. At no time do we find in geological epochs a species spread all over the surface of our globe. Every type of animal—every variety of animal, occupies in the geological epochs only a small portion of the surface of the globe. This fact holds true in all geological times. Before the animals now living were created—when races entirely different from them existed, every species was circumscribed within narrow limits, and in no case occupied the whole surface of the globe. No one of the species of former epochs was superior to the whole type of its time. At no geological epoch do we find one species standing preëminent above others. But at this present epoch, we find not only that Man stands preëminent above all other species, but that he occupies the whole surface of our globe; and in this respect he appears to be of a superior organization and endowed with privileges which no type ever enjoyed before him.

But I will not dwell on those general questions without some more precise foundation. I shall at once proceed to call your attention to the varied types which exist in Nature, so as to have actual facts upon which to reason. I desire that the statements with which I set out may be regarded as the results of investigation and not as matter of mere speculative opinion.

There is an astonishing variety of animals upon the surface of our globe. This variety is such that it is very difficult for the student who for the first time directs his attention to the subject, to perceive any order. It is impossible at first to perceive the intimate affinities and the near relations which subsist between all these varied formations.

I have here some diagrams giving outlines of a few of these formations. I just name the subjects before passing to their characteristics. Here we have the common star-fish of the Mediterranean Sea. Here we have one of those jelly-fish so common in temperate and warm latitudes. This is a species common in the Atlantic—one of the species whose substance is more or less phosphorescent. Here is a coral of the Red Sea—a very common species. Here is a cuttle-fish, common on the western shores of France. Here are different species of snakes, some from the East Indies and one from Central America. Here is a clam very common on the south-west shores of Africa—not the common species. Here is the common lobster. Here is a worm, of that species having colored blood. Here is a spider. Here are several skeletons of vertebrated animals—an hyena—an ostrich—a crocodile—an enlarged skeleton of the bat. I do not mention two of these animals, because although represented so perfectly, they are not now in existence. They are nowhere to be found on the surface of the globe; but

these representations have been made from preparations
most skillfully completed by attaching together isolated
bones collected in the neighborhood of Paris, and arranged
into a complete animal by the wonderful attainments of
Cuvier in comparative anatomy. Thus these long extinct
species of animals are as well known to us as if we had
perfect specimens of them in our museums.

Now, on looking at these diagrams the beginner in Natural History will be struck by the great apparent dissimi-
larity between animals which yet belong to the same family. Thus, how little apparent resemblance between the
star-fish and the coral! Then again, the cuttle-fish, the snail
and the clam appear to have little in common, and yet the
affinity between them is so close that they appear to the
naturalist as members of one and the same family. And
again, the worm, the lobster, the spider and the butterfly
belong to one and the same tribe. The common earth-
worm is more intimately allied to the crab or the butterfly
than to a snail or slug. One might think that the leech and
the slug were of a very similar class. Not so. Mere external
appearance alone conveys an idea of identity. There is by
no means any actual relation between them. The animals
represented in the other diagrams constitute a fourth great
division all ultimately allied. The fish and the bat—the
crocodile and the ostrich, belong to one great type; and
the characters by which they may be defined are not artificial characters. They are not distinctions introduced by
Man in order to facilitate his understanding of those subjects and to make his classification easy. This intimate relation between them is a natural one, derived from their
internal character.

It is very obvious that here in this star-fish, the star-like
rays constitute the prominent characteristic. The rays proceed from the centre.— The same character is perceived in
the coral and jelly-fish. Here you perceive a similar radiated arrangement of the parts. The common characteristic
of this order of animals is this radiated arrangement from
the common centre, the mouth.— The star-fish has at the

lower surface an opening through which the food is introduced: precisely the same arrangement is seen in the jelly-fish, which has a quadrangular mouth; so, also, in the case of the polyp, surrounded by these fringes or tentaculæ. In consequence of this peculiarity these animals have been denominated *Radiated* animals.

The next type contains animals which have very soft bodies and have the power of contracting themselves very much. If you see a snail contract itself and entirely disappear at the bottom of its shell and again, if you see it grow out enlarging and expanding itself so as to have apparently twice the size of the shell itself, you will consider that this is a faculty which no other type of animals possesses in such a degree. No bird can swell its body to twice or three times its natural size. No quadruped can do that; no insect can do it. It is only in these animals that we see so considerable expansion and contraction. Again, the movements of this type are very sluggish. No one of them can jump or run; they can only creep upon the soil by successive contractions of the body. A few can swim, but when swimming they are moved in a peculiar mode by means of those appendages round the head. Even these have the power of contraction in a degree which no other type of animal possesses, and even here [pointing to the cuttle-fish] the locomotion is owing to this contraction.

The whole body of this class is covered by a dense mucosity, and this mucosity makes these animals very unpleasant to the touch; and it is a peculiarity of this substance to contain a great deal of mucus, which, to some, has a very agreeable taste, so that a great many of this type are among the eatable animals. Nevertheless, a great majority of them please only in consequence of the beauty and value of their covering. For instance, shells, for many centuries, have been one of the subjects of greatest attention among naturalists, and extensive collections of these coverings have been made everywhere, while the animals themselves have been much neglected; and we do not possess in our collections the soft parts of these animals, which would

enable us to know them perhaps better than we do by
their shells. In fact, when we attempt to classify them from
the shell, it is not more reasonable than if we should attempt to form a correct notion of the character of a people
by looking at their coats! (Laughter.) . . .

DOCUMENT 15

The Good Astronomy

Just as the selection from Agassiz gives something of the flavor and the tone of the biological sciences, so does the selection printed below from Olmsted for the physical sciences. Professor Denison Olmsted (1791–1859) was an astronomer at Yale College and a substantial scholar. Like Agassiz he upheld the theological order of his time but did not let it get in the way of his scientific data. For instance, in his *Letters on Astronomy* (1840) he assured his reader that the heavens testified to the power and wisdom of their Creator, but the assurance came only after four hundred pages of scientific matter. The letters though ostensibly to an inquiring lady are actually an attempt to reach the public and share information with the largest possible group. It is an interesting sidelight on the growing status of women that Olmsted uses a woman's request as his vehicle. His style is plain and clear, his explanations lucid. In "Letter I," given below, he expatiates on what he calls "this noble science"—and does so in a tone of moral enthusiasm that scientists seem not to employ today.

"Letter I" is, in fact, a remarkable example of how the position of science and the attitude toward science have altered since a century ago. We now live in a so-called age of science but none of its votaries would make the fervent claims for it that Olmsted did. "Letter I" shows a love of science, in this case astronomy, that has all the ingenuous ardor of youth. "The emotion felt by the astronomer," Olmsted asserts, "is a continued glow of exalted feeling, which gives the sensation of breathing in a purer atmosphere than others enjoy." It is a sensation that, to all appearances, Olmsted himself felt. Given this devotion it is no wonder that his claims

for astronomy are emphatic. He maintains that it is a
dignified study, appealing to the most refined and cultivated minds. He maintains that it elevates and increases
the mental powers, for it is well known that contemplating large things enlarges the mind just as contemplating
small ones shrinks it. He even maintains that it will
improve health and stamina. He has the grace, however,
not to say this flatly. He merely suggests that "it is a
singular fact, that distinguished astronomers, as a class,
have been remarkable for longevity."

Olmsted obviously hopes that his enthusiasm will be
contagious. Though he addresses his anonymous lady,
he wants everyone to share in astronomy's joys. And,
appropriately to a democratic society, he stoutly affirms
that everyone can enjoy them. Everyone can learn.
Though it has taken some of our greatest minds to
formulate the truths of astronomy, anybody can comprehend them once they are found. The key to the heavens
is waiting for us; all we have to do is to reach out and
take it.

SOURCE: Denison Olmsted, *Letters on Astronomy, Addressed to a
Lady, in Which the Elements of the Science are Familiarly Explained* (Boston, 1840), pp. 9–16.

Letter I

To Mrs. C—— M——.

DEAR MADAM,—In the conversation we recently held on
the study of Astronomy, you expressed a strong desire to
become better acquainted with this noble science, but said
you had always been repelled by the air of severity which
it exhibits, arrayed as it is in so many technical terms, and
such abstruse mathematical processes: or, if you had taken
up some smaller treatise, with the hope of avoiding
these perplexities, you had always found it so meager and
superficial, as to afford you very little satisfaction. You
asked, if a work might not be prepared, which would convey to the general reader some clear and adequate knowledge of the great discoveries in astronomy, and yet require

for its perusal no greater preparation, than may be presumed of every well-educated English scholar of either sex.

You were pleased to add the request, that I would write such a work,—a work which should combine, with a luminous expositon of the leading truths of the science, some account of the interesting historical facts with which it is said the records of astronomical discovery abound. Having, moreover, heard much of the grand discoveries which, within the last fifty years, have been made among the *fixed stars*, you expressed a strong desire to learn more respecting these sublime researches. Finally, you desired to see the argument for the existence and natural attributes of the Deity, as furnished by astronomy, more fully and clearly exhibited, than is done in any work which you have hitherto perused. In the preparation of the proposed treatise, you urged me to supply, either in the text or in notes, every *elementary principle* which would be essential to a perfect understanding of the work; for although, while at school, you had paid some attention to geometry and natural philosophy, yet so much time had since elapsed, that your memory required to be refreshed on the most simple principles of these elementary studies, and you preferred that I should consider you as altogether unacquainted with them.

Although, to satisfy a mind, so cultivated and inquisitive as yours, may require a greater variety of powers and attainments than I possess, yet, as you were pleased to urge me to the trial, I have resolved to make the attempt, and will see how far I may be able to lead you into the interior of this beautiful temple, without obliging you to force your way through the "jargon of the schools."

Astronomy, however, is a very difficult or a comparatively easy study, according to the view we take of it. The investigation of the great laws which govern the motions of the heavenly bodies has commanded the highest efforts of the human mind; but profound truths, which it required the mightiest efforts of the intellect to disclose, are often, when once discovered, simple in their complexion, and may be expressed in very simple terms. Thus, the creation of that element, on whose mysterious agency depend all the forms of beauty and loveliness, is enunciated in these few monosyllables, "And God said, let there be light, and there was light;" and the doctrine of universal gravitation, which is the key that unlocks the mysteries of the universe, is simply this,—that every portion of matter in the universe tends towards every other. The three great laws of motion, also, are, when stated, so plain, that they seem hardly to assert any thing but what we knew before. That all bodies, if at rest, will continue so, as is declared by the first law of motion, until some force moves them; or, if in motion, will continue so, until some force stops them, appears so much a matter of course, that we can at first hardly see any good reason why it should be dignified with the title of the first great law of motion; and yet it contains a truth which it required profound sagacity to discover and expound.

It is, therefore, a pleasing consideration to those who have not either the leisure or the ability to follow the astronomer through the intricate and laborious processes, which conducted him to his great discoveries, that they may fully avail themselves of the *results* of this vast toil, and easily understand truths which it required ages of the severest labor to unfold. The descriptive parts of astronomy, or what may be called the natural history of the heavens, is still more easily understood than the laws of the celestial motions. The revelations of the telescope, and the wonders it has disclosed in the sun, in the moon, in the planets, and especially in the fixed stars, are facts not difficult to be understood, although they may affect the mind with astonishment.

The great practical purpose of astronomy to the world is, enabling us safely to navigate the ocean. There are indeed many other benefits which it confers on man; but this is the most important. If, however, you ask, what advantages the study of astronomy promises, as a branch of education, I answer, that few subjects promise to the mind so much profit and entertainment. It is agreed by writers on the human mind, that the intellectual powers are enlarged and strengthened by the habitual contemplation of great objects, while they are contracted and weakened by being constantly employed upon little or trifling subjects. The former elevate, the latter depress, the mind, to their own level. Now, every thing in astronomy is great. The magnitudes, distances, and motions, of the heavenly bodies; the amplitude of the firmament itself; and the magnificence of the orbs with which it is lighted, supply exhaustless materials for contemplation, and stimulate the mind to its noblest efforts. The emotion felt by the astronomer is not that sudden excitement or ecstasy, which wears out life, but it is a continued glow of exalted feeling, which gives the sensation of breathing in a purer atmosphere than others enjoy. We should at first imagine, that a study which calls upon its votaries for the severest efforts of the human intellect, which demands the undivided toil of years, and which robs the night of its accustomed hours of repose, would abridge the period of life; but it is a singular fact, that distinguished astronomers, as a class, have been remarkable for longevity. I know not how to account for this fact, unless we suppose that the study of astronomy itself has something inherent in it, which sustains its votaries by a peculiar aliment.

It is the privilege of the student of this department of Nature, that his cabinet is already collected, and is ever before him; and he is exempted from the toil of collecting his materials of study and illustration, by traversing land and sea, or by penetrating into the depths of the earth. Nor are they in their nature frail and perishable. No sooner is the veil of clouds removed, that occasionally conceals the firmament by night, than his specimens are displayed to view, bright and changeless. The renewed pleasure which he feels, at every new survey of the constellations, grows into an affection for objects which have so often ministered to his happiness. His imagination aids him in giving them a personification, like that which the ancients gave to the constellations; (as is evident from the names which they have transmitted to us;) and he walks abroad, beneath the evening canopy, with the conscious satisfaction and delight of being in the presence of old friends. This emotion becomes stronger when he wanders far from home. Other objects of his attachment desert him; the face of society changes; the earth presents new features; but the same sun illumines the day, the same moon adorns the night, and the same bright stars still attend him.

When, moreover, the student of the heavens can command the aid of telescopes, of higher and higher powers, new acquaintances are made every evening. The sight of each new member of the starry train, that the telescope successively reveals to him, inspires a peculiar emotion of pleasure; and he at length finds himself, whenever he sweeps his telescope over the firmament, greeted by smiles, unperceived and unknown to his fellow-mortals. The same personification is given to these objects as to the constellations, and he seems to himself, at times, when he has penetrated into the remotest depths of ether, to enjoy the high prerogative of holding converse with the celestials.

It is no small encouragement, to one who wishes to acquire a knowledge of the heavens, that the subject is embarrassed with far less that is technical than most other branches of natural history. Having first learned a few definitions, and the principal circles into which, for convenience, the sphere is divided, and receiving the great laws of astronomy on the authority of the eminent persons who have investigated them, you will find few hard terms, or technical distinctions, to repel or perplex you; and you will, I hope, find that nothing but an intelligent mind and fixed attention are requisite for perusing the Letters which I propose to address to you. I shall indeed be greatly disappointed, if the perusal does not inspire you with some portion of that pleasure, which I have described as enjoyed by the astronomer himself.

The dignity of the study of the heavenly bodies, and

its suitableness to the most refined and cultivated mind, has been recognised in all ages. Virgil celebrates it in the beautiful strains with which I have headed this Letter, and similar sentiments have ever been cherished by the greatest minds.

As, in the course of these Letters, I propose to trace an outline of the history of astronomy, from the earliest ages to the present time, you may think this the most suitable place for introducing it; but the successive discoveries in the science cannot be fully understood and appreciated, until after an acquaintance has been formed with the science itself. We must therefore reserve the details of this subject for a future opportunity; but it may be stated, here, that astronomy was cultivated the earliest of all the sciences; that great attention was paid to it by several very ancient nations, as the Egyptians and Chaldeans, and the people of India and China, before it took its rise in Greece. More than six hundred years before the Christian era, however, it began to be studied in this latter country. Thales and Pythagoras were particularly distinguished for their devotion to this science; and the celebrated school of Alexandria, in Egypt, which took its rise about three hundred years before the Christian era, and flourished for several hundred years, numbered among its disciples a succession of eminent astronomers, among whom were Hipparchus, Eratosthenes, and Ptolemy. The last of these composed a great work on astronomy, called the 'Almagest,' in which is transmitted to us an account of all that was known of the science by the Alexandrian school. The 'Almagest' was the principal text-book in astronomy, for many centuries afterwards, and comparatively few improvements were made until the age of Copernicus. Copernicus was born at Thorn, in Prussia, in 1473. Previous to his time, the doctrine was held, that the earth is at rest in the centre of the universe, and that the sun, moon, and stars, revolve about it, every day, from east to west; in short, that the *apparent* motions of the heavenly bodies are the same with their *real* motions. But Copernicus expounded what is now known to be the true theory of the celestial motions, in which the sun is placed in the centre of the solar system, and the earth and all the planets are made to revolve around him, from west to east, while the apparent diurnal motion of the heavenly bodies, from east to west, is explained by the revolution of the earth on its axis, in the same time, from west to east; a motion of which we are unconscious, and which we erroneously ascribe to external objects, as we imagine the shore is receding from us, when we are unconscious of the motion of the ship that carries us from it.

Although many of the appearances, presented by the motions of the heavenly bodies, may be explained on the former erroneous hypothesis, yet, like other hypotheses founded in error, it was continually leading its votaries into difficulties, and blinding their minds to the perception of truth. They had advanced nearly as far as it was practicable to go in the wrong road; and the great and sublime discoveries of modern times are owing, in no small degree, to the fact, that, since the days of Copernicus, astronomers have been pursuing the plain and simple path of truth, instead of threading their way through the mazes of error.

Near the close of the sixteenth century, Tycho Brahe, a native of Sweden, but a resident of Denmark, carried astronomical observations (which constitute the basis of all that is valuable in astronomy) to a far greater degree of perfection than had ever been done before. Kepler, a native of Germany, one of the greatest geniuses the world has ever seen, was contemporary with Tycho Brahe, and was associated with him in a part of his labors. Galileo, an Italian astronomer of great eminence, flourished only a little later than Tycho Brahe. He invented the telescope, and, both by his discoveries and reasonings, contributed greatly to establish the true system of the world. Soon after the commencement of the seventeenth century, (1620,) Lord Bacon, a celebrated English philosopher, pointed out the true method of conducting all inquiries into the phenomena of Nature, and introduced the *inductive method of philosophizing*. According to the inductive method, we are to begin our inquiries into the causes of any events by first examining and classifying all the *facts* that relate to it, and, from the comparison of these, to deduce our conclusions.

But the greatest single discovery, that has ever been made in astronomy, was the law of universal gravitation, a discovery made by Sir Isaac Newton, in the latter part of the seventeenth century. The discovery of this law made us acquainted with the hidden forces that move the great machinery of the universe. It furnished the key which unlocks the inner temple of Nature; and from this time we may regard astronomy as fixed on a sure and immovable basis. I shall hereafter endeavor to explain to you the leading principles of universal gravitation, when we come to the proper place for inquiring into the causes of the celestial motions, as exemplified in the motion of the earth around the sun.

DOCUMENT 16

Know-How

The wealth of knowledge being heaped up in the 1840s was important for its own sake, certainly. But if any generalizations about Americans can be made easily, one is that they are a practical people. They want results. They ask what things are good for. When they became aware of the studies of the scientists, they wished to use them. Not always of course and not always promptly, but consistently enough so that by the 1840s American technology was already making a place for itself in American civilization. The full title of Jacob Bigelow's two-volume work is indicative: *The Useful Arts Considered in Connexion with the Applications of Science*. Bigelow (1787–1879) published the work as part of a series of books sponsored by the Board of Education of Massachusetts for school libraries in that state. The section reprinted here is on "The Arts of Illumination" and takes us from something as time-hallowed as the torch to something as modern as hydro-oxygen light.

Bigelow's fact-filled pages give us a precise picture of the status of American technology at one moment in time. They reveal that there was much more technical data available, both foreign and domestic, than we might think. Our own mental picture of lighting in the 1840s, if we have one, is apt to go little beyond the candle and the oil lamp—or young Lincoln studying by the flickering fire. Yet there are nearly a dozen kinds of illuminating devices described. Bigelow's pages reveal a working knowledge of physics and chemistry more than respectable for that period and he shares the knowledge with his readers in a direct expository style. These pages, furthermore, possess cultural as well as economic significance. To have decent light meant to extend the day. And that in turn meant many things, from easier reading after dark to a more extensive social life. Better light stood out both as an economic and a social benefit. Bigelow's succinct explanations show how it can be secured. Today we take good light for granted everywhere. But let our electricity be cut off and Bigelow's book can regain much of its old interest.

SOURCE: Jacob Bigelow, *The Useful Arts Considered in Connexion with the Applications of Science* (Boston, 1840), I, 333-39.

The Arts of Illumination

Lamps.—When the combustible used is fluid, at common temperatures, a vessel is necessary to contain this fluid, and supply it to the flame. In this country, and in England, whale oil is the principal fluid which is burnt in lamps. In France, and the south of Europe, the oil of poppies, of nuts, rape seed, and the inferior kinds of olive oil, are used for this purpose. The volatile oils are but seldom burnt, since they exhale a strong odor, and throw off soot, during their combustion. They are also liable to take fire, over their whole surface, unless guarded with great care. Naphtha, however, as it is found native, or as it is distilled from pitcoal, is used for supplying street lamps, in some of the cities of Europe.

Reservoirs.—As the flame of a lamp is intended to consume no more oil, than is attracted upward by the capillary action of the wick, it is necessary that a sufficient body of oil should be so placed, as to keep its surface, permanently, at a small distance below the level of the flame. The Greeks and Romans employed lamps of various forms, having the wick projecting from a sort of beak, at the side, nearly on a level with the surface of the oil. A similar plan is now practised in our street lamps. At the present day, portable lamps, of small size, are made with a central wick, having the reservoir of oil immediately below the flame. These reservoirs, if small, require frequent filling, and if large, cast an inconvenient shadow. All closed lamps require a minute hole, for the admission of air; otherwise, the pressure of the atmosphere will prevent the oil from ascending the wick. If this hole be obstructed, the oil will also sometimes overflow, from the expansion of the confined air, when heated. . . .

Argand Lamp.—This name is applied, after one of the inventors, to all lamps with hollow or circular wicks; and, of course, most of the lamps already described, may be also Argand lamps, if furnished with a circular burner. The intention of the Argand burner is, to furnish a more rapid supply of air to the flame, and to afford this air to the centre, as well as the outside, of the flame. It is constructed by forming a hollow cylindrical cavity, which receives oil from the main body of the lamp, and, at the same time, transmits air through its axis, or central hollow. In this cavity is placed a circular wick, attached at bottom to a movable ring. This ring is capable of being elevated, or depressed, by means of a rack and pinion, or, more commonly, by a screw; so that the height of the wick may be varied, to regulate the size of the flame. On the outside is placed a glass chimney, which is capable of transmitting a current of air, on the same principles as a common smoke-flue. When this lamp is lighted, the combustion is vivid, and the light intense, owing to the free and rapid supply of air. The flame does not waver, and the smoke is wholly consumed. The brilliancy of the light is still further increased, if the air be made to impinge laterally against the flame. This is done, either by contracting the glass chimney, near the blaze, so as to direct the air inwards, or by placing a metallic button over the blaze, so as to spread the internal current outward.

Submarine Lamp.—A lamp, ingeniously contrived to burn under water, has been connected with a diving apparatus, for examining the Thames tunnel. A box, containing the lamp, is made air-tight, with a glass in front, and a reflector behind. A quantity of alkali is placed in the box, and a reservoir of condensed oxygen is attached. The oxygen is admitted in a small stream, to support the flame. The products of the combustion are water, and carbonic acid. The water is condensed, and the carbonic acid combines with the alkali, so that room is continually made for the fresh supply of oxygen.

A common lamp may be made to burn under water, by enclosing it in a lantern, through which a current of air is continually forced, by means of a pump, and an elastic pipe.

Hydro-oxygen Light.—If a stream of oxygen and hydrogen be directed, while in combustion, upon a mass of quicklime, the result is an intense degree of ignition, attended with a most brilliant light, which is said to be visible at a greater distance than any other artificial light. It has been modified, in various ways, by conducting a stream of oxygen through alcohol, or oil of turpentine, and by using it in the combustion of common oil.

Spirit Lamp.—It has been found, that certain volatile and inflammable liquids are capable of burning with a bright light, but are objectionable, on account of the generation of smoke and lampblack, during their combustion. This defect has been obviated, by burning them in combination with other fluids, and in a lamp of particular construction. Oil of turpentine, when mixed with a certain proportion of alcohol, and, perhaps, with other fluids, burns with a clear, white light, in a lamp properly constructed. As these liquids are cheaper than common sperm oil, lamps for burning them were at one time extensively introduced. But they were found objectionable, on account of the volatility and extreme inflammability of the liquid, by which serious accidents occurred, when it was spilt upon the dress, and took fire. A mixture, which appears to resemble the foregoing, in some respects, has been introduced under the name of "chemical oil," for the use of light houses. It gives an intense and brilliant light, much exceeding that of common oil.

DOCUMENT 17

(PLATES 11–15)

Shaping the American Mind

Of all the influences that made the American mind what it was in the 1840s, the common school was plainly the principal one. It existed in town and country both. It taught reading, writing, arithmetic, and morality. It held its classes in the little red schoolhouse of American legend, which stood for learning on the most local and democratic level. It instructed the people. But it should be said again that it did not instruct all the people. For some there was no school whatsoever. For others, unusually fortunate, there was the more advanced, more specialized education provided by academies, high schools, Latin schools, and the like. For still others, a tiny but influential handful, there was college. Our first picture, of the Poughkeepsie Female Academy, can represent the special school. Its imposing portico and its classical pediment supported by Ionic columns prepare us for the classical education given to the starchy young ladies within. If the drawing of the academy in a sense represents the past, the next picture, of Franklin and his kite, points to the future. For it was in the progress of American experimental science that one of the main contributions to knowledge was to be made. This progress, however, was only beginning to be realized in the 1840s. Later decades would see an astounding increase in the amount of scientific discovery. Meanwhile, science was making itself felt not so much in the rudimentary laboratories as in the shrewd application of its findings to our material welfare. The American public was being influenced especially by science as technology.

Perhaps the most influential of technological achievements was the improvement in printing. American enterprise quickly appropriated from abroad the latest press designs and incorporated them into its own ideas. The result was more and cheaper books, magazines, and newspapers. Hand in hand with cheaper print went greater literacy. During the 1840s the value of books printed more than doubled and the number of persons who were literate came close to doubling. The illustration of the printing press, given here, shows one of the major agents in shaping the American mind.

The spread of print meant not only a wider distribution of the products of American culture but also an easier access to foreign culture. The world of English literature moved still nearer to us than it had been before. The relatively new world of continental European literature showed itself over the horizon. Through the pioneering efforts of professors and critics the riches of Spain, Germany, and Italy were increasingly accessible. French culture was already fairly well known; our affiliations with France had existed since the Revolutionary War. The sum total was a much greater awareness throughout the United States of what European civilization had to offer. The linecut "Faust and Margaret," reproduced here, testifies to the knowledge of Goethe in America not only among the elite but also among the middle class; for the picture appeared in the *Illustrated Monthly Courier*, a rather blowzy Philadelphia journal. The lack of sophistication in its readers is best suggested by the grotesqueness of the drawing.

The last of this group of pictorial documents shows education at its most idyllic. The season is spring, late spring. A pretty girl and a handsome youth study their lessons on a hilltop. The young man reads to the girl, who sits as near him as she can. Some schoolbooks, strapped together, lie on the ground. Everything looks placid and lovely. Surely education is going on, even though it is pedantry to point it out. Here the American mind is being shaped, no doubt without knowing it, and under extremely pleasant conditions.

PLATE 11. *Poughkeepsie Female Academy*. Engraving by Dossing[?].

SOURCE: *American Magazine*, II (February 1842), 56. Library of Congress.

The picture of the village school comes so automatically to the American mind that there is little need to include it here. We all know the stereotype, complete with the faithful dog waiting outside for his little master. So it is a good idea if we remind ourselves that a substantial minority of other, more special schools also existed. One was the Poughkeepsie Female Academy. Its handsome, austere building harked back to classical models. All in the architecture is order, discipline, balance, just as in the education administered within. As the *American Magazine* put it, "The discipline adopted is believed to be such as must ensure to diligent, docile pupils, the acquirement of superior mental and moral attainments." The tone desired in the Poughkeepsie Academy was the tone desired in most of the academies, whether for boys or girls.

Although the founders of the Poughkeepsie Academy announced that their curriculum would include innovations—there was some talk about education for the "business of life"—at this distance the result appears to be a largely traditional classical schooling. There is more novelty in the fact that this is a girls' school; for education for girls and women, as opposed to training, was only beginning to make much progress. Despite the efforts of such outspoken feminists as the Transcendentalist Margaret Fuller, women remained the second-class sex.

The style of drawing nicely matches the subject. The composition stands firm and foursquare. The lines themselves are mainly straight ones; the broken masses of the trees and the modest curvatures of the clouds serve merely to set off the straightness of the building, fence, and street.

There is no softness or sentiment in this picture; no dog ever loitered on this portico.

PLATE 12. *The Philosopher & his Kite.* Designed by J. L. Morton and engraved by H. S. Sadd.

SOURCE: *Columbian Magazine,* III (February 1845), frontispiece. Library of Congress.

During the 1840s Benjamin Franklin was still considered the greatest American scientific figure. His homely experiments, with the kite and key for instance, could be easily understood by the average man. He brought the mysteries of science close to us. His experiments, moreover, were only one aspect of his many-sided career. Franklin was a man of affairs, a shrewd enterpriser and innovator, and this meant that his science was also in the popular mind tinged with practicality. His science included not only the renowned electrical experiments but also the invention of the exceedingly useful Franklin stove. Pure and applied science were both in his province.

The state of science in this decade is unwittingly indicated by the title of the picture. It is the "philosopher" and his kite. Science had not yet realized the manifold resources of the laboratory or of the experimental method. It still retained the flavor of pure thought, of the scientist sitting and simply thinking through the problem he wished to solve. As has been noted before, science still kept the name of "natural philosophy" and the implications of the name were clear.

The engraving itself, soft, dark, and sentimentalized, shows a feeling about science compounded of wonder and respect. The admiration for the already legendary Franklin, the great but unpretentious man, includes his experiment; the marveling boy represents us all in this tableau. The composition with its stagy highlighting attracts the eye at once and the general effect appears appropriately dramatic.

PLATE 13. *Cylinder Printing Press*. Artist and engraver unknown.

SOURCE: *Scientific American*, II (December 1846), 86. Smithsonian Institution.

No other machine had as profound cultural implications as the rotary press. The Hoe press, capable as the explanation below says of "throwing off from four to five thousand impressions an hour," meant that publishing of nearly every kind had reached a new dimension. The presses were multiplying the books, magazines, and newspapers to read; and the schools were multiplying the number of readers. The census figures of 1840 and 1850 paint a vivid picture of the progress made during the 1840s. In 1840 the population was, in round numbers, 17,000,000; in 1850 it rose to 23,000,000. The number of literate rose from 6,440,000 to 11,000,000. The value of books manufactured rose from $2,850,000 to $5,900,000. The number of magazines cannot be determined well but it certainly increased. The number of daily newspapers rose from 138 to 254 and the number of weeklies from 1266 to 2048. All this in a single decade.

The engraving of the Hoe press provides a good example of American illustrative art. The purpose is to make clear rather than to adorn, and the intricacies of the machine show up well. The balance and symmetry of the engraving are perfectly functional.

PLATE 14. *Faust and Margaret*. Drawn[?] by Abraham Woodside.

SOURCE: *Illustrated Monthly Courier*, I (October 1848), 61. Library of Congress.

Perhaps the salient development of the cultural life of the 1840s was the new access to continental European culture. Books, periodicals, and pictures came to us from across the ocean in greatly increasing numbers. The same improvements in printing that we saw in America occurred on the Continent as well, and sometimes earlier. The American publishers' new presses also expedited the pirating of English materials in particular and, on a much more limited scale, the reprinting of European works in general. Foreign languages and literatures now made their way into the American consciousness. They began to play a role in the shaping of the American mind. Their introduction was not only a matter of cheaper printing, of course. It was also the result of ardent propagandizing on the part of a few strategically placed and dedicated scholars. Chief among them was the poet Longfellow. In his teaching at Harvard from 1836 to 1854 and in his writing thoughout his long career, he did more than any other person to popularize European literature in this country. He opened the door wide to such great writers as Dante and Goethe. He delivered one of his first college lectures on Goethe's *Faust*.

In this picture, which would be seen not by the Harvard elite but by a wider, less sophisticated group, a properly evil Faust is seducing a rather dubious Margaret. The drawing doubtless would have made Goethe wince. The picture also represents the interest in the medieval, in the distant exotic past, which was one of the elements in American Romanticism.

PLATE 15. *Spring-Time*. Designed by T. H. Matteson and engraved by M. Osborne.

SOURCE: *Union Magazine*, II (May 1848), opposite p. 229. Library of Congress.

Faust, in the previous picture, was evil and alien. The learning he personified was bought at the cost of sin and suffering. In "Spring-Time" we see an innocent American education, pleasantly romantic. It is enough that the boy and girl are gazing at the book, not each other. The mood of leisurely isolation is set by the hilltop, by the dog which looks away, and by the far-off farmer busy at his plowing. We cannot tell what is being read. It may not be a school-book but a bundle of schoolbooks, strapped, lies on the ground.

Much of American education was routine and by rote; some of it was dull. But here is a picture which suggests not only spring and young love but also a love of learning. The emphasis is more on the heart than on the mind but the mind is involved. To education this picture gives a grace note.

PART IV

The House of Worship

I Love the Church

Religion in America had an importance a century ago that is hard for us to imagine. Its functions were varied; so were its forms. The house of worship had many mansions. On the left were the Unitarians, individualistic, often intellectual, and innocent of dogma. They were not sure in their own minds about the divinity of Christ though they united in praising his achievement. Universalists, Congregationalists, and other similarly liberal but more minor sectarians were somewhat closer to the center. In the center stood the great Protestant denominations, the Baptists, the Methodists, and the Presbyterians. They dominated American religion though each had its own internal troubles. Just to the right of them came the Episcopalians, already dividing into low church and high church groups but managing to stay within the Anglican communion. At their right came the Roman Catholics, swelling in numbers thanks to Irish and German immigration and already centralized and disciplined beyond any of the Protestant denominations. Off to one side the eccentric sects were arranged, the religious splinter groups. The Shakers in their austere abode could exemplify them. They aptly demonstrated the dissidence of dissent.

Despite the many differences in doctrine and attitude, there was in American religion a common bond. It was not an intellectual but an emotional one. It was love: love of God, love of Christ, love of the church which represented them. We can see that it was much more openly and ingenuously expressed than it would be today. When the Reverend Arthur Coxe (1818–96) composed "I Love the Church" he breathed into it a fervor and an old-fashioned directness that have a pastoral air to them. The book it appeared in, *Christian Ballads*, was issued anonymously, and we can be justified in assuming that Coxe spoke for a host of other unnamed Christians. He informs the lyric with his feeling not only for the Church itself but also of course for the Saviour and the Lord. The church, to Coxe's mind, is religion richly institutionalized and he describes its ritual with affection. His high church leanings can be seen in much of the poem.

The measures he writes in are regular, heavily accented; his metrics are in fact quite simple. His imagery impresses us as being nondescript and unoriginal. What distinguishes the poem is the unabashed outpouring of the poet's emotion.

SOURCE: Anonymous (Arthur C. Coxe), *Christian Ballads* (New York, 1840), pp. 93–96.

I Love the Church

I love the Church—the holy Church,
    The Saviour's spotless bride;
And oh, I love her palaces
    Through all the land so wide!
The cross-topp'd spire amid the trees,
    The Holy bell of prayer;
The music of our mother's voice,
    Our mother's home is there.

The village tower—'tis joy to me,
    I cry the LORD is here!
The village bells—they fill my soul:
    They more than fill mine ear!
O'er kingdoms to the Saviour won,
    Their triumph-peal is hurled;
Their sound is now in all the earth,
    Their words throughout the world.

And here—eternal ocean cross'd,
    And long, long ages past;

In climes beyond the setting sun,
   They preach the LORD at last;
And here, Redeemer, are thy priests
   Unbroken in array,
Far from thine Holy Sepulchre,
   And thine Ascension-day!

Unbroken in their lineage;
   Their warrants clear as when
Thou, Saviour, didst go up on high,
   And give good gifts to men;
Here, clothed in innocence they stand,
   To shed thy mercy wide,
Baptizing in thy holy name,
   With waters from thy side.

And here, confessors of thy cross,
   Thine holy Orders three,
The bishop, and the elders too,
   And lowly deacons be;
To rule and feed the flock of CHRIST,
   To wage a noble strife,
And to the host of GOD'S elect,
   To break the bread of Life.

Here rises, every Sabbath morn
   Their incense unto Thee,
With bold confession Catholic,
   And high Doxology:
Soul-melting litany, is here,
   And Holy Gospel's sound;
And GLORY, LORD, they cry to thee,
   In all thy temples round.

Then comes the message of our King,
   Delivered from on high;
How beautiful the feet of them
   That on the mountain cry!
And then the faithful sons of CHRIST,
   With CHRIST are left alone:

And gather to the sacred feast,
　　Which JESUS' love hath strewn.

And kneeling by the chancel's side,
　　With blessings all divine,
As from the Saviour's hand, they take
　　The broken bread, and wine;
In one communion with the saints,
　　With angels and the blest,
And looking for the blessed hope
　　Of an eternal rest.

The peace of GOD is on their heads,
　　And so they wend away,
To homes all cheerful with the light,
　　Of love's inspiring ray!
And through the churchyard and the graves,
　　With kindly tears they fare,
Where every turf was decent laid,
　　And hallowed by a prayer.

The dead in CHRIST—they rest in hope;
　　And o'er their sleep sublime,
The shadow of the steeple moves,
　　From morn to vesper-chime:
On every mound, in solemn shade,
　　Its imaged cross doth lie,
As goes the sunlight to the west,
　　Or rides the moon on high.

I love the Church—the holy Church,
　　That o'er our life presides,
The birth, the bridal, and the grave,
　　And many an hour besides!
Be mine, through life, to live in her,
　　And when the LORD shall call,
To die in her—the spouse of CHRIST,
　　The Mother of us all.

DOCUMENT 19

Learning from Christ

One of the most noteworthy things about American religion was the constant attempt to apply it to daily life. It was religion for use, sanctifying American pragmatism. Throughout the nation, Sunday after Sunday, in pulpit after pulpit, the clergy preached about what Emerson once called "The Conduct of Life." True, many of the preachments were as easily forgotten or ignored then as now, but the fact remains that the standards embodied in religious teaching were not only the chief ones acknowledged in the United States, they were the only ones. Today, with the effect of religious teaching apparently on the wane, there is no ethic to take its place; there is nothing like the moral certainty of the 1840s. Among the many different denominations there was a large amount of agreement on what these standards should be, for the common bases were the Bible and the example of Christ.

The love of Christ is central to the Reverend Orville Dewey's discourse "The Problem of Life Resolved in the Life of Christ." His discourse is broader than a sermon, is largely devoid of doctrinal restrictions, and can perhaps represent as well as any document the essence of American religion in the 1840s.

In the ministry of this decade Dewey (1794–1882) enjoyed a nationwide reputation. He occupied prominent pulpits in Boston and New York, lectured widely before lyceums, and typified the active, dedicated urban clergyman. No frontier evangelist, he appeals in his many sermons and addresses to reason more than to emotion. But the office of reason is to bring about an emotional response; the mind is enlisted in the cause of love. The great design of this lucidly developed discourse is to arouse in us the love of Christ. Without it we are helpless; with it the truth is ours, and the truth will make us not only free but good. We "cannot *view* the truth," Dewey insists, "but through the medium of love." Only love can allow us to perceive, truly perceive, our most basic problem.

That problem is selfishness. If we learn to love Christ we can renounce our self-seeking. With self-renunciation will come a love of others and a happiness which only the unselfish can know. Dewey does not minimize the struggles before selflessness can be attained. But he firmly believes that it is possible, and possible for all.

Throughout the discourse he looks directly at us. He addresses his hearers simply and personally. His sentences are short, their rhythms flexible. His vocabulary is familiar, with a minimum of theological language. Perhaps it can be said that the effect of "The Problem of Life Resolved in the Life of Christ" will be dull to us only if we consider our problem already solved.

To some modern readers this will be nothing but a long homily. But if they will use their imagination it will tell them more about the aspirations, and limitations, of the 1840s than any other document in this book.

SOURCE: Orville Dewey, *Discourses on Human Nature, Human Life, and the Nature of Religion* (New York and Boston, 1847), pp. 255–69.

The Problem of Life Resolved in the Life of Christ

The words, "life and light," are constantly used by the Apostle John, after a manner long familiar in the Hebrew writings, for spiritual happiness, and spiritual truth. The inmost and truest life of man, the life of his life, is spiritual life—is, in other words, purity, love, goodness; and this inward purity, love, goodness, is the very light of life; that which brightens, blesses, guides it.

I have little respect for the ingenuity that is always

striving to work out from the simple language of Scripture, fanciful and far-fetched meanings; but it would seem, in the passage before us, as if John intended to state one of the deepest truths in the very frame of our being; and that is, *that goodness is the fountain of wisdom.*

Give me your patience a moment, and I will attempt to explain this proposition. "In it, was life;" that is, in this manifested and all-creating energy, this outflowing of the power of God, was a divine and infinite love and joy; and this life was the light of men. That is to say—love first, then light. Light does not create love; but love creates light. The good heart only can understand the good teaching. The doctrine of truth that guides a man, comes from the divinity of goodness that inspires him. But, it will be said, does not a man become holy or good, *in view* of truth? I answer, that he cannot *view* the truth, but through the medium of love. It is the loving view only, that is effective; that is any view at all. I must desire you to observe that I am speaking now of the primary convictions of a man, and not of the secondary influences that operate upon him. Light may *strengthen* love; a knowledge of the works and ways of God may have this effect, and it is properly presented for this purpose. But light cannot *originate* love. If love were not implanted in man's original and inmost being; if there were not placed there, the moral or spiritual feeling, that loves while it perceives goodness; all the speculative light in the universe, would leave man's nature, still and forever cold and dead as a stone. In short, loveliness is a quality which nothing but love can perceive. God cannot be known in his highest, that is, in his spiritual and holy nature, except by those who love him.

Now of this life and light, as we are immediately afterwards taught, Jesus Christ, not as a teacher merely, but as a being, is to us the great and appointed source. And therefore when Thomas says, "how can we know the way of which thou speakest," Jesus answers, "I *am* the way, and the truth and the life; no man cometh to the Father but by me." That is, no man can truly come to God, but in that spirit of filial love, of which I am the example.

In our humanity there is a problem. In Christ only is it perfectly solved. The speculative solution of that problem, is philosophy. The practical solution is a good life; and the only perfect solution is, the life of Christ. "In him was life, and the life was the light of men."

In him, I say, was solved the problem of life. What is that problem? What are the questions which it presents? They are these: Is there anything that can be achieved in life, in which our nature can find full satisfaction and sufficiency? And if there be any such thing, any such end of life; then is there any adaptation of things to that end? Are there any means or helps provided in life, for its attainment? Now the end must be the highest condition of our highest nature; and that end, we say, is virtue, sanctity, blessedness. And the helps or means are found in the whole discipline of life. But the end was perfectly accomplished in Christ, and it was accomplished through the very means which are appointed to us. "He was tempted in all points as we are, yet without sin;" and "he was made thus perfect through sufferings."

Our Saviour evidently regarded himself as sustaining this relation to human life; the enlightener of its darkness, the interpreter of its mystery, the solver of its problem. "I am the light of the world," he says; "he that followeth me, shall not walk in darkness, but shall have the light of life." And again: "I am come a light into the world, that whosoever believeth on me, should not abide in darkness." It was not for abstract teaching to men that he came, but for actual guidance in their daily abodes. It was not to deliver doctrines alone, nor to utter or echo back the intuitive convictions of our own minds, but to live a life and to die a death; and so to live and to die, as to cast light upon the dark paths in which we walk.

I need not say that there *is* darkness in the paths of men; that they stumble at difficulties, are ensnared by temptations, are perplexed by doubts; that they are anxious and troubled and fearful; that pain and affliction and sorrow often gather around the steps of their earthly pilgrimage. All this is written upon the very tablet of the human heart. And I *do* not say that all this is to be erased; but only that it is to be seen and read in a new light. I *do* not say that ills and trials and sufferings are to be removed from life; but only that over this scene of mortal trouble a new heaven is to be spread; and that the light of that heaven is Christ, the sun of righteousness.

To human pride, this may be a hard saying; to human philosophy, learning, and grandeur, it may be a hard saying; but still it is true, that the simple life of Christ, studied, understood and imitated, would shed a brighter light than all earthly wisdom can find, upon the dark trials and mysteries of our lot. It is true that whatever you most need or sigh for, whatever you most want, to still the troubles of your heart or compose the agitations of your mind, the simple life of Jesus can teach you.

To show this, I need only take the most ordinary admissions from the lips of any Christian, or I may say, of almost any unbeliever.

Suppose that the world were filled with beings like Jesus. Would not all the great ills of society be instantly relieved? Would you not immediately dismiss all your anxieties concerning it; perfectly sure that all was going on well? Would not all coercion, infliction, injury, injustice, and all the greatest suffering of life, disappear at once? If, at the stretching out of some wonder-working wand, that change could take place, would not the change be greater far, than if every house, hovel and prison on earth, were instantly turned into a palace of ease and abundance and splendour? Happy then would be these "human years;" and the eternal ages would roll on in brightness and beauty! The "still, sad music of humanity," that sounds through the world, now in the swellings of grief, and now in pensive melancholy, would be exchanged for anthems, lifted up to the march of time, and bursting out from the heart of the world!

But let us make another supposition, and bring it still nearer to ourselves. Were any one of us a perfect imitator of Christ; were any one of us clothed with the divinity of his virtue and faith; do you not perceive what the effect would be? Look around upon the circle of life's ills and trials, and observe the effect. Did sensual passions assail you? How weak would be their solicitation to the divine beatitude of your own heart! You would say, "I have meat to eat that ye know not of." Did want tempt you to do wrongly, or curiosity to do rashly? You would say to the one, "man shall not *live* by bread alone; there is a higher life which I must live;" and to the other, "thou shalt not tempt the Lord thy God." Did ambition spread its kingdoms and thrones before you, and ask you to swerve from your great allegiance? Your reply would be ready: "Get thee hence, Satan, for it is written, thou shalt worship the Lord thy God, and him only shalt thou serve." Did the storm of injury beat upon your head, or its silent shaft pierce your heart? In meekness you would bow that head, in prayer, that heart; saying, "Father forgive them, for they know not what they do." What sorrow could reach you; what pain, what anguish, that would not be soothed by a faith and a love like that of Jesus? And what blessing could light on you, that would not be brightened by a filial piety and gratitude like his? The world around you would be new, and the heavens over you would be new; for they would be all, and all around their ample range, and all through their glorious splendours, the presence and the visitation of a Father. And you yourself, would be a new creature; and you would enjoy a happiness new, and now scarcely known on earth.

And I cannot help observing here, that if such be the spontaneous conviction of every mind at all acquainted with Christianity, what a powerful independent argument there is for receiving Christ as a guide and example! It were an anomaly, indeed, to the eye of reason, to reject the solemn and self-claimed mission of one, whom it would be happiness to follow, whom it would be perfection to imitate. Yet if the former, the special mission, *were* rejected; if it were, as it may be, by possibility, honestly rejected; what is a man to think of himself, who passes by, and discards the latter, the teaching of the life of Christ? Let it be the man, Rousseau, or the man, Hume, or any man in these days, who says that he believes nothing in churches or miracles or missions from heaven. But he admits, as they did and as every one must, that in Jesus Christ was the most perfect unfolding of all divine beauty and holiness that the world ever saw. What, I say, is he to do with this undeniable and undenied Gospel of the *life* of Jesus? Blessed is he, if he receives it; that is unquestionable. All who read of him, all the world, admits that. But what shall we say if he rejects it? If any one could be clothed with the eloquence of Cicero or the wisdom of Socrates, and would not, all the world would pronounce him a fool, would say that he had denied his humanity. And surely if any one could be invested with all the beauty and grandeur of the life of Jesus, and would not; he must be stricken with utter moral fatuity; he must be accounted to have denied his highest humanity. The interpretation of his case is as plain as words can make it; and it is this: "light has come into the world, and men have loved darkness rather than light, because their deeds are evil."

"In him was life," says our text, "and the life was the light of men."

I have attempted to bring home the conviction of this, simply by bringing before your minds the supposition that the world, and we ourselves, were like him. But as no conviction, I think, at the present stage of our Christian progress, is so important as this, let me attempt to impress it, by another course of reflections. I say of *our* Christian progress. We have cleared away many obstacles, as we think, and have come near to the simplicity of the Gospel. No complicated ecclesiastical organization nor scholastic creed, stands between us and the solemn verities of Christianity. I am not now pronouncing upon those accumulations of human devices; but I mean especially to say, that no mystical notions of their necessity or importance, mingle themselves with *our* ideas of acceptance. We have come to stand before the simple, naked shrine of the original Gospel. We have come, through many human teachings and human admonitions, to Christ himself. But little will it avail us to have come so far, if we take not one step farther. *Now*, what I think we need is, to enter more deeply into the study and understanding of what Christ was.

This, let us attempt. And I pray you and myself, Brethren, not to be content with the little that can now be said; but let us carefully read the Gospels for ourselves, and lay the law of the life of Christ, with rigorous precision to our own lives, and see where they fail and come short. It is true indeed, and I would urge nothing beyond the truth, that the life of Jesus is not, in every respect, an example for us. That is to say, the manner of his life was, in some respects, different from what ours can, or should be. He was a teacher; and the most of us are necessarily and lawfully engaged in the business of life. He was sent on a peculiar mission; and none of us have such a mission. But the spirit that was in him, may be in us. To some of the traits of this spirit, as the only sources of light and help to us, let me now briefly direct your attention.

And first, consider his self-renunciation. How entire that self-renunciation was; how completely his aims went beyond personal ease and selfish gratification; how all his thoughts and words and actions were employed upon the work for which he was sent into the world; how his whole life, as well as his death, was an offering to that cause; I need not tell you. Indeed, so entirely is this his accredited character; so completely is he set apart in our thoughts not only to a peculiar office, but set apart too and separated from all human interests and affections, that we are liable to do his character in this respect, no proper justice. We isolate him, till he almost ceases to be an example to us; till he almost ceases to be a *virtuous* being. He stands alone in Judea; and the words—society, country, kindred, friendship, home—seem to have, to him, only a fictitious application. But these ties bound him as they do others; the gentleness and tenderness of his nature made him peculiarly susceptible to them; no more touching allusions to kindred and country can be found in human language, than his; as when he said, "Oh! Jerusalem! Jerusalem!" in foresight of her coming woes; as when he said on the cross, "behold thy mother! behold thy son!" Doubtless he desired to be a benefactor to his country, an honour to his family; and when Peter, deprecating his dishonour and degradation, said, "be it far from thee, Lord! this shall not be unto thee," and he turned and said unto Peter, "get thee behind me, Satan, thou savourest not the things that be of God, but those that be of men," it has been beautifully suggested that the very energy of that repulse to his enthusiastic and admiring disciple, shows perhaps that he felt that there was something in his mind that was leaning that way; that the things of men were contending with the things of God in him; that he too much dreaded the coming humiliation and agony, to wish to have that feeling fostered in his heart.

But he rejected all this; he renounced himself, renounced all the dear affections and softer pleadings of his affectionate nature, that he might be true to higher interests than his own, or his country's, or his kindred's.

Now I say that the same self-renunciation would relieve us of more than half of the difficulties and of the diseased and painful affections of our lives. Simple obedience to rectitude, instead of self-interest, simple self-culture, instead of ever cultivating the good opinion of others; how many disturbing and irritating questions would these single-hearted aims, take away from our bosom meditations! Let us not mistake the character of this self-renunciation. We are required, not to renounce the nobler and better affections of our natures, not to renounce happiness, not to renounce our just dues of honour and love from men. It is remarkable that our Saviour, amidst all his

meekness and all his sacrifices, always claimed that he deserved well of men, deserved to be honoured and beloved.
It is not to vilify ourselves that is required of us; not to
renounce our self-respect, the just and reasonable sense of
our merits and deserts; not to renounce our own righteousness, our own virtue, if we have any; such falsehood
towards ourselves gains no countenance from the example
of Jesus; but it is to renounce our sins, our passions, our
self-flattering delusions; and it is to forego all outward advantages which can be gained only through a sacrifice of
our inward integrity, or through anxious and petty con-
trivances and compliances. What we have to do, is to
choose and keep the better part; to secure that, and let
the worst take care of itself; to keep a good conscience,
and let opinion come and go as it will; to keep high, self-
respect, and to let low self-indulgence go; to keep inward
happiness, and let outward advantages hold a subordinate
place. Self-renunciation, in fine, is, not to renounce ourselves in the highest character; not to renounce our moral
selves, ourselves as the creatures and children of God;
herein rather it is to cherish ourselves, to make the most
of ourselves, to hold ourselves inexpressibly dear. What
then is it precisely to renounce ourselves? It is to renounce
our selfishness; to have done with this eternal self-considering which now disturbs and vexes our lives; to cease that
ever asking "and what shall we have?"—to be content with
the plenitude of God's abounding mercies; to feast upon
that infinite love, that is shed all around us and within
us; and so to be happy. I see many a person, in society,
honoured, rich, beautiful, but wearing still an anxious and
disturbed countenance; many a one upon whom this simple principle, this simple self-forgetting, would bring a
change in their appearance, demeanour, and the whole
manner of their living and being; a change that would
make them tenfold more beautiful, rich and honoured.
Yes; strange as it may seem to them; what they want, is,
to commune deeply, in prayer and meditation, with the
spirit of Jesus, to be clothed, not with outward adorning,

but with the simple self-forgetting, single-hearted truth and beauty of his spirit. This is the change, this is the conversion that they want, to make them lovely and happy beyond all the aspirations of their ambition, and all their dreams of happiness.

Have you never observed how happy is the mere visionary schemer, quite absorbed in his plans, quite thoughtless of everything else? Have you never remarked how easy and felicitous, is the manner in society, the eloquence in the public assembly, the whole life's action, of one who has forgotten himself? For this reason in part it is, that the eager pursuit of fortune is often happier than the after enjoyment of it; for now the man begins to *look about* for happiness, and *to ask* for a respect and attention which he seldom satisfactorily receives; and many such are found, to the wonder and mortification of their families, looking back from their splendid dwellings, and often referring to the humble shop in which they worked; and wishing in their hearts, that they were there again.

It is our inordinate self-seeking, self-considering, that is ever a stumbling-block in our way. It is this which spreads questions, snares, difficulties around us. It is this that darkens the very ways of Providence to us, and makes the world a less happy world to us, than it might be. There is one thought that could take us out from all these difficulties; but we cannot think it. There is one clue from the labyrinth; there is one solution of this struggling philosophy of life within us; it is found in that Gospel, that life of Jesus, with which we have, alas! but little deep, heart-acquaintance. Every one must know, that if he could be elevated to that self-forgetting simplicity and disinterestedness, he would be relieved from more than half of the inmost trials of his bosom. What then can be done for us, but that we be directed, and that too with a concern as solemn as our deepest wisdom and welfare, to the Gospel of Christ? "In him was life; and the life was the light of men."

In him was the life of perfect love. This is the second

all-enlightening, all-healing principle that the Gospel of
Christ commends to us. It is indeed the main and positive
virtue, of which self-renunciation is but the negative side.

Again, I need not insist upon the pre-eminence of this
principle in the life of our Saviour. But I must again remind you that this principle is not to be looked upon as
some sublime abstraction, as merely a love that drew him
from the bliss of heaven, to achieve some stupendous and
solitary work on earth. It was a vital and heartfelt love to
all around him; it was affection to his kindred, tenderness
to his friends, gentleness and forbearance towards his disciples, pity to the suffering, forgiveness to his enemies,
prayer for his murderers; love flowing all round him as the
garment of life, and investing pain and toil and torture and
death, with a serene and holy beauty.

It is not enough to renounce ourselves, and there to
stop. It is not enough to wrap ourselves in our close garment of reserve and pride, and to say, "the world cares
nothing for us, and we will care nothing for the world;
society does us no justice, and we will withdraw from it
our thoughts, and see how patiently we can live within
the confines of our own bosom, or in quiet communion,
through books, with the mighty dead." No man ever found
peace or light in this way. The misanthropic recluse is
ever the most miserable of men, whether he lives in cave
or castle. Every relation to mankind, of hate or scorn or
neglect, is full of vexation and torment. There is nothing
to do with men, but to love them; to contemplate their
virtues with admiration, their faults with pity and forbearance, and their injuries with forgiveness. Task all the ingenuity of your mind to devise some other thing, but you
never can find it. To all the haughtiness and wrath of men,
I say—however they may disdain the suggestion—the spirit
of Jesus is the only help for you. To hate your adversary
will not help you; to kill him will not help you; nothing
within the compass of the universe can help you, but to
love him. Oh! how wonderfully is man shut up to wis-

dom—barred, as I may say, and imprisoned and shut up to wisdom; and yet he will not learn it.

But let that love flow out upon all around you, and what could harm you? It would clothe you with an impenetrable, heaven-tempered armour. Or suppose, to do it justice, that it leaves you, all defencelessness, as it did Jesus; all vulnerableness, through delicacy, through tenderness, through sympathy, through pity; suppose that you suffer, as all must suffer; suppose that you be wounded, as gentleness only can be wounded; yet how would that love flow, with precious healing, through every wound! How many difficulties too, both within and without a man, would it relieve! How many dull *minds* would it rouse; how many depressed minds would it lift up! How many troubles, in society, would it compose; how many enmities would it soften; how many questions, answer! How many a knot of mystery and misunderstanding would be untied by one word spoken in simple and confiding truth of heart! How many a rough path would be made smooth, and crooked way be made strait! How many a solitary place would be made glad, if love were there; and how many a dark dwelling would be filled with light! "In him was life, and the life was the light of men."

Once more: there was a sublime spirituality in the mind of Jesus, which must come into our life, to fill up the measure of its light. It is not enough in my view, to yield ourselves to the blessed bonds of love and self-renunciation, in the immediate circles of our lives. Our minds must go into the infinite and immortal regions, to find sufficiency and satisfaction for the present hour. There must be a breadth of contemplation in which this world shrinks, I will not say to a point, but to the narrow span that it is. There must be aims, which reign over the events of life, and make us feel that we can resign all the advantages of life, yea, and life itself; and yet be "conquerors and more than conquerors through him who has loved us."

There is many a crisis in life when we need a faith like the martyr's to support us. There are hours in life like martyrdom—as full of bitter anguish, as full of utter earthly desolation; in which more than our sinews, in which we feel as if our very heart-strings were stretched and lacerated on the rack of affliction; in which life itself loses its value, and we ask to die; in whose dread struggle and agony, life might drop from us, and not be minded. Oh! then must our cry, like that of Jesus, go up to the pitying heavens for help, and nothing but the infinite and the immortal can help us. Calculate, then, all the gains of earth, and they are trash; all its pleasures, and they are vanity; all its hopes, and they are illusions; and then, when the world is sinking beneath us, must we seek the everlasting arms to bear us up, to bear us up to heaven. Thus was it with our great Example, and so must it be with us. "In him was life;" the life of self-renunciation, the life of love, the life of spiritual and all-conquering faith; and that life is the light of men. Oh! blessed light! come to our darkness; for our soul is dark, our way is dark, for want of thee; come to our darkness, and turn it into day; and let it shine brighter and brighter, till it mingles with the light of the all-perfect and everlasting day!

Document 20

Shouting for Christ

American religion permeated the fabric of American life. It comprehended town and country, North and South, rich and poor, old and young; it could be found as well on the frontier as in the city. In point: the contribution of Peter Cartwright.

If the Reverend Orville Dewey typifies the dedicated city minister, the Reverend Peter Cartwright (1785–1872) typifies the tireless frontier evangelist. He tells much of his story in the *Autobiography of Peter Cartwright*, which was edited by W. P. Strickland and published in 1857. It found a wide response, reaching its twenty-third thousand by the next year and qualifying as a best seller. No hardships could deter Cartwright from his mission. As a matter of fact, the relish he took in it made the hardships seem slight. In the winter of 1845/46, which is the time of the selection printed below, he had many days like the one he described just before the selection opens. On that day he ended his labors by looking for a lodging for the night. He felt cold, tired, hungry. But he fortunately found a cabin where an old acquaintance welcomed him and fed him a "good backwoods supper." Then Cartwright prayed with his host and the host's family until most of them "got shouting happy." When the evening was over, Cartwright slept the sleep of peace, he reported, though he was still wakeful enough to note that one young man in the family "shouted and praised God nearly all night." When morning came Cartwright left, and the selection continues the story of his lively labors for Christ.

The selection is useful not only because it testifies to the power of the Christian religion but also because it reminds us that the ungodly were likewise known to be among us. Cartwright's tart comment, for instance, on Waynesville, Illinois, is revealing: "a very wicked little village."

SOURCE: Peter Cartwright, *Autobiography of Peter Cartwright, the Backwoods Preacher*, ed. W. P. Strickland (New York and Cincinnati, 1857), pp. 445–50.

[Winter of 1845/46]

Next morning I started on to my quarterly meeting, and just as I got to the bridge, on the main Sangamon River, the high water had surrounded it, but not deep enough to swim my horse, who waded through, and I passed over safely, and got to my quarterly meeting in good time; and although the weather was disagreeable, yet the people crowded out. The word of God took hold on sinners, many of them wept, and cried for mercy, and found by happy experience, that Christ had power on earth to forgive sins. About twenty-eight were soundly converted to God, the most of whom joined the Church, and Methodism was planted here firmly, never to be destroyed, I humbly trust. I have often thought of this scene, and many similar scenes through which I have passed, during my protracted ministry; and when I look back on them my heart grows warm, and swells with gratitude to my heavenly Father for the sanction he has given to my poor little ministry amid all the sacrifices and sufferings through which I have passed, as a Methodist itinerant preacher; and to his holy name be all the glory, both now and forever!

In the Bloomington District I had many warm personal friends, many members that I had received into the Church in Kentucky, and some, in whose houses I had preached in the days of my comparative youth; and although it was a hard district for me to travel, my family living entirely beyond its bounds, yet I was much attached to this field of labor and the brethren, preachers, and people. Some of these old members had fought side by side with me in Kentucky and Western Tennessee, where and when Methodism had many glorious triumphs over slavery, whisky, and superfluous dressing. These were her internal foes; but she not only triumphed over these enemies, but she triumphed over her combined hosts of inveterate and uncompromising sectarian enemies, and attained an elevated position in the affections of very many of the best citizens of those states. Now, many of those brethren who sung, prayed, and preached to and with us, have fallen asleep in Jesus, and sing and shout in heaven; while a few, and comparatively very few of us old soldiers, linger on the shores of time, still fighting under the banners of Christ; and our motto is, "Victory, or death!"

Our next annual conference sat in Paris, Edgar County, Illinois, September 23d, 1846; Bishop Hamline presiding. Our next, at Jacksonville, Morgan County, Illinois, September 22d, 1847; Bishop Waugh presiding. During the three years I was on the Bloomington District we had general peace and some considerable prosperity. During the last conference year that I was on this district, some incidents occurred, which I will relate.

My winter's round of quarterly meetings commenced at Bloomington; Brother Samuel Elliott was preacher in charge, and it was his second year. There had fallen a very deep snow, which had greatly blocked up the roads; and by some strange forgetfulness in me, I started for my Bloomington quarterly meeting a week too soon; it was very cold, and I had an open bleak prairie to travel through. The first day, I rode about forty miles, and late in the evening I arrived at a very friendly brother's house, but, behold! when I went in, I found a large company, consisting of parts of several families, that had taken shelter under this friendly roof, from the severe cold and pitiless storm of snow that had fallen; but all was as pleasant as could be expected in a crowd, in very cold weather. When we came to retire to rest, it was found that all the beds had to be put into requisition, to accommodate the females; what was to be done with the five or six men of us that composed a part of the company? Our accommodation was cared for in something like the following way. A large fire was made up, and plenty of wood brought in to keep it up all night. Large buffalo robes and quilts were spread down before the fire, and plenty of blankets and quilts for covering; and after praying together, we all retired to rest, and though our bedding was hard, we slept soundly.

Rising early next morning, I mounted my horse, and started on my way to Waynesville, a little village which gave name to one of my circuits. Brother John A. Brittenham was preacher in charge. He saluted me in good brotherly style, and inquired which way I was traveling. I informed him I was bound for the Bloomington quarterly meeting. He said, "That meeting is not till Saturday week; so Brother Elliott informs me."

I was surprised, and immediately turned to the District Book, and found it even so. Well, what was now to be done? Shall I retrace my steps, two days back home; and then travel over this dreary cold road here again? Or what shall I do? Said Brother Brittenham,

"Stay with us, and let us have meeting every night till just time for you to reach your quarterly meeting in Bloomington."

"Agreed," said I.

This was a very wicked little village. The Church was feeble, and greatly needed a revival. We sent out, and gathered a small congregation, and tried to preach to them; and there were some signs of good. Next night our congregation was considerably larger, with increasing evidences of good. The third night our house was not sufficient to hold the congregation; and there were mighty displays of the power of God. Some shouted aloud the praise of God; some wept. Our altar was crowded with mourners, and several souls were converted; but, notwithstanding, the place was made awful by reason of the power of God; some mocked, and made sport. Among these were two very wicked young men, ringleaders in wickedness. After interrupting the congregation, and profanely cursing the religious exercises of the people of God, they mounted their horses, and started home. After, or about the time of their starting home, they made up a race for a trifling sum, or a bottle of whisky, and started off, under whip, at full speed; but had not run their horses far, till the horse of the most daring and presumptuous of those young men flew the track, and dashed his rider against a tree, knocked the breath out of him, and he never spoke again. Thus, unexpectedly, this young man, with all his blasphemous oaths still lingering on his lips, was suddenly hurried into eternity, totally unprepared to meet his God.

The tidings of this awful circumstance ran with lightning speed through the village and country round; an awful panic seized upon the multitude, and such weeping and wailing among his relatives and people at large, I hardly ever beheld before. There was no more persecution during the protracted meeting, which lasted for many days; and it seemed, at one time, after this calamity had fallen on this young man, that the whole country was in an agony for salvation. Many, very many, professed religion and joined the Church, but the exact number I do not now recollect.

Before our meeting closed here, Brother Elliott, who had kept up a series of meetings in Bloomington preparatory to the quarterly meeting—which meetings had been greatly blessed—met me in Waynesville, and we returned to the battle-field in Bloomington again. Our meetings were recommenced, and, with constantly increasing interest, were kept up night and day for a considerable length of time. Many were convicted, reclaimed, converted, and built up in the most holy faith. Of the number of conversions and accessions to the Church I do not now remember, but it occurs to me that it was seventy or eighty. Brother Elliott's labors were greatly blessed in this charge, the last year of his pastoral labors there.

Another incident occurred, while I was on this district,

which I feel disposed to name. There were a good many settlements and neighborhoods in the bounds of the district where the people had become, in opinion, Universalists, and, judging from their morality, or rather their immorality, this doctrine suited them well; and it is a little strange, but no stranger than true, I say, without any fear of contradiction, the most of these Universalists had been members of some Christian Church, and had backslidden and lost their religion, if ever they had any. In the course of my peregrinations I fell in with one of their preachers, who really thought himself a mighty smart, talented man, and was ready for debate, in public or private, on all occasions. His assumed boldness gave him great consequence with his hoodwinked disciples. He was very loquacious, and had some clumsy play on words. After conversing with him a few minutes, I took my line, common sense, and sounded him. He affected to have great veneration for my gray hairs; but I soon found his veneration for my gray hairs arose more from a fear of my gray arguments than otherwise. He was a man of slender constitution, and had been, and was then, greatly afflicted with sore eyes, and was threatened with the total loss of sight. He, in the course of our conversation, said there could not be any such being as a personal devil, who could be everywhere present at one and the same time, tempting mankind to evil; and as for a future place of punishment called hell, there was no such place; that the temptations of man arose from his fallen nature and not from the devil, and the punishment that man would suffer for his evil doings he suffered in this life, and these sufferings consisted in the compunctions of conscience for his moral delinquencies, and in his bodily afflictions.

"Well," said I, "my dear sir, if your argument is a sound one, I must draw very unfavorable conclusions in reference to the magnitude of your crimes."

"Why so?" responded he.

"Well, sir, for a very good reason. As to your moral delinquencies, and your compunctions of conscience, they are best known, perhaps, to yourself; but as to your bodily afflictions, as a punishment, I think I can draw very fair inferences, for I cannot conceive of a greater bodily affliction than the loss of sight; and as your vision is almost gone, and you have expressed your firm belief that you will lose your sight altogether, I must, if your doctrine be true, number you among the greatest sinners on earth, for God is too wise to err, and too good to inflict undeserved punishment." I tell you his stars and stripes were not only dropped to half mast, but trailed in the dust.

DOCUMENT 21

The Church of Rome

In 1830 there were some 600,000 Catholics in the United States. By 1850 there were 3,500,000. Behind the remarkable increase, most of which came during the 1840s, lay the potato famine in Ireland, the social revolts in Germany, and cheaper fares across the Atlantic. In both 1845 and 1846 Ireland was plagued by the potato rot. The result was something not far from mass starvation. Irishmen by the hundreds of thousands streamed across the ocean throughout the last half of the decade. The German immigrants were fewer in number; but especially at the end of the decade, the revolt of 1848 having failed, the proportion of intellectuals among them was considerable. During all this time the Catholics already in this country, most notably in Maryland, Massachusetts, and New York, were increasing too.

Perhaps the clearest picture of the appeal of the Catholic faith can be painted by a convert. Unlike the "cradle Catholic" he sees with a fresh eye, taking nothing for granted. If that convert is also a man of exceptional intelligence, breadth, and—sometimes—belligerence, his account of the process of his conversion should be exceptionally informative. Such a man was the one-time Transcendentalist Orestes Brownson (1803–76). He published his book *The Convert* in 1857. In it he traced his path from the most permissive of Protestantisms to the discipline of the Catholic church. A key chapter, "Become a Catholic," deals with his official conversion in 1844, under the instruction of the Right Reverend J. B. Fitzpatrick, and his rationale for it.

Brownson addresses himself both to those without and those within the fold. He bases his new allegiance, as he explains, on faith and reason. In the selection below he calmly but firmly presents his case. For a diehard controversialist he argues with unexpected coolness. He begins by referring to the fact that he has now made public, by means of his book, the rationale for his new allegiance. To him it is so logical that he feels his non-Catholic friends *should* not object to it and his Catholic friends *will* not object.

The rationale can be summed up something like this. Fully aware that he is speaking in an age of skepticism, Brownson asserts that revelation and faith are the foundations of religion. Reason, or philosophy, must build upon them. Principles must come first, not method. The trouble with current philosophy is that it begins with method. As a result it is "cold, lifeless, and offers only dead forms." Yet the modern skeptic clings to it and avoids the true reality based on religious belief in general and on Catholic doctrine in particular. In the course of his argument Brownson proceeds to consider one of the chief obstacles to belief, the presence of evil in this world. He tries to explain to the skeptic why a good God allowed evil to appear in His creation. Brownson concludes the argument, and the chapter, with a call to the Catholic philosophers to expound systematically the kind of logical principles which have led him to the Catholic church.

SOURCE: Orestes A. Brownson, *The Convert; or, Leaves from my Experience* (New York, 1857), pp. 385–96.

Become a Catholic

My Catholic friends cannot look upon my doing so [that is, publishing the rationale for his conversion], after years of probation, as indicative of any departure from the diffidence and humility which at first restrained me from putting it forth. The doctrine is new only in form, not in substance, and is only a development and application of principles which every Catholic theologian does and must hold. The fact that it was first developed and applied by one outside of the Church, and served to bring him to the Church, since it is not repugnant to any principle of Catholic faith or theology, is rather in its favor, for it creates a presumption that it really contains something fitted to reach a certain class of minds at least, and to remove the obstacles they experience in yielding assent to the claims of the Church. Non-Catholics do not, indeed, know Catholicity as well as Catholics know it, but they know better their own objections to it, and what is necessary to remove them. If in investigating questions before them, in attempting to establish a system of their own, with no thought of seeking either to believe Catholicity, or to find an answer to the objections they feel to the Church, they find these objections suddenly answered, and themselves forced, by principles which they have adopted, to recognize the Church as authority for reason, it is good evidence that these principles, and the methods of reasoning they authorize, are well adapted to the purpose of the defenders of the faith, and not unworthy of the attention of Catholic controversialists, when, as in my case, they neither supersede nor interfere with the ordinary methods of theologians.

Motives of credibility or methods of proof should be adapted to the peculiar character and wants of the age, or class of persons addressed. Philosophy could never have attained to Christian revelation, or the sacred mysteries of our holy religion; but now that the revelation is made, that the mysteries are revealed, we know that all sound philosophy does and must accord with them; must, as far as it goes, prepare the mind to receive them; and taken in connection with the historical facts in the case, must demand them as its own complement. Now, if I am not mistaken, a philosophy of this sort has become indispensable. The age is skeptical, I grant, but its skepticism relates rather to the prevailing philosophy than to reason, of which that philosophy professes to be the exponent. It distrusts reasoning rather than reason. It has no confidence in the refinements and subtilties of schoolmen, and though often sophistical, it is in constant dread of being cheated out of its wits by the sophistry of the practised logician. Conclusions in matters of religion, which are arrived at only by virtue of a long train of reasoning, even when it perceives no defect in the premises and no flaw in the reasoning, do not command its assent, for it fears there may still be something wrong either in the reasoning or the premises, which escapes its sagacity. The ordinary motives of credibility do not move non-Catholics to believe, because these motives start from principles which they do not accept, or accept with so much vagueness and uncertainty, that they do not serve to warrant assent even to strictly logical conclusions drawn from them. Moreover, they do not reach their peculiar difficulties, do not touch their real objections; and though they seem overwhelming to Catholics, they leave all their objections remaining in full force, and their inability to believe undiminished.

The reason is in the fact that the philosophy which prevails, and after which the modern mind is, in some sense, moulded, is opposed to Christian revelation, and does not recognize as fundamental the principles or premises which warrant the conclusions drawn in favor of Christianity. The prevalent philosophy with very nearly the whole scientific culture of the age, is not only un-Christian, but anti-Christian, and if accepted, renders the Christian faith an impossibility for a logical mind. There is always lurking in the mind a suspicion of the antecedent improbability of the whole Evangelical doctrine. Apologists may say, and say truly, that there is and can be no contradiction between philosophy and faith, but, unhappily, the philosophy between which and faith there is no contradiction, is not generally recognized. Between the official and prevalent philosophy of the day, between the principles which have passed from that philosophy into the general mind, and Catholic faith, there is a contradiction, and not a few Catholics even retain their faith only in spite of their philosophy. The remedy is in revising our philosophy, and in placing it in harmony with the great principles of Catholic faith. I will not say with Bonetty that the method of the Scholastics leads to rationalism and infidelity, for that is not true; but I will say that that method, as developed and applied in the modern world, especially the non-Catholic world, does not serve as a preamble to faith, and does place the mind of the unbeliever in a state unfitted to give to the ordinary motives of credibility their due weight, or any weight at all.

Modern philosophy is mainly a method, and develops a method of reasoning instead of presenting principles to intellectual contemplation. It takes up the question of method before that of principles, and seeks by the method to determine the principles, instead of leaving the principles to determine the method. Hence it becomes simply a doctrine of science, *Wissenschaftslehre*, a doctrine of abstractions, or pure mental conceptions, instead of being, as it should be, a doctrine of reality, of things divine and human. It is cold, lifeless, and offers only dead forms, which satisfy neither the intellect nor the heart. It does not, and cannot move the mind towards life and reality. It obscures first principles, and impairs the native force and truthfulness of the intellect. The evil can be remedied only by returning from this philosophy of abstractions,—from modern psychology, or subjectivism, to the philosophy of reality, the philosophy of life, which presents to the mind the first principles of all life and of all knowledge as identical.

Herein is the value of the process by which I arrived at the Church. I repeat again and again, that philosophy did not conduct me into the Church, but just in proportion as I advanced towards a sound philosophy, I did advance towards the Church. As I gained a real philosophy, a philosophy which takes its principles from the order of being, from life, from things as they are or exist, instead of the abstractions of the schools, faith flowed in, and I seized with joy and gladness the Christian Church and her dogmas. The non-Catholic world is far less in love with heresy or infidelity than is commonly supposed, and our arguments, clear and conclusive as they are to us, fail because they fail to meet their objections, and convince their reason. They are not addressed to reason as it is developed in them, and answer not their objections as they themselves apprehend them. The non-Catholic world is not deficient in logical force or mental acuteness, but it expresses itself in broad generalizations, rather than in precise and exact statements. Its objections are inductions from particulars, vaguely apprehended and loosely expressed, are more subjective than objective, and rarely admit of a rigid scientific statement or definition. To define them after the manner of the schools, and to reduce them to a strictly logical formula, is in most cases to refute them; but the non-Catholic is not thus convinced that they are untenable, for he feels them still remaining in his mind. He attributes their apparent refutation to some logical sleight-of-hand, or dialectic jugglery, which escapes his detection. He remains unconvinced, because his objection has been met by a refutation which has given no new light to his understanding, or made him see any higher or broader principles than he was before in possession of.

An external refutation of the unbeliever's objections effects nothing, because the real objection is internal, and the refutation leaves the internal as it was before. The secret of convincing is not to put error out of the mind, but truth into it. There is little use in arguing against the objections of non-Catholics, or in laboring directly for their refutation. We can effectually remove them only by correcting the premises from which the unbeliever reasons, and giving him first principles, which really enlighten his reason, and as they become operative, expel his error by their own light and force. This can be done only by bringing the age back, or up to a philosophy which conforms the order of knowledge to the order of being, the logical order to the order of reality, and gives the first principles of things as the first principles of science. If Catholicity be from God, it does and must conform to the first principles of things, to the order of reality, to the loss of life or intelligence, and hence a philosophy which conforms to the same order will conform to Catholicity, and supply all the rational elements of Catholic theology. Such a philosophy is the desideratum of the age, and we must have it, not as a substitute for faith, but as its preamble, as its hand-maid, or we cannot recall the non-believing world to the Church of God; because it is only by such a philosophy that we can really enlighten the mind of the unbeliever, and really and effectually remove his objections, or show that it is in fact true that there is no contradiction between Catholicity and philosophy.

The greatest and most serious difficulty in the way of the unbeliever, is his inability to reconcile faith and reason, that is, the Divine plan in the order of grace with the Divine plan evident in the order of nature. The Christian order appears to him as an after-thought, as an anomaly, if not a contradiction, in the general plan of Divine Providence, incompatible with the perfections of God, which we must admit, if we admit a God at all. It strikes him as unforeseen, and not contemplated by the Divine Mind in the original intention to create, and as brought in to remedy the defects of creation, or to make amends for an unexpected and deplorable failure. The two orders, again, seem to stand apart, and to imply a dualism, in fact, an antagonism, which it is impossible to reconcile with the unity and perfections of God. If God is infinite in all his attributes, in wisdom, power, and goodness, why did he not make nature perfect, or all he desired it, in the beginning, so as to have no need to interfere, to repair, or to amend it, or to create a new order in its place, or even to preserve it, and avert its total ruin? It is of no use to decry such thoughts and questions as irreverent, as impious, as blasphemous; for they arise spontaneously in the unbelieving mind, and denunciation will not suppress them. It will serve no purpose to bring in here the ordinary motives of credibility, drawn from the wants of nature, the insufficiency of reason, prophecies, miracles, and historical monuments, for these only create new and equally grave difficulties. What is wanted is not argument, but instruction and explanation. It is necessary to show, not merely assert, that the two orders are not mutually antagonistic, that one and the same principle of life runs through them both, that they correspond one to the other, and really constitute but two parts of one comprehensive whole, and are equally embraced in the original plan and purpose of God in creating. God could have created man, had he chosen, in a state of pure nature; but in point of fact he did not, and nature has never for a single instant existed as pure nature. It has, from the first moment of its existence, been under a supernatural Providence; and even if man had not sinned, there would still have been a sufficient reason for the Incarnation, to raise human nature to union with God, to make it the nature of God, and to enable us, through its elevation, to enjoy endless beatitude in heaven.

The doctrine that all dependent life is life by communion of the subject with the object, shows that this is possible, shows the common principle of the two orders, and thus prepares the mind to receive and yield to the arguments drawn from the wants of nature, the insufficiency of reason, prophecies, miracles, and historical monuments; for it shows these to be in accordance with the original intent of the Creator, and that these wants and this insufficiency, are wants and insufficiency, not in relation to the purely natural order, but in relation to the supernatural. Natural reason is sufficient for natural reason, but it is not sufficient for man; for man was intended from the beginning to live simultaneously in two orders, the one natural and the other supernatural.

Taking into consideration the fact that the skepticism of our age lies further back than the ordinary motives of credibility extend—further back than did the skepticism our ancestors had to meet, and shows itself under a different form, I believe the process by which I was conducted towards the Church is not only a legitimate process in itself, but one which, in these times, in abler hands than mine, may be adopted with no little advantage. The present non-Catholic mind has as much difficulty in admitting the motives of credibility, as usually urged, as it has in accepting Christianity without them. Prior to adducing them, we must, it seems to me, prepare the way for them, by rectifying our philosophy, and giving to our youth a philosophical doctrine which reproduces the order of things, of reality, of life; not merely an order of dead abstractions. Such a philosophy, I think, will be found in that which underlies the process I have detailed; and I hope it is no presumption or lack of modesty on my part, to recommend it to the attention of the schools, as well as to the consideration of all whose office or vocation it is to combat the unbelief of the age and country.

The Sects: In Particular the Shakers

The great major denominations, Methodist, Baptist, and Presbyterian, held the center of the stage. However, there also existed an almost bewildering variety of minor sects. It is hard to select one to represent the rest but perhaps the Shakers will do, for they carried sectarianism to an ultimate. In the first volume of the *Lowell Offering*, published by the mill girls in 1841, one C.B. told the story of her two trips to a Shaker village in upstate New York. Her account is praiseworthy for its fairness, since the Shakers were a highly controversial group. C.B. penetrates the sensational surface of Shakerism and stresses the fact that the Shakers were trying to apply some of the basic principles of Christianity. Certain of her friends at the mills must have thought the account of her first visit overly favorable, and so she adds to her report of the second visit a touch of apology. She realizes, she says, that she may have spoken too well of Shaker life; on the other hand she affirms that her facts are still facts. Her reports are reprinted below, the first being entitled "Visit to the Shakers."

She writes of two things that especially impress her. One is the orderly deportment of the Shakers. They conduct themselves with a propriety so strict that it borders on the singular. The other—and a factory girl would notice it—is their diligence. They work longer and harder than the paid employees at the Lowell mills. They work in fact during most of their waking moments. They interrupt their labors only for the religious meetings (when they shake) and for the so-called union meetings. These last are brief social periods, one each evening, when in small groups they visit together. But the Shaker pattern still holds: the men sit stiffly in one row of chairs and the women, facing them, sit in the other. Their spit-boxes stand in a line between them—this is the era of expectoration. Order continues to rule.

SOURCE: "C.B.," "Visit to the Shakers," *Lowell Offering*, I (? 1841), 279–81; and "A Second Visit to the Shakers," I (? 1841), 337–40.

Visit to the Shakers

Sometime in the summer of 18—, I paid a visit to one of the Shaker villages in the State of New York. Previously to this, many times and oft had I (when tired of the noise and contention of the world, its erroneous opinions, and its wrong practices) longed for some retreat, where, with a few chosen friends, I could enjoy the present, forget the past, and be free from all anxiety respecting any future portion of time. And often had I pictured, in imagination, a state of happy society, where one common interest prevailed—where kindness and brotherly love were manifested in all of the every-day affairs of life—where liberty and equality would live, not in name, but in very deed—where idleness in no shape whatever would be tolerated—and where vice of every description would be banished, and neatness, with order, would be manifested in all things.

Actually to witness such a state of society, was a happiness which I never expected. I thought it to be only a thing among the airy castles which it has ever been my delight to build. But with this unostentatious and truly kind-hearted people, the Shakers, I found it; and the reality, in beauty and harmony, exceeded even the picturings of imagination.

No unprejudiced mind could, for a single moment, resist the conviction that this singular people, with regard to their worldly possessions, lived in strict conformity to the teachings of Jesus of Nazareth. There were men in this society who had added to the common stock thousands and tens of thousands of dollars; they nevertheless labored, dressed, and esteemed themselves as no better and fared in all respects, like those who had never owned, neither added to the society, any worldly goods whatever. The cheerfulness with which they bore one another's burdens, made even the temporal calamities, so unavoidable among the inhabitants of the earth, to be felt but lightly.

This society numbered something like six hundred persons, who in many respects were differently educated, and who were of course in possession of a variety of prejudices; and were of contrary dispositions and habits. Conversing with one of their Elders respecting them, he said, "You may say that these were rude materials of which to compose a church, and speak truly: but here (though strange it may seem) they are worked into a building, with no sound of axe or hammer. And however discordant they were in a state of nature, the square and the plumbline have been applied to them, and they now admirably fit the places which they were designed to fill. Here the idle become industrious, the prodigal contracts habits of frugality, the parsimonious become generous and liberal, the intemperate quit the tavern and the grog-shop, the debauchee forsakes the haunts of dissipation and infamy, the swearer leaves off his habits of profanity, the liar is changed into a person of truth, the thief becomes an honest man, and the sloven becomes neat and clean."

The whole deportment of this truly singular people, together with the order and neatness which I witnessed in their houses, shops and gardens, to all of which I had free access for the five days which I remained with them, together with the conversations which I held with many of the people of both sexes, confirmed the words of the Elder. Truly, thought I, there is not another spot in the wide earth where I could be so happy as I could be here, provided the religious faith and devotional exercises of the Shakers were agreeable to my own views. Although I could not see the utility of their manner of worship, I felt not at all disposed to question that it answered the end for which spiritual worship was designed, and as such is accepted by our heavenly Father. That the Shakers have a love for the gospel exceeding that which is exhibited by professing christians in general, cannot be doubted by any one who is acquainted with them. For on no other principle could large families, to the number of fifty or sixty, live together like brethren and sisters. And a number of these families could not on any other principles save those of the gospel, form a society, and live in peace and harmony, bound together by no other bond than that of brotherly love, and take of each other's property, from day to day, and from year to year, using it indiscriminately, as every one hath need, each willing that his brother should use his property, as he uses it himself, and all this without an equivalent.

Many think that a united interest in all things temporal, is contrary to reason. But in what other light, save that of common and united interest, could the words of Christ's prophecy or promise be fulfilled? According to the testimony of Mark, Christ said, "There is no man who hath left house, or brethren, or sisters, or father, or mother, or wife, or children, or lands, for my sake and the gospel's, but he shall receive an hundred fold now in this time, houses, and brethren, and sisters, and mothers, and children, and lands, with persecutions, and in the world to come eternal life." Not only in fact, but in theory, is an hundred fold of private interest out of the question. For a believer who forsook all things, could not possess an hundred fold of all things, only on the principle in which he could possess *all that* which his brethren possessed, while they also possessed the same in a united capacity.

In whatever light it may appear to others, to me it appears beautiful indeed, to see a just and an impartial equality reign, so that the rich and the poor may share an equal privilege, and have all their wants supplied. That the Shakers are in reality what they profess to be, I doubt not. Neither do I doubt that many, very many lessons of wisdom might be learned of them, by those who profess to be wiser. And to all who wish to know if "any good thing can come out of Nazareth," I would say, you had better "go and see."

A Second Visit to the Shakers

I was so well pleased with the appearances of the Shakers, and the prospect of quietness and happiness among them, that I visited them a second time. I went with a determination to ascertain as much as I possibly could of their forms and customs of worship, the every-day duties devolving on the members, &c.; and having enjoyed excellent opportunities for acquiring the desired information, I wish to present a brief account of what "I verily do know" in relation to several particulars.

First of all, justice will not permit me to retract a word in relation to the industry, neatness, order, and general good behavior, in the Shaker settlement which I visited. In these respects, that singular people are worthy of all commendation—yea, they set an example for the imitation of Christians every-where. Justice requires me to say, also, that their hospitality is proverbial, and deservedly so. They received and entertained me kindly, and (hoping perhaps that I might be induced to join them) they extended extra-civilities to me. I have occasion to modify the expression of my gratitude in only one particular—and that is, one of the female elders made statements to me concerning the requisite confessions to be made, and the forms of admission to their society, which statements she afterwards denied, under circumstances that rendered her denial a most aggravated insult. Declining farther notice of this matter, because of the indelicacy of the confessions alluded to, I pass to notice,

1st. The domestic arrangements of the Shakers. However strange the remark may seem, it is nevertheless true, that our factory population work fewer hours out of every twenty-four, than are required by the Shakers, whose bell to call them from their slumbers, and also to warn them that it is time to commence the labors of the day, rings much earlier than our factory bells; and its calls were obeyed, in the family where I was entertained, with more punctuality than I ever knew the greatest "workey" among my numerous acquaintances (during the fourteen years in which I have been employed in different manufacturing establishments) to obey the calls of the factory-bell. And not until nine o'clock in the evening were the labors of the day closed, and the people assembled at their religious meetings.

Whoever joins the Shakers with the expectation of relaxation from toil, will be greatly mistaken, since they deem it an indispensable duty to have every moment of time profitably employed. The little portions of leisure which the females have, are spent in knitting—each one having a basket of knitting-work for a constant companion.

Their habits of order are, in many things, carried to the extreme. The first bell for their meals rings for all to repair to their chambers, from which, at the ringing of the second bell, they descend to the eating-room. Here, all take their appropriate places at the tables, and after locking their hands on their breasts, they drop on their knees, close their eyes, and remain in this position about two minutes. Then they rise, seat themselves, and with all expedition swallow their food; then rise on their feet, again lock their hands, drop on their knees, close their eyes, and in about two minutes rise and retire. Their meals are taken in silence, conversation being prohibited.

Those whose chambers are in the fourth story of one building, and whose work-shops are in the third story of another building, have a daily task in climbing stairs, which is more oppressive than any of the rules of a manufacturing establishment.

2d. With all deference, I beg leave to introduce some of the religious views and ceremonies of the Shakers.

From the conversation of the elders, I learned that they considered it doing God service, to sever the sacred ties of husband and wife, parent and child—the relationship existing between them being contrary to their religious views

—views which they believe were revealed from heaven to "Mother Ann Lee," the founder of their sect, and through whom they profess to have frequent revelations from the spiritual world. These communications, they say, are often written on gold leaves, and sent down from heaven to instruct the poor, simple Shakers in some new duty. They are copied, and perused, and preserved with great care. I one day heard quite a number of them read from a book, in which they were recorded, and the names of several of the brethren and sisters to whom they were given by the angels, were told me. One written on a gold leaf, was (as I was told) presented to Proctor Sampson by an angel, so late as the summer of 1841. These "revelations" are written partly in English, and partly in some unintelligible jargon, or unknown tongue, having a spiritual meaning, which cannot be understood only by those who possess the spirit in an eminent degree. They consist principally of songs, which they sing at their devotional meetings, and which are accompanied with dancing, and many unbecoming gestures and noises.

Often in the midst of a religious march, all stop, and with all their might set to stamping with both feet. And it is no uncommon thing for many of the worshipping assembly to crow like a parcel of young chanticleers, while others imitate the barking of dogs; and many of the young women set to whirling round and round—while the old men shake and clap their hands; the whole making a scene of noise and confusion, which can be better imagined than described. The elders seriously told me that these things were the outward manifestations of the spirit of God.

Apart from their religious meetings, the Shakers have what they call "union meetings." These are for social converse, and for the purpose of making the people acquainted with each other. During the day, the elders tell who may visit such and such chambers. A few minutes past nine, work is laid aside; the females change, or adjust, as best suits their fancy, their caps, handkerchiefs, and pin-ners, with a precision which indicates that they are not *altogether* free from vanity. The chairs, perhaps to the number of a dozen, are set in two rows, in such a manner that those who occupy them may face each other. At the ringing of a bell, each one goes to the chamber where either he or she has been directed by the elders, or remains at home to receive company, as the case may be. They enter the chambers *sans ceremonie*, and seat themselves—the men occupying one row of chairs, the women the other. Here, with their clean, checked, home-made pocket-handkerchiefs spread in their laps, and their spit-boxes standing in a row between them, they converse about raising sheep and kine, herbs and vegetables, building wall and raising corn, heating the oven and pearing apples, killing rats and gathering nuts, spinning tow and weaving sieves, making preserves and mending the brethren's clothes,—in short, every thing they do will afford some little conversation. But beyond their own little world, they do not appear to extend scarcely a thought. And why should they? Having so few sources of information, they know not what is passing beyond them. They however make the most of their own affairs, and seem to regret that they can converse no longer, when, after sitting together from half to three-quarters of an hour, the bell warns them that it is time to separate, which they do by rising up, locking their hands across their breasts, and bowing. Each one then goes silently to his own chamber.

It will readily be perceived, that they have no access to libraries, no books, excepting school-books, and a few relating to their own particular views; no periodicals, and attend no lectures, debates, Lyceums, &c. They have none of the many privileges of manufacturing districts—consequently their information is so very limited, that their conversation is, as a thing in course, quite insipid. The manner of their life seems to be a check to the march of mind and a desire for improvement; and while the moral and perceptive faculties are tolerably developed, the intellectual, with a very few exceptions, seem to be below the average.

I have considered it my duty to make the foregoing statement of facts, lest the glowing description of the Shakers, given in the story of my first visit, might have a wrong influence. I then judged by outward appearances only—having a very imperfect knowledge of the true state of the case. Nevertheless, the *facts* as I saw them in my first visit, are still facts; my error is to be sought only in my inferences. Having since had greater opportunities for observation, I am enabled to judge more righteous judgment.

DOCUMENT 23

The Word in Print

Any picture of religion in the culture of the 1840s would be incomplete without testimony to the power of printed materials. The Bible was of course the most popular book ever issued. Publishers, bookstores, and traveling agents all sold it. But the major means for distributing Bibles everywhere in America was the American Bible Society. Its grand aim was to see that each household had a Bible, whether it could pay for it or not. Besides the Bible many other religious works appeared; they could be found in substantial numbers in most of the book lists of the time. There was also a host of printed sermons. In fact the published sermon, both as a means to instruction and as a literary form, enjoyed a vogue entirely lost today.

Of other religious documents the most popular was the tract. It typically consisted of a brief religious anecdote followed by an even briefer homily. Its strength lay in the fact that it was vivid and succinct. To a nation that, even then, ran as it read, tracts had considerable merit. The outstanding publisher of them was the American Tract Society, which also issued a good many religious volumes. Its tracts were useful weapons for the Christian cause. They were distributed throughout the United States in numbers running to the millions. Churches, benevolent societies, and a phalanx of agents called "colporteurs" saw to it that tracts were passed out, free or for a few cents, to people in all parts of the country. The colporteurs prided themselves on bringing the Word to the least accessible places—to the remotest village, the loneliest frontier cabin. The leading tract was "Quench Not the Spirit"; 908,000 copies were issued by the end of the 1840s. Other leaders included

"The Lost Soul" and "Procrastination." Some of the most effective were gathered together in J. A. Ackley's *Pictorial Narratives*. From it comes the grim one given below.

SOURCE: Anonymous, "Warning to Sabbath Breakers," *Pictorial Narratives*, compiled by J. A. Ackley (New York, n.d.), pp. 1–4.

Warning to Sabbath Breakers

As I was walking down —— street, on my way to church, I saw a party of young people going on before me, whose volatile manners ill accorded with the sanctity of the day; and just as I was passing them I heard one say, "Indeed I think we shall do wrong—my conscience condemns me—I must return." "There can be no harm," replied another, "in taking an excursion on the water; especially as we have resolved to go to church in the evening." "I must return," rejoined a female voice, "my conscience condemns me. What will father say, if he hear of it?" By this time they had reached the river, and one of the party was busily engaged with a waterman, while the rest stood in close debate for the space of five minutes, when they all moved forward towards the water.

I watched them going down the stairs, and thought I perceived an air of peculiar melancholy in the countenance of the female who had objected to the excursion, but whose firmness gave way to the ardor of importunity. Two of the gentlemen stepped into the boat, two more stood at the water's edge, and the females were handed in, one after another; but still I could perceive great reluctance on the part of the one who had previously objected; till, at length, being surrounded by all the gentlemen of the party, she yielded, and the boat was pushed off.

It was a fine morning, though rather cold; the tide was running in at its usual rate; many were gazing on them, like myself, when a naval officer, standing near to me, called to them and said, "A pleasant voyage to you." One of the gentlemen suddenly arose to return the compliment; but, from some cause which I could not perceive, he unfortunately fell into the water. This disaster threw the whole party into the utmost consternation; and each one, instead of retaining his seat, rushed to the side of the boat over which their companion had fallen, which upset it, and all were instantaneously plunged into the deep. The shriek which the multitude of spectators gave, when they beheld this calamity, exceeded any noise I had ever heard; several females fainted; boats immediately put off; and in a few minutes I had the gratification of seeing the watermen rescuing one—and another—and another, from a premature grave. Having picked up all that they could find, the different boats rowed to shore, where some medical gentlemen were in waiting; but when the party met together, no language can describe the horror which was depicted on every countenance, when they found that two were still missing. "Where's my sister?" said the voice which had said, only a few minutes before, "There can be no harm in taking an excursion on the water; especially as we have resolved to go to church in the evening." "Where's my Charles?" said a female, who had appeared the most gay and sprightly when I first saw them.

At length, two boats, which had gone a considerable distance up the river, were seen returning; and, on being asked if they had picked up any, they replied, "Yes, two." This reply electrified the whole party; they embraced each other with the tenderest emotions; they wept for joy, and so did many others who stood around them. "Here's a gentleman," said the waterman, as he was coming up to the foot of the stairs, "but I believe he's dead." "Where's the lady?" said her brother, "is she safe?" "She is in the other boat, sir!" "Is she alive? Has she spoken?" "No sir, she has not spoken, I believe." "Is she dead? O tell me!" "I fear she is, sir."

The bodies were immediately removed from the boats to a house in the vicinity, and every effort was employed to restore animation; and some faint hopes were entertained by the medical gentlemen that they should succeed. In the space of little more than ten minutes they announced the joyful news that the gentleman began to breathe, but they made no allusion to the lady. Her brother sat motionless, absorbed in the deepest melancholy, till the actual decease of his sister was announced, when he started up, and became almost frantic with grief; and, though his companions tried to comfort him, yet he refused to hear the words of consolation. "O my sister! my sister! would to God I had died for thee!" They were all overwhelmed in trouble, and knew not what to do. "Who will bear the heavy tidings to our father?" said the brother, who paced backwards and forwards the room, like a maniac broke loose from the cell of misery—"O, who will bear the heavy tidings to our father?" He paused—a deathlike silence pervaded the whole apartment: he again burst forth, in the agonies of despair—"I forced her to go against the dictates of her conscience—I am her murderer—I ought to have perished, and not my sister. Who will bear the heavy tidings to our father?" "I will," said a gentleman who had been unremitting in his attention to the sufferers. "Do you know him, sir?" "Yes, I know him." "O, how can I ever appear in his presence? I enticed the best of children to an act of disobedience which has destroyed her!"

How the old man received the intelligence, or what moral effect resulted from the disaster, I never heard; but it may furnish me with a few reflections, which I wish to press upon the attention of my readers. As the Sabbath is instituted for the purpose of promoting your moral improvement and felicity, never devote its sacred hours to the recreations of pleasure. He who has commanded you to keep it holy, will not suffer you to profane it with impunity. He may not bring down upon you the awful expressions of his displeasure while you are in the act of setting at open defiance his authority; but there is a day approaching when you must stand before him. And can you anticipate the solemnities of that day, while going on in a course of sin, but with the most fearful apprehensions?

You may, like many others, suppose that that day is very
far off; but you may be undeceived by a sudden visitation
of Providence, and in a moment be removed from amongst
your gay companions to appear in his presence. If you
should, with what terror-struck amazement will you look on
the awful scene around you! with what agonizing despair
will you listen to the final sentence—*Depart!*

Resist the *first* temptation to evil, or your ruin may be
the inevitable consequence. "Indeed, I think we shall do
wrong—my conscience condemns me—I must return," said
the unfortunate female, when she got near the edge of the
water; but, having yielded to the first temptation, she was
induced to overcome all her scruples—and, within the space
of half an hour from that time she entered the eternal
world. Had she refused when her brother solicited her to
leave her father's house, she had still lived to bless and
comfort him in his old age; but, by complying, she lost her
strength to withstand temptation—and then her life. What
a warning!

And is this the only one which the history of crime has
given us? Alas, no! Have not many, who have ended their
days on the gallows, traced up their ruin to their profana-
tion of the Sabbath? This is the day in which the foul
spirits are abroad, enticing the young and the thoughtless
to evil; and if you wish to avoid the misery and degradation in which others have been involved, devote its sacred
hours to the purpose for which they were appointed.
Attend some place of worship, where the pure evangelical
truth of the Scriptures is preached with pathos and with
power; and attend regularly. He who regularly attends a
place of worship—who engages with reverence in its devotional exercises, and receives the truth which is preached,
under a deep conviction of its excellence and importance,
enjoys a high mental feast on the Sabbath, and becomes
imperceptibly fortified to resist the fascinating seductions
of the world; while he who spends the consecrated hours
in the society of the impure, amidst scenes of gayety and

dissipation, becomes an easy prey to the worst of temptations—often retires to rest reproaching himself for his folly and impiety; and is gradually led on, from one crime to another, till "iniquity proves his ruin."

The Departing Missionary

The evangelistic impulse throve in American religion. The urge was pervasive to make converts to Christ, to waken the sluggish sleepers, to snatch the brands from the burning. It can be felt in the reasoned persuasion of Orville Dewey; and it is plain in the lusty prayer of Peter Cartwright, in the thoughtful urgency of Orestes Brownson, and in the hard-hitting homilies of the tracts. It was natural that the denominations should wish to carry the word of God beyond the borders of the United States. They sent their missionaries out farther and farther. Armed in righteousness these missionaries traveled to Africa, Asia, and the South Seas. To them, or more literally to one of them, the Reverend George Bethune addressed one of his popular poems, "The Departing Missionary." It was collected in his *Lays of Love and Faith*.

Bethune puts his highly emotional valedictory into a rolling measure which makes the poem easier to declaim but harder to appreciate. To the reader of today the most impressive quality about it is the poet's absolute confidence in the rightness and need of the mission itself. There are "glad tidings to bear, / To the desolate isles in their night of despair." It is doubtful that the South Sea islanders would have recognized that description of their home.

SOURCE: George W. Bethune, *Lays of Love and Faith, with Other Fugitive Poems* (Philadelphia, 1848), pp. 170–71.

The Departing Missionary

Farewell to thee, brother! We meet but to part,
And sorrow is struggling with joy in each heart;
There is grief—but there's hope, all its anguish to quell;
The Master goes with thee—Farewell! oh, farewell!

Farewell! Thou art leaving the home of thy youth,
The friends of thy God, and the temples of truth,
For the land where is heard no sweet Sabbath bell;
Yet the Master goes with thee—Farewell! oh, farewell!

Farewell! for thou treadest the path that He trod;
His God is thy Father, His Father thy God;
And if ever with doubtings thy bosom shall swell,
Remember He's with thee—Farewell! oh, farewell!

Farewell! and God speed thee, glad tidings to bear,
To the desolate isles in their night of despair;
On the sea, on the shore, all the promises tell,
His wings shall enfold thee. Farewell! oh, farewell!

Farewell! but in spirit we often shall meet
(Though the ocean divide us) at one mercy-seat;
And above, ne'er to part, but for ever to dwell
With the Master in glory—Till then, oh! farewell!

The Christian Consolation

To the American of the 1840s death seemed far more natural than it does today. It was nearer; it was faced more readily, almost more matter-of-factly. Today the life span is much longer, death less often observed. When it occurs the undertaker and probably the minister are summoned; the body goes to the undertaking establishment; the final ceremonies are held there or, more often, at the church. In the 1840s death was a frequent visitor. The earliest extensive data we have comes from Massachusetts in 1850: there the male life expectancy was thirty-eight years, the female forty years. Infant mortality was high enough so that a baby had more than one chance in ten of dying before the end of his first year. And this was in Massachusetts, where the medical facilities were much better than most. In the slums of New York and other big cities, everywhere on the frontier, throughout the South, the death rates were astronomical.

When death took place the body was prepared at home and viewed there before the church service and interment. Frequently the family held a wake; this was a Protestant as well as a Catholic custom. Once the body was buried, family and friends often visited the grave. Strange as it may appear now, cemeteries were in themselves highly regarded as places to see. A stranger visiting in some community in the 1840s might well stop to inspect its cemetery.

Death's closest relation in our culture was to religion. In Bible and sermon, in prayer and ritual, in advice and exhortation, the forces of religion in America strove to cope with the omnipresent fact of death. Providing the Christian consolation was one of the church's great services.

In the literature of the time the natural concern with death became even an interest in it. The death-bed scene grew to be a staple of fiction and drama. Death provided the theme for many a poem, the suggestion for many a song. It offered the subject for many a picture. Here, emblematic of the interest in death in art and letters, is a poem published in 1844 in *The Cypress Wreath*. The compiler was that literary man-of-all-work, the Reverend Rufus Griswold (1815–57). Between the covers of his little book he put the poetry and brief passages of prose which he had culled from the writing of others, for "the consolation of those who mourn." "Thou art Gone to the Grave!" is one of the anonymous items he included. Its mournful message is delivered in much too rolling a rhythm, the same one employed in "The Departing Missionary," but the facts of death and loss still lend strength to the poem. Its appeal was doubtless powerful.

SOURCE: *The Cypress Wreath; a Book of Consolation for Those Who Mourn,* ed. Rufus W. Griswold (Boston, 1844), pp. 110–11.

Thou art Gone to the Grave!

Thou art gone to the grave, but we will not deplore thee,
  Though sorrows and darkness encompass the tomb;
Thy Saviour has pass'd through its portal before thee,
  And the lamp of his love is thy guide through the gloom!

Thou art gone to the grave!—we no longer behold thee,
  Nor tread the rough paths of the world by thy side;
But the wide arms of mercy are spread to enfold thee,
  And sinners may die, for the sinless have died!

Thou art gone to the grave—and its mansion forsaking,
  Perchance thy weak spirit in fear linger'd long;
But the mild rays of Paradise beam'd on thy waking,
  And the sound which thou heard'st was the seraphim's song!

Thou art gone to the grave!—but we will not deplore thee,
    Whose God was thy ransom, thy guardian and guide;
He gave thee—He took thee—and He will restore thee,
    And death has no sting, for the Saviour has died.

DOCUMENT 26

(PLATES 16–19)

Testaments of Faith

The powerful presence of religion in the 1840s can be seen in numberless ways. The testaments of faith are manifold. One way to illustrate this is in terms of the individual and the group, the few and the many, the family and the world outside, the solitary communion and the church meeting. In each of these related rubrics we can find evidence of a strength in religion no longer discernible today.

A memorable illustration of that strength is the Currier lithograph "Search the Scriptures." It shows an old man and his daughter gazing at a passage in their folio Bible. Evidently they are seeking advice among the sacred writings; they do not know what to do about some problem and they turn automatically to Scripture. It is worth asking ourselves how many Americans today would do the same thing; the chances are considerably better that they would write to the "Advice" column of their local newspaper. Another lithograph, very popular in the late 1840s, was "Our Father." It was designed to be pasted in the family Bible or else to be put on the wall. It consisted essentially of an elaborately lettered text of the Lord's Prayer but it also had space for the recording of the family's births, marriages, and deaths. Like "Search the Scriptures" this lithograph helps to document the strength of religion for the family. It is domestic evidence of Christianity's effectiveness.

The church and the church service represent religion for the group, for the many, religion in the world outside the home. The church building was often depicted in lithographs and in engravings for books and periodicals. There were pictures of everything from rustic chapels to urban cathedrals. In "The Floating Chapel of the Holy Comforter" we see a structure with several aspects. First of all it is a rather nondescript edifice used for Episcopal church services. But it floats and so, secondly, it is a special chapel to take religion to the sailors in the port of New York. It was ordinarily anchored on the East River, in fact. Lastly, it symbolizes the missionary efforts everywhere of a given denomination. It stands for religion taken over the oceans to the far corners of the earth.

One of the most widely publicized examples of religion in relation to the group was the camp meeting. Most of us have heard about the fervent evangelizing that went on there. Most of us have seen a picture somewhere of the preacher exhorting his listeners from an improvised pulpit in the frontier clearing and the crowd clustered around to hear his message. But there were other, more general and systematic, meetings that we are apt to overlook. They can be exemplified in the "Indiana Yearly Meeting of Friends" for 1844. This orderly, decorous lithograph shows the meeting house in the background. Before it and around it are gathered carriages, wagons, and carts. Among them the Quakers stand or walk soberly. Such assemblies too had their function; they too testified to the vigor of the religious impulse of this decade.

The Bible, the Lord's Prayer, the floating chapel, and the Quaker meeting all indicate the range and extent of the faith of the 1840s.

PLATE 16. *Search the Scriptures.* Issued by N. Currier, n.d.

SOURCE: Library of Congress.

To say that the Bible ranked as the most popular book in America is true but demeans the Bible's significance. For it was to many people the literal word of God. To many, perhaps to a majority of Americans, it constituted a guide to conduct, a source of inspiration, and a link with divinity. To some it was, in all reverence, even a magical book.

This lithograph has all the appeal of Currier's most widely circulated works. The light and shade are strongly marked but no harshness mars the delineations. Strong horizontals hold their place at the bottom of the picture. The composition like the message is based on the Book. With one exception (the top line of the sofa) the lines of the upper two-thirds of the composition point downward. They all direct our attention to the Bible itself. The eye does not travel straight down; that would be too obvious. Instead after first angling one way and then another, it stops at the horizontals and rests there. The downcast eyes of both figures and the contemplative expression on their faces suggest that the problem they bring to the Scriptures is no major one. If this is true, it is in harmony with the usual subject matter of the Currier lithographs: moments of mood, solemn or joyful, rather than times of crisis.

PLATE 17. *Our Father*. Designed and executed by Rice & Pratt. Issued by Sarony & Major, 1847.

SOURCE: Library of Congress.

Much popular religious art appeared in the 1840s in response to the widespread religious impulse. This particular lithograph represents the attempt to create something both artistic and useful. In it are portraits, human and divine, with all the sugariness characteristic of popular religious art. And it has a family register, surrounded by the words of the Lord's Prayer lettered with loving Victorian elaboration. The lettering itself is also an example of the popular art of the time; it is noted on the lithograph that the lettering was originally executed with a pen (that is, written rather than drawn). Of the various vignettes the lowest in the picture is perhaps the most interesting since we can only speculate on whether it is the Virgin Mary and infant Jesus or a mortal mother and child. The adornments to the lithograph are unusually varied, including

the eye, the Bible opened to Isaiah, and the basket of agricultural produce.

PLATE 18. *The Floating Chapel of the Holy Comforter.*
Drawn by J. F. Badeau and engraved by J. H. G.

SOURCE: *Holden's Dollar Magazine*, IV (October 1849), frontispiece. Library of Congress.

During the 1840s the Episcopal Church performed relatively few actions that attracted popular attention. One of
them was to build and set afloat a chapel for seamen.
Anchored off Manhattan, it was seen by thousands and became the subject of a number of articles and pictures. The
picture, reproduced here from *Holden's Dollar Magazine,*
has a certain pawky charm. The public notice which the
structure received was a tribute to its novelty. At the same
time hundreds of other churches were being erected on
every side during the decade—a matter of prime importance. One of the plainest signs of the flourishing of
religion in America was in fact the amount of new construction. It took place at all economic levels; it evidenced
itself in churches as crude as a cabin or as finished as a
marble monument. At the most popular level, the widely
used carpenters' and builders' manuals ordinarily included designs for two typical churches. One was in the
simple classical style, with reminiscences of New England
meeting houses and Southern Colonial structures. The other
was a version of "carpenter Gothic" with its scrolls and
curlicues. Above the rather humble styles of the manuals
came the architect-planned churches of the middle class
in every part of the country. Though more ornate, their
designs usually fell into the same two categories with the
occasional addition of a Tuscan pattern with its hooded
tower and bracketed roof. Above these in turn, considerably
above them in fact, came the elegant edifices of the rich
urban congregations. For example: the lofty structure
James Renwick designed to house the congregation of
Grace Church on Broadway in New York.

"The Floating Chapel of the Holy Comforter," amateurish in execution though its drawing is, has a feeling of both action and rest. Boats circle around the chapel, while it stays still in the middle, as it should. It has a sense of haven to it, enhanced by the long windows which show a dark interior.

PLATE 19. *Indiana Yearly Meeting of Friends 1844.* Drawn by Mote. Issued by John Pease and Jer. Hubbard.

SOURCE: The Harry T. Peters "America on Stone" Lithography Collection, the Smithsonian Institution.

Subject and form, content and style, harmonize in this lithograph. It is in a way Quakerish. At first glance the picture appears naïvely conceived and crudely drawn. Though the scene is crowded, the initial impression it gives is one of a large space with figures simply stuck into it. However, there is more to the picture than shows on the surface. The composition is actually arranged with some art. Three great diagonals divide it, giving an ample perspective and a pleasing alternation of light with shade. The first diagonal is provided by the road which starts in the lower lefthand corner. The second is provided by the mass of carriages, dark to light, from the upper end of the road to the barn at the middle left. The last is provided by part of the roof line of the meeting house and the upper outline of the towering trees in the upper righthand corner. Along these diagonals the eye travels pleasantly. The attenuated figures too have their charm, among them the man in the light beaver who seems nearly eight feet tall. We look at him and his quiet colleagues first; then our eye is taken by the group of three men to the right. They all appear to be looking at and talking about us. Then our eye naturally follows the path upward and we give the meeting house due attention. Turning from the meeting house, we gaze above the trees, appropriately enough, at the heavens.

PART V

The Enjoyment of Life

Document 27

The Appreciation of Literature

Reading for recreation's sake enjoyed an unparalleled boom. We may remember that the value of books manufactured rose from $2,850,000 at the start of the decade to $5,900,000 ten years later, that the number of newspapers and magazines climbed, and that the potential public of readers nearly doubled during the decade. Much of the reading was for practical purposes, reading for the sake of information, but the amount of reading for pleasure was also great and becoming greater. The favorite forms of recreational reading were the domestic novel and short story, the travel book, the personal essay, and the sentimental poem. For example: Mrs. E. D. E. N. Southworth's novel *The Curse of Clifton*, Poe's short stories, Bayard Taylor's *Views A-Foot, or Europe Seen with Knapsack and Staff*, Henry Tuckerman's Lamb-like essays, and Mrs. L. H. Sigourney's sugared verse.

Yet, the climate of the 1840s being what it was, even this leisure-time reading had a tinge of practicality to it. That is, it was often done to improve the mind a little as well as to relax it. For the prejudice against mere reading, against any cultural recreation in fact, which had originated in Puritan times, continued to exist though with lessened intensity right down to the end of the nineteenth century. During the 1840s it was still strong but embattled. Its most noted, most articulate opponent was Edgar Allan Poe (1808–49). He spoke with the voice of the future; time was on his side.

As might be expected Poe took a position which was both cogent and compelling. Not only did he defend enjoyment as the aim of literature, he attacked what he characterized as the heresy of the didactic. He found

Longfellow his best target. In *Graham's Magazine* for
April 1842 he printed a long, analytical review of Longfellow's *Ballads and Other Poems*. He knew what was
wrong with Longfellow's verses and defined it carefully.
He criticized him more for obtrusive didacticism than
for didacticism as such. Poe's approach had both positive and negative aspects. He both criticized Longfellow's practice and provided for the reader a fresh theory
on the enjoyment of literature. In presenting his theory
Poe showed a subtleness which made its own demands
on the intellect and spirit of the reader. The strategy of
enjoyment Poe proposed was far from the simple defense of reading as a relaxer.

Most of the review is printed below. Poe starts with a
reference to previous remarks about the *Ballads* and in
particular their all too evident attempts to teach.

SOURCE: [Edgar Allan Poe], Review of Longfellow's *Ballads and
Other Poems*, *Graham's Magazine*, XX (April 1842), 248–50,
abridged.

In Praise of Beauty, Not Instruction

We have said that Mr. Longfellow's conception of the
aims of poesy is erroneous; and that thus, laboring at a
disadvantage, he does violent wrong to his own high powers;
and now the question is, what *are* his ideas of the aims
of the muse, as we gather these ideas from the *general*
tendency of his poems? It will be at once evident that, imbued with the peculiar spirit of German song (a pure
conventionality) he regards the inculcation of a *moral* as
essential. Here we find it necessary to repeat that we have
reference only to the *general* tendency of his compositions; for there are some magnificent exceptions, where, as
if by accident, he has permitted his genius to get the better of his conventional prejudice. But didacticism is the
prevalent *tone* of his song. His invention, his imagery, his
all, is made subservient to the elucidation of some one or
more points (but rarely of more than one) which he looks

upon as *truth*. And that this mode of procedure will find stern defenders should never excite surprise, so long as the world is full to overflowing with cant and conventicles. There are men who will scramble on all fours through the muddiest sloughs of vice to pick up a single apple of virtue. There are things called men who, so long as the sun rolls, will greet with snuffing huzzas every figure that takes upon itself the semblance of truth, even although the figure, in itself only a "stuffed Paddy," be as much out of place as a toga on the statue of Washington, or out of season as rabbits in the days of the dog-star.

Now with as deep a reverence for "the true" as ever inspired the bosom of mortal man, we would limit, in many respects, its modes of inculcation. We would limit to enforce them. We would not render them impotent by dissipation. The demands of truth are severe. She has no sympathy with the myrtles. All that is indispensable in song is all with which she has nothing to do. To deck her in gay robes is to render her a harlot. It is but making her a flaunting paradox to wreathe her in gems and flowers. Even in stating this our present proposition, we verify our own words—we feel the necessity, in enforcing this *truth*, of descending from metaphor. Let us then be simple and distinct. To convey "the true" we are required to dismiss from the attention all inessentials. We must be perspicuous, precise, terse. We need concentration rather than expansion of mind. We must be calm, unimpassioned, unexcited —in a word, we must be in that peculiar mood which, as nearly as possible, is the exact converse of the poetical. He must be blind indeed who cannot perceive the radical and chasmal difference between the truthful and the poetical modes of inculcation. He must be grossly wedded to conventionalisms who, in spite of this difference, shall still attempt to reconcile the obstinate oils and waters of Poetry and Truth.

Dividing the world of mind into its most obvious and immediately recognisable distinctions, we have the pure intellect, taste, and the moral sense. We place *taste* between the intellect and the moral sense, because it is just this intermediate space which, in the mind, it occupies. It is the connecting link in the triple chain.

It serves to sustain a mutual intelligence between the extremes. It appertains, in strict appreciation, to the former, but is distinguished from the latter by so faint a difference, that Aristotle has not hesitated to class some of its operations among the Virtues themselves. But the *offices* of the trio are broadly marked. Just as conscience, or the moral sense, recognises duty; just as the intellect deals with *truth*; so is it the part of taste alone to inform us of BEAUTY. And Poesy is the handmaiden but of Taste. Yet we would not be misunderstood. This handmaiden is not forbidden to moralise—in her own fashion. She is not forbidden to depict—but to reason and preach, of virtue. As, of this latter, conscience recognises the obligation, so intellect teaches the expediency, while taste contents herself with displaying the beauty: waging war with vice merely on the ground of its inconsistency with fitness, harmony, proportion. . . .

An important condition of man's immortal nature is thus, plainly, the sense of the Beautiful. This it is which ministers to his delight in the manifold forms and colors and sounds and sentiments amid which he exists. And, just as the eyes of Amaryllis are repeated in the mirror, or the living lily in the lake, so is the mere *record* of these forms and colors and sounds and sentiments—so is their mere oral or written repetition a duplicate source of delight. But this repetition is not Poesy. He who shall merely sing with whatever rapture, in however harmonious strains, or with however vivid a truth of imitation, of the sights and sounds which greet him in common with all mankind —he, we say, has yet failed to prove his divine title. There is still a longing unsatisfied, which he has been impotent to fulfil. There is still a thirst unquenchable, which to allay he has shown us no crystal springs. This burning thirst belongs to the *immortal* essence of man's nature. It is equally a consequence and an indication of his perennial life. It is the desire of the moth for the star. It is not the mere appreciation of the beauty before us. It is a wild effort to reach the beauty above. It is a forethought of the loveliness to come. It is a passion to be satiated by no sublunary sights, or sounds, or sentiments, and the soul thus athirst strives to allay its fever in futile efforts at *creation*. Inspired with a prescient ecstasy of the beauty beyond the grave, it struggles by multiform novelty of combination among the things and thoughts of Time, to anticipate some portion of that loveliness whose very elements, perhaps, appertain solely to Eternity. And the result of such effort, on the part of souls fittingly constituted, is alone what mankind have agreed to denominate Poetry.

We say this with little fear of contradiction. Yet the spirit of our assertion must be more heeded than the letter. Mankind have *seemed* to define Poesy in a thousand, and in a thousand conflicting definitions. But the war is one only of words. Induction is as well applicable to this subject as to the most palpable and utilitarian; and by its sober processes we find that, in respect to compositions which have been really received as poems, the *imaginative*, or, more popularly, the creative portions *alone* have ensured them to be so received. Yet these works, on account of these portions, having once been so received, and so named, it has happened, naturally and inevitably, that other portions totally unpoetic have not only come to be regarded by the popular voice as poetic, but have been made to serve as false standards of perfection, in the adjustment of other poetical claims. Whatever has been found in whatever has been received as a poem, has been blindly regarded as *ex statu* poetic. And this is a species of gross error which scarcely could have made its way into any less intangible topic. In fact that license which appertains to the Muse herself, it has been thought decorous, if not sagacious to indulge, in all examination of her character.

Poesy is thus seen to be a response—unsatisfactory it is true—but still in some measure a response, to a natural and irrepressible demand. Man being what he is, the time could

never have been in which Poesy was not. Its first element
is the thirst for supernal BEAUTY—a beauty which is not
afforded the soul by any existing collocation of earth's
forms—a beauty which, perhaps, *no possible* combination
of these forms would fully produce. Its second element
is the attempt to satisfy this thirst by *novel* combinations,
*of those combinations which our predecessors, toiling in
chase of the same phantom, have already set in order.*
We thus clearly deduce the *novelty*, the *originality*, the
invention, the *imagination*, or lastly the *creation* of BEAUTY,
(for the terms as here employed are synonymous) as the
essence of all Poesy. Nor is this idea so much at variance
with ordinary opinion as, at first sight, it may appear. A
multitude of antique dogmas on this topic will be found,
when divested of extrinsic speculation, to be easily resolu-
ble into the definition now proposed. We do nothing more
than present tangibly the vague clouds of the world's idea.
We recognise the idea itself floating, unsettled, indefinite,
in every attempt which has yet been made to circumscribe
the conception of "Poesy" in words. A striking instance
of this is observable in the fact that no definition exists,
in which either "the beautiful," or some one of those qualities which we have above designated synonymously with
"creation," has not been pointed out as the *chief* attribute
of the Muse. "Invention," however, or "imagination," is by
far more commonly insisted upon. . . . But here we must,
perforce, content ourselves with mere suggestion; for this
topic is of a character which would lead us too far. We
have already spoken of Music as one of the moods of poetical development. It is in Music, perhaps, that the soul
most nearly attains that end upon which we have commented—the creation of supernal beauty. It may be, indeed,
that this august aim is here even partially or imperfectly
attained, *in fact*. The *elements* of that beauty which is
felt in sound, *may be* the mutual or common heritage of
Earth and Heaven. In the soul's struggles at combinations
it is thus not impossible that a harp may strike notes not
unfamiliar to the angels. And in this view the wonder

may well be less that all attempts at defining the character or sentiment of the deeper musical impressions have been found absolutely futile. Contenting ourselves, therefore, with the firm conviction, that music (in its modifications of rhythm and rhyme) is of so vast a moment in Poesy, as *never* to be neglected by him who is truly poetical—is of so mighty a force in furthering the great aim intended that he is mad who rejects its assistance—content with this idea we shall not pause to maintain its absolute essentiality, for the mere sake of rounding a definition. We will but add, at this point, that the highest possible development of the Poetical Sentiment is to be found in the union of song with music, in its popular sense. The old Bards and Minnesingers possessed, in the fullest perfection, the finest and truest elements of Poesy; and Thomas Moore, singing his own ballads, is but putting the final touch to their completion as poems.

To recapitulate, then, we would define in brief the Poetry of words as the *Rhythmical Creation of Beauty*. Beyond the limits of Beauty its province does not extend. Its sole arbiter is Taste. With the Intellect or with the Conscience it has only collateral relations. It has no dependence, unless incidentally, upon either Duty or *Truth*. That our definition will necessarily exclude much of what, through a supine toleration, has been hitherto ranked as poetical, is a matter which affords us not even momentary concern. We address but the thoughtful, and heed only their approval—with our own. If our suggestions are truthful, then "after many days" shall they be understood as truth, even though found in contradiction of *all* that has been hitherto so understood. If false shall we not be the first to bid them die? . . .

Of the poets who have appeared most fully instinct with the principles now developed, we may mention *Keats* as the most remarkable. He is the sole British poet who has never erred in his themes. Beauty is always his aim.

We have thus shown our ground of objection to the general *themes* of Professor Longfellow. In common with all who claim the sacred title of poet, he should limit his endeavors to the creation of novel moods of beauty, in form, in color, in sound, in sentiment; for over all this wide range has the poetry of words dominion. To what the world terms *prose* may be safely and properly left all else. The artist who doubts of his thesis, may always resolve his doubt by the single question—"might not this matter be as well or better handled in *prose?*" If it *may*, then is it no subject for the Muse. In the general acceptation of the term *Beauty* we are content to rest; being careful only to suggest that, in our peculiar views, it must be understood as inclusive of *the sublime*.

Of the pieces which constitute the present volume, there are not more than one or two thoroughly fulfilling the idea above proposed; although the volume as a whole is by no means so chargeable with didacticism as Mr. Longfellow's previous book. We would mention as poems *nearly true*, "The Village Blacksmith;" "The Wreck of the Hesperus;" and especially "The Skeleton in Armor." In the first-mentioned we have the *beauty* of simple-mindedness as a genuine thesis; and this thesis is inimitably handled until the concluding stanza, where the spirit of legitimate poesy is aggrieved in the pointed antithetical deduction of a *moral* from what has gone before. In "The Wreck of the Hesperus" we have the *beauty* of child-like confidence and innocence, with that of the father's stern courage and affection. But, with slight exception, those particulars of the storm here detailed are not poetic subjects. Their thrilling *horror* belongs to prose, in which it could be far more effectively discussed, as Professor Longfellow may assure himself at any moment by experiment. There *are* points of a tempest which afford the loftiest and truest poetical themes—points in which pure beauty is found, or, better still, beauty heightened into the sublime, by terror. But when we read, among other similar things, that

> The salt sea was frozen on her breast,
> The salt tears in her eyes,

we feel, if not positive disgust, at least a chilling sense of the inappropriate. In the "Skeleton in Armor" we find a pure and perfect thesis artistically treated. We find the beauty of bold courage and self-confidence, of love and maiden devotion, of reckless adventure, and finally of life-contemning grief. Combined with all this we have numerous *points* of beauty apparently insulated, but all aiding the main effect or impression. The heart is stirred, and the mind does not lament its malinstruction. The metre is simple, sonorous, well-balanced and fully adapted to the subject. Upon the whole, there are few truer poems than this. It has but one defect—an important one. The prose remarks prefacing the narrative are really *necessary*. But every work of art should contain within itself all that is requisite for its own comprehension. And this remark is especially true of the ballad. In poems of magnitude the mind of the reader is not, at all times, enabled to include, in one comprehensive survey, the proportions and proper adjustment of the whole. He is pleased, if at all, with particular passages; and the sum of his pleasure is compounded of the sums of the pleasurable sentiments inspired by these individual passages in the progress of perusal. But, in pieces of less extent, the pleasure is *unique*, in the proper acceptation of this term—the understanding is employed, without difficulty, in the contemplation of the picture *as a whole*; and thus its effect will depend, in great measure, upon the perfection of its finish, upon the nice adaptation of its constituent parts, and especially, upon what is rightly termed by Schlegel *the unity or totality of interest*. But the practice of prefixing explanatory passages is utterly at variance with such unity. By the prefix, we are either put in possession of the subject of the poem; or some hint, historic fact, or suggestion is thereby afforded, not included in the body of the piece, which, without the hint, is incomprehensible. In the latter case, while perusing the poem, the reader must revert, in mind at least, to the prefix, for the necessary explanation. In the former, the poem being a mere paraphrase of the prefix, the interest is divided between the prefix and the paraphrase. In either instance the totality of effect is destroyed.

Of the other original poems in the volume before us, there is none in which the aim of instruction, or *truth*, has not been too obviously substituted for the legitimate aim, *beauty*. . . .

Of the translations we scarcely think it necessary to speak at all. We regret that our poet will persist in busying himself about such matters. *His* time might be better employed in original conception. Most of these versions are marked with the error upon which we have commented. This error is, in fact, essentially Germanic. "The Luck of Edenhall," however, is a truly beautiful poem; and we say this with all that deference which the opinion of the "Democratic Review" demands. This composition appears to us *one of the very finest*. It has all the free, hearty, *obvious* movement of the true ballad-legend. The greatest force of language is combined in it with the richest imagination, acting in its most legitimate province. Upon the whole, we prefer it even to the "Sword-Song" of Körner. The pointed moral with which it terminates is so exceedingly natural—so perfectly fluent from the incidents—that we have hardly heart to pronounce it in ill taste. We may observe of this ballad, in conclusion, that its subject is more *physical* than is usual in Germany. Its images are rich rather in physical than in moral beauty. And this tendency, in Song, is the true one. It is chiefly, if we are not mistaken—it is chiefly amid forms of physical loveliness (we use the word *forms* in its widest sense as embracing modifications of sound and color) that the soul seeks the realization of its dreams of BEAUTY. It is to her demand in this sense especially, that the poet, who is wise, will most frequently and most earnestly respond.

DOCUMENT 28

Art for Almost Everyone

It is true that the pleasures of art were not so widely appreciated as those of literature. Nevertheless, art made greater advances during this decade than it ever had before. It did so on two levels. On the popular level it showed itself especially in the low-priced, shrewdly designed lithographs of such firms as Sarony & Major and Nathaniel Currier (later to be Currier & Ives). The chief subjects for these lithographs were human-interest scenes and landscapes. As the 1840s went along, the methods of distribution improved and sales surged forward. The real prosperity for the lithograph publishers would not start till the 1850s but there was no doubt in the 1840s that it was on the way. The retail prices of the pictures varied from seller to seller but fifteen to twenty-five cents a piece was probably the average range. Popular art had never been as cheap before and would seldom be as cheap thereafter.

At the middle- and upper-class level, art advanced remarkably thanks to the emergence of the so-called art-unions, and one in particular, the American Art-Union, whose headquarters was in New York. It acted as the honest broker between the artist and the potential buyer of the 1840s. It helped to arouse and then satisfy a taste for art which had not been very noticeable before. The Art-Union's plan was to buy paintings from professional artists and raffle them off to the society's members in an annual lottery. The approach was unorthodox but the results were spectacular. The annual drawing of prizes proved to be as exciting as a horse race. Of course only a minority of members won but as the years passed, the Art-Union was able to give the losers more and more in the way of consolation prizes. By the end of the decade each of the nearly nineteen thousand members of the society received an ornate steel engraving annually as well as a fine etching. The engraving for 1849, for example, was "Sparking" by F. W. Edmonds and the etching was "The Escape of Captain Wharton" by Thomas Hoppin.

At the same cultural level there was one other major source of art: the magazines. Most of them were illustrated and some were illustrated handsomely, in particular, *Graham's Magazine*, John Sartain's *Union Magazine*, and *Godey's Lady's Book*. No wonder that the Reverend George Bethune could look back happily on all these developments and write in 1852, "Especially within the last ten years, large advances have been made and Art has fairly begun to flourish among us."

Two excerpts from the yearly *Transactions* of the American Art-Union are reprinted here. The first, from the "Annual Report" in the volume for 1844, is a description of the pleasures of art as seen by the managers of the society; these pleasures are marked by the didacticism typical of the time. The second, from the "Annual Report" in the volume for 1849, describes with pride the increasingly important role of the Art-Union in bringing art to the American public. The excerpts offer between them the best single statement, for the time, of the middle-class view on the delights and profits of art.

SOURCE: *Transactions of the American Art-Union for the Promotion of the Fine Arts in the United States for the Year 1844* (New York, n.d.), pp. 6–8; and *Transactions of the American Art-Union for the Year 1849* (New York, 1850), pp. 29–35.

Annual Report [1844]

Before we can have good works of art, we must feel the need of them; it is the universal rule; men cannot seek to satisfy a want which they have never felt; good taste is of all things the most gradual in its development, and of all pleasures it can with most propriety be said to grow by what it feeds on. It is only, then, by distributing works of art of some kind, that the people will ever gain a relish for them, whether good or bad. Though a love of art is a universal feeling, which has been manifested in all ages and by all races, yet among the ill-informed and unthinking, paintings and statues are regarded as luxuries to be indulged in only by the rich and effeminate; and in this misconception is found one of the greatest obstacles to success in an undertaking like this of the Art-Union. And when it is remembered that works of art are rarely found but in the houses of the rich, or else shut up carefully in galleries, where the inquiring glances of the vulgar poor rarely penetrate, it cannot be wondered at that such a feeling should exist. But, it is the aim of the Art-Union to dispel such errors as these, and to convey to the abodes of common life works of intrinsic merit, which wealth does not always possess the discrimination to appropriate to its own use. It would be a sorry labor were we moved by no higher motives than to provide elegant ornaments for the parlors and halls of our citizens: if such were the case we might as well extend our purchases to the shops of the upholsterer and cabinet maker, as to the studios of our artists. But paintings and statues, are the palpable expressions of thinking minds; they lead us to something better than themselves, or they are of little worth. They are the servants of nature calling us to her side. It may seem paradoxical, but it is nevertheless true, that men are first led to a contemplation of nature by the blandishments of art.

Of all the pleasures that we derive from material things, none are more innocent, more enduring, or less likely to be perverted to evil, than those which we find in a love of art. "A thing of beauty is a joy for ever," because the idea that it creates endures for ever: the work may be destroyed but the thought will remain.

To the inhabitants of cities, as nearly all of the subscribers to the Art-Union are, a painted landscape is almost essential to preserve a healthy tone to the spirits, lest they forget in the wilderness of bricks which surrounds them the pure delights of nature and a country life.

Those who cannot afford a seat in the country to refresh their wearied spirits, may at least have a country seat in their parlors; a bit of a landscape with a green tree, a distant hill, or low-roofed cottage;—some of those simple objects, which all men find so refreshing to their spirits after being long pent up in dismal streets and in the haunts of business—that even in the noisome air of the city they may see if not feel "the breezy call of incense-breathing morn." Such a sight must improve the digestion of the dyspeptic merchant as he sits at his pampered table, after a day of harassing labor, the labor that wearies without strengthening the body, because it makes the inside instead of the outside of the head sweat. But if pictures are needed in the houses of the rich, how much more are they needed on the walls of our public schools, for the daily contemplation of the little souls that are just beginning to taste of the good and evil, the beauty and deformity of the world; something to teach them not only that loveliness is better, but that it is cheaper than deformity. The education of the young is the legitimate and acknowledged duty of the State; but what is education, if not to refine and expand the mind? Not that the man may better acquire wealth, but that his sources of enjoyment may be increased, and the goods which God has provided for his use be rightly enjoyed. Is it not then a legitimate branch of education to distil into the minds of the youth of our common schools a love for beautiful things, and a veneration for what is good and holy? And how could this be done with surer effect, or in a more economical manner, than by a pictured representation, hung up for their daily contemplation, upon the walls which are now a cheerless blank, of some of the instructive incidents of our own history; or of the great truths of holy writ? There would be little danger of books like these touching the sectarian sores of Jew or Gentile. If the pious Doddridge learned his first lessons in divine truth from the pictured tiles which surrounded the fire-place of his mother's parlor, might not the tender minds of the young people in our common schools receive good impressions from lessons like these? The stewards of our public wealth are too apt to forget that man lives not by bread alone; that his mind, like his body, is omniverous, and must be nourished by all the aids of art as well as of letters. It is not our wish to interfere in affairs with which we have no legitimate connexion, but as the Art-Union has been established for the promotion of the Fine Arts in the United States, we may be allowed the privilege of indicating to the stewards of the commonwealth one of the legitimate means of aiding in this work, without offence.

But art should not be encouraged by our people solely with a view to refined enjoyment, but as a source of national wealth. France has long cherished the arts as among the chief of her national resources. Of the enormous amount of manufactured articles which we receive from her, the greatest part owe their sole value, to the ingenuity of her artists, who have been educated at the national expense. She thus creates her wealth out of the imagination of her people; a source of national prosperity which yet lies fallow with us.

It is sometimes urged that we are too young as a nation —have too many important affairs to heed, to give our attention to works of art. But it must be remembered, that we produced some of our best artists in our extreme youth, when our fields were bordered by the primitive forest, and a red or a white foe was always at the door. But in truth, the great business in life, that of providing food for the people, weighs less heavily upon us than upon any other nation in the world. No nation in Europe has half the leisure to bestow upon the arts that we have, or an historical background richer in materials of which a nation should be proud, or less occupied by the pencil of the artist. . . .

Annual Report [1849]

The growth of the American Art-Union, as exhibited in its vast subscription list, and the enlargement of its

simple and appropriate accommodations, offers gratifying
evidences of progress, but represents rather the means of
usefulness than the objects for which it was established.
Its purpose is to advance the cause of American Art—to
develope talent, to encourage merit, and to diffuse among
the people a love of Art, refinement of taste, and general
æsthetic culture; and in all these respects, it claims to
have achieved results at least commensurate with its business success.

During these eleven years, more than two hundred
thousand dollars has been expended directly upon Works
of Art. There is little reason to doubt, that this enormous
amount has been secured to the promotion of American
Art solely by the establishment of this Union. The purchases, which it has made, have not diminished in the
least degree, but have greatly augmented, individual patronage. The sum requisite to constitute membership
interferes with no man's ability, and surely does not diminish the disposition of any one to encourage Art, as a
matter of personal taste or liberality. On the contrary, the
friends of the American Art-Union maintain, that it has
created both artists and purchasers, and that its direct
patronage is far exceeded by that, which, indirectly, it has
called into existence. There are artists, who once depended
mainly upon us, but now rarely send us their works, being
fully occupied with private orders. It is only necessary,
in support of this view, to advert to the position of
American Art now, compared with what it was when this
Association was founded. Undoubtedly, with the general
progress of the nation in wealth and refinement, it would
have made some advancement. It had been advancing before that period, but how slowly, contrasted with its progress since! From what studios, could such a gallery of
American works, as the collection which is to be distributed among you this night, have been gathered, eleven
years ago?

Each year has exhibited indications of an advance in
Art, as well as a rapid increase in the number of artists

and of their productions. That now terminating presents no exception. Those who are familiar with the collections made in previous years, should compare them with the present, not by singling out some remembered favorite, perhaps a gem of peerless beauty, perhaps a production seen to great advantage in the midst of surrounding works of inferior merit, but by picturing before the mind the Gallery, as it was hung from year to year. It is the unanimous opinion of the Committee of Management, that the present exhibition is greatly superior to any of its predecessors; that it contains a larger number of productions of a high order of excellence, and a far less proportion of inferior works.

Our collections exhibit characteristics that betoken the rise of a new school of Art. The pictures have an American aspect, in the subjects, in the landscapes, in the treatment, in the sentiment, and in various other particulars. We are all ready to acknowledge our inferiority, in many respects, to the best schools of modern Art, and to hail our successes as the dawnings of a glorious meridian. Yet, in its actual condition, American Art presents indications of originality, beauty, and power, that are exceedingly interesting to contemplate. It is especially pleasing to dwell upon the healthfulness and purity of sentiment that distinguish it. It is not a nursery of false and affected sentiment. It delights not in the expression of impure ideas. It does not portray the human form with a pencil dipped in voluptuousness, nor does it surround its subjects with an enchanted, sensual atmosphere. Let this ever be the motto of American Art, inscribed in golden characters upon a snow-white scroll, "*Truth and Purity.*"

It is to the development of such an elevated school of Art that this Union of American sympathies, and the associated power of its multitudinous contributions, are directed.

American Art is advancing. It has its advantages, and it has great disadvantages. It does not imitate the vices, nor copy the style, of any mannered school. It is left in an especial degree to the study of nature, and to its own development in the exercise of original thought. Our artists lack high examples, and especially the influence and the teachings of the works of the great painters. But they may overcome this difficulty by aiming at the same standard which the authors of these immortal works strove to reach; for they may create in fancy forms of beauty, and summon, if they choose, legions of angels, infinitely excelling anything that earthy pigments can represent. But they will never become the masters of American Art, if they imitate low examples, or rest contented with low attainments. They must resolve never to be satisfied with any excellence they can reach. Above all, they must not consent to barter away piecemeal a popular reputation that has been gained. No man shall hang the *spolia opima* in the Temple of Art, unless with self-denying devotion he give himself away to the one great earthly object of his life; unless he resist the seductions of flattery, of indolence, and of luxury;—unless he paint for posterity rather than for the passing taste of the day; unless he labor, as all the great minds who have left their impress upon the world, have labored, from the impulses of genius, and in obedience to its inspirations.

There is one pleasant recollection connected with the operations of the Art-Union, which the Committee of Management desire that the members shall share with them. It is a consideration of the joy that is sent by its instrumentality into the bosom of the struggling artist;— for it does not reserve all its favors until the artist can dispense with its aid. It patterns, too, the hospitable spirit of the whole people, in the liberal welcome it extends to artists from abroad. It is American to the heart's core, but it practices the principles of true international courtesy. There are many paintings in this exhibition, the work of artists, born and trained in Europe, who, but for its potent introduction, would probably have been unknown and unemployed. They have been naturalized at once, as American artists.

The statuettes, which make a novel figure in our list of prizes,—those twenty copper-colored Indians, beautiful as Apollo, and armed with bow and arrow, like him as he pursued the children of Niobe, which we are about to send out as scouts into the haunts of civilized life,—were cast in bronze by artists recently from France, who have chosen this country as their home.

The American Art-Union has accomplished results which the local patronage of wealthy centres of population could not accomplish at all. It has scattered its engravings and distributed its prizes over the whole length and breadth of the land. The taste of the people has been cultivated, and the latent germ of Art unfolded in the mind of many a youth. The mode of distribution we have adopted for disposing of our accumulated treasures, by the awards of Fortune's wheel, is a convenient method of scattering them with impartial hand. The works we send out are messengers and missionaries of Art. Genius speaks from the canvas, and awakens responses like that which fell from the lips of young Correggio, as he stood before a picture of Raphael, "*I, too, am a painter.*"

Our Association is, for our country, the mother of Art-Unions. The Western Art-Union, located in that beautiful city of the West, where Art seems to have sprung out of the ground, and where it well may choose its Western home, is modeled on precisely the same plan. It has been in operation three years, and gives promise of great usefulness and future importance. We cannot relinquish to our fair daughter the whole dowry of the West, but will claim the privilege of sharing with her the contributions of Art, and the contributions to Art, from the extensive field she has chosen. The Philadelphia Art-Union is also successfully established, upon the scheme of the London Art-Union, distributing money prizes to be expended in pictures. Our Union hails with pleasure the success of similar institutions, conducted upon public principles, and for public ends. It welcomes all fellow laborers in its great purpose of promoting Art, and the love of refined Art, among the whole people.

The managers and members of the London Art-Union seem to be entirely satisfied with the working of their scheme, and to deprecate a change. The Committee of Management, and a large majority unquestionably of the members of the American Art-Union, are as fully convinced of the excellence of our plan. We think that their scheme would be impracticable with us, by reason of the wide diffusion of our subscribers. The injudicious selections that would be made, arising from the necessity of trusting to a great extent to agents unacquainted with Art, might prove of real disservice, by the encouragement that would be given to bad artists, and the consequent neglect of the meritorious. We should lose, too, that most interesting feature in our operations—the means of aiding deserving artists who are in circumstances of temporary need, or who have not yet achieved a reputation. But there is one objection which outweighs all others—we should lose our beautiful free Gallery.

The Gallery is one of the prominent characteristics of our plan, and it is one of the most interesting. It is the most effective means that could be devised for making known the merits of American artists. Besides the large number of works purchased for distribution, it affords the opportunity of exhibiting many that are to find other purchasers, and gives them the benefit of a free, and daily renewed advertisement. It is a useful school for our artists, too, not such a school as the great galleries of Europe offer with their inimitable works, but still highly instructive, suggestive of many bright imaginings, affording opportunities of comparison, and teaching the willing and careful student, even by its short comings and errors.

It is also a school of æsthetic education for the people, not merely in creating an appreciative taste in one or two departments of the fine arts, but as developing the love of the Beautiful. Its lessons are full of refinement. The influence of the cultivation of a taste for Art will be felt in social life, and will add fresh charms to the family circle. It tends to impart beauty to all the objects and appliances that a refined society needs for its comfort and gratification. It must have been just this sort of training that the artizans of the ancient world enjoyed, and which moulded in graceful and elegant forms all the productions of useful Art, even as we see them disentombed from the ashes of Vesuvius, where every object discovered is a gem of taste, and the very domestic implements, and the handles of the commonest kitchen utensils, are fashioned with artistic skill.

The deportment of the large and miscellaneous multitudes who frequent the Gallery shows that they visit it from refined motives. It is estimated that the number of visitors during the present year amounts to seven hundred and fifty thousand; and yet there has been no disorder or impropriety; and there never has been a single article injured.

The principles by which the Committee of Management are guided in the purchase of Works of Art are happily, and very distinctly, set forth in the May number of the Bulletin, to which the members, and all interested in the subject, are respectfully and particularly referred. To apply all the considerations there presented, in the case of every work submitted, is certainly no light task, especially when the number offered is taken into view. During the course of the year, over eighteen hundred paintings have been offered, out of which the four hundred and sixty in your catalogue of prizes were purchased.

During the present year, a monthly Bulletin has been published, containing a list of works purchased and on exhibition, general information on the subject of Art, notices and criticisms. This publication will be the means of diffusing widely sound views and principles, and will undoubtedly be of great service to the cause of Art. It is sent regularly to the Honorary Secretaries, and to every member who wishes to receive it, and constitutes a strong inducement to subscribe early. The entire aggregate of the

various numbers of the Bulletin issued is one hundred and
seventy thousand. As a means of communication with the
Honorary Secretaries and distant subscribers, its value can
scarcely be over-estimated, and it has met with so much
favor, and seems to promise so much advantage, that it
will be continued, enlarged, and improved, hereafter. It
is hoped that the discriminating taste, the liberal spirit,
and the scholar-like finish, which characterize this paper,
are appreciated.

The Power of Music

The development of culture is never uniform on all sides, and yet during the 1840s there was an advance in the appreciation of music that resembled the advances in the appreciation of literature and art. It can be epitomized in the achievements of three gifted men.

The first was the Bostonian Lowell Mason, who became the dominating musical figure of the decade. His influence went further than anyone else's. He acted as the nation's choirmaster. His forte was the composing, collecting, and publishing of hymns. He also composed, collected, and arranged many secular songs. He compiled more than fifty books of music, issuing the first one in 1822. The most popular, *Carmina Sacra*, and its supplement sold half a million copies by 1858. One of the main virtues of Mason's volumes lies in the fact that they are not only collections of highly singable tunes but also brief courses in how to sing them. *Carmina Sacra*, for instance, opens with thirty helpful pages on "The Elements of Vocal Music."

The second man was Stephen Foster. The sound of his music lingers even today. Though most of the melodies he composed and published in the middle and late 1840s have been forgotten, every now and then we still hear "There's a Good Time Coming," "Oh! Susanna," and "Nelly was a Lady." The most famous songs came in the next decade, however. The winning charm of Foster's music lies most perhaps in its air of plaintive simplicity. The songs are carefully designed, notwithstanding, to achieve that simplicity. They often capture a mood of nostalgia, a regretful recollection of a kinder, easier world, whose appeal is almost timeless. The 1840s enjoyed the songs of Stephen Foster; we enjoy some of them still.

The third man was the enormously popular violinist Ole Bull. The most widely admired instrumentalist to visit America during the 1840s, he was hailed by his audiences as the Viking of the violin. He arrived in New York late in 1843 for what developed into a long triumphal tour. He traveled as far south as New Orleans and as far west as the upper Mississippi. By the time he sailed home to his native Norway he had covered a hundred thousand miles and had given over two hundred concerts. He would return four more times. James Gordon Bennett's *Herald* reported his initial appearance in New York. The lavish praise accorded Bull in this and many other newspaper reports shows that his coming filled a need. The *Herald's* ecstatic description is reproduced below.

SOURCE: New York *Herald*, November 26, 1843.

Extraordinary Sensation at the Park Theater.—Ole Bull's Reception.—

One of the most extraordinary excitements that we ever saw in the musical world in this country took place last evening at the Park Theater. The celebrated Ole Bull, the greatest artist on the violin in the world, made his first appearance before an American audience. It was a tempest—a torrent—a very Niagara of applause, tumult, and approbation throughout his whole performances. The house was crammed from top to bottom, with one of the most fashionable, scientific, and critical audiences that we have ever seen.

We cannot describe Ole Bull's playing—it is beyond the power of language. Its effects on others may be indicated. Some of his unearthly, his heavenly, passages work on the feelings and the heart till the very tears flow. Others it makes vociferous, mad, and terrible in their applauses. At the close of some of his wonderful cadences the very musicians in the orchestra flung down their instruments and stamped and applauded like madmen.

This extraordinary being, this Ole Bull, will produce an excitement throughout the republic unlike any thing that ever took place in our day. He is young, unmarried, tall and elegantly formed—as beautiful as the Apollo, with an affectionate simplicity of manner that wins all hearts and all souls. He is the most extraordinary being, the most perfect genius in his art that ever yet crossed the broad Atlantic and rose upon the bright horizon of the new world.

DOCUMENT 30

A *Spring Day*

The discovery of nature was one of the delightful
contributions of the mid-nineteenth century. Though
the woods and trees had certainly been appreciated by
some before, by the 1840s they were preparing to become a vogue. They could do so because nature as an
opponent was gradually disappearing. As long as nature
could chill us throughout a long winter or frighten us
at night or savage us like an animal, we were not very
mindful of her beauty. Snow seems splendid only if we
are not freezing; the forest looks sublime only if we
are not lost in it. But as America's control over the
natural environment grew, the climate for a sentimental
or romantic view of nature appeared. It was aided by
the fact that growing numbers of Americans, even
though still a minority, were living in cities. The more
they walked on pavements, the better a meadow looked
to them; the more they sniffed city smoke, the purer a
country breeze appeared.

The artist began to paint nature more, especially nature when smiling. The poet increasingly celebrated her
felicities. And the essayist found in her an engaging
topic. No one would celebrate nature more brilliantly
than Henry Thoreau but his finest essays would come
out after the end of this decade. Meanwhile he had more
than one predecessor in print. Among them: the New
York artist and journalist Charles Lanman (1819–95).

A painter with a flair for writing, he published some
readable essays from time to time. In 1845 he issued a
volume called *Letters from a Landscape Painter*. "A
Spring Day," reprinted from it, seems too exclamatory
and rhapsodic for our present taste, yet the emotion is
strong though naïvely expressed and a tinge of humor

keeps the composition from being mawkish. The style to us seems almost gushing; nevertheless, every now and then a glint of Izaac Walton comes through. The essay is animated by the author's joy in life and distinguished by his painterly eye for descriptive detail.

SOURCE: [Charles Lanman], *Letters from a Landscape Painter* (Boston, 1845), pp. 19–33, abridged.

A Spring Day

May is near its close, and I am still at work in the valley of the Hudson. Spring is indeed come again, and this, for the present year, has been its day of triumph. The moment I awoke, at dawn, this morning, I knew by intuition that it would be so, and I bounded from my couch like a startled deer, impatient for the cool delicious air. Spring is upon the earth once more, and a new life is given me of enjoyment and hope. The year is in its childhood, and my heart clings to it with a sympathy, that I feel must be immortal and divine. What I have done to-day, I cannot tell: I only know that my body has been tremulous with feeling, and my eyes almost blinded with seeing. Every hour has been fraught with a new emotion of delight, and presented to my vision numberless pictures of surpassing beauty. I have held communion with the sky, the mountains, the streams, the woods, and the fields: and these, if you please, shall be themes of my present letter.

The sky! It has been of as deep an azure, and as serene, as ever canopied the world. It seemed as if you could look *through* it, into the illimitable home of the angels—could almost behold the glory which surrounds the Invisible. Three clouds alone have attracted my attention. One was the offspring of the dawn, and encircled by a rim of gold; the next was the daughter of noon, and white as a pearl; and the last, of evening, and robed in deepest crimson. Wayward and coquettish creatures were these clouds! Their chief ambition seemed to be to display their charms to the best advantage, as if conscious of their loveliness; and, at sunset, when the light lay pillowed on the mountains, it was a joyous sight to see them, side by side, like three sweet sisters, as they were, *going home.* Each one was anxious to favor the world with its own last smile, so that, by their changing places so often, you would have thought they were all unwilling to depart. But they were the ministers of the Sun, and he would not tarry for them; and, while he beckoned them to follow on, the Evening Star took his station in the sky, and bade them depart: and when I looked again, they were gone. Never more, thought I, will those clouds be a source of joy to a human heart. And in this respect, also, they seemed to me to be the emblems of those beautiful but thoughtless maidens, who spend the flower of youth trifling with the affections of all whom they have the power to fascinate.

The mountains! In honor of the season which has just clothed them in the richest green, they have displayed every one of their varied and interesting charms. At noon, as I lay under the shadow of a tree, watching them "with a look made of all sweet accord," my face was freshened by a breeze. It seemed to come from the summit of South Peak, and to be the voice of the Catskills. I listened, and these were the words which echoed through my ear.

"Of all the seasons, oh, Spring! thou art the most beloved, and to us, always the most welcome. Joy and gladness ever attend thy coming, for we know that the 'winter is past, the rains are over and gone, the time of the singing of birds is come, and the voice of the turtle is heard in our land.' And we know, too, that from thy hands flow unnumbered blessings. Thou softenest the earth, that the husbandman may sow his seed, which shall yield him a thousand fold at the harvest. Thou releasest the rivers from their icy fetters, that the wings of commerce may be unfurled once more. Thou givest food to the cattle upon a thousand hills, that they, in their turn, may furnish man with necessary food, and also assist him in his domestic labors. Thou coverest the earth with a garniture of freshest loveliness, that the senses of man may be gratified, and his thoughts directed to Him who hath created all things, and pronounced them good. And, finally, thou art the hope of the year, and thine admonitions, which are of the future, have a tendency to emancipate the thoughts of man from this world, and the troubles which may surround him here, and fix them upon that clime where an everlasting spring abides." "The voice in my dreaming ear melted away," and I heard the roaring of the streams as they fretted their way down the rocky steeps.

The streams! Such "trumpets" as they have blown to-day, would, I am afraid, have caused Mr. Wordsworth to exclaim:

The cataracts—*make a devilish noise up yonder.*

The fact is, "all the earth is gay," and all the springs among the mountains "giving themselves up to jollity," the streams are full to overflowing, and rush along with a "vindictive looseness," because of the burden they have to bear. The falls and cascades, which make such exquisite pictures in the summer months, are now fearful to behold, for, in their anger, every now and then they toss some giant tree into an abyss of foam, which makes one fear the effects of an earthquake. But, after the streams have left the mountains, and are running through the bottom lands, they still seem to be displeased at something, and at *every turn* they take, *delve* into the "bowels of the harmless earth," making it dangerous for the angler to approach too near, but rendering the haunt of the trout more spacious and commodious than before. The streams are about the only things I cannot praise to-day, and I hope it will not *rain* for a month to come, if this is the way they intend to act whenever we have a number of delightful showers.

The woods! A goodly portion of the day have I spent in one of their most secret recesses. I went with Shakspeare under my arm, but could not read, any more than fly, so I stretched myself at full length on a huge log, and kept a sharp look-out for anything that might send me a waking dream. The brotherhood of trees clustered around me, laden with leaves just bursting into full maturity, and possessing that delicate and peculiar green, which lasts but a single day, and never returns. A fitful breeze swept through them, so that ever and anon I fancied a gushing fountain to be near, or that a company of ladies fair were come to visit me, and that I heard the rustle of their silken kirtles. And now my eyes rested on a tree, that was entirely leafless, and almost without a limb. Instead of grass at its foot, was a heap of dry leaves, and not a bush or vine grew anywhere near it, but around its neighbors they grew in great abundance. It seemed branded with a curse, alone, forsaken of its own, and despised by all. Can this, thought I, be an emblem of any human being? Strange that it should be, but it is nevertheless too true. Only one week ago, I saw a poor miserable maniac, bound hand and foot, driven from "home and all its treasures," and carried to a dark, damp prison-house in a neighboring town. We can be reconciled to the mystery of a poisonous reptile's existence, but it is very hard to understand for what good purpose a maniac is created. But to return. Another object I noticed was a little tree about five feet high, completely covered with blossoms of a gaudy hue. At first, I tried to gather something poetical out of this thing, but could not to save my life. It caused me a real hearty laugh as the idea expanded, for it reminded me of a certain maiden lady of my acquaintance, who is *old*, *stunted*, very fond of *tall men*, and always strutting round under a weight of *jewelry*. But oh, what beautiful flowers did I notice in that shady grove, whose whispering thrilled me with delight! Their names? I cannot tell them to you—they *ought* to have no names, any more than a cloud or a foam-bell on the river. Some were blue, some white, some purple, and some scarlet. There were little parties of them on every side, and as the wind swayed their delicate stems, I could not but fancy they were living creatures, the personified thoughts perhaps of happy and innocent children. Occasionally, too, I noticed a sort of straggler peeping at me from beside a hillock of moss, or from under the branches of a fallen tree, as if surprised at my temerity in entering its secluded haunt. Birds also were around me in that greenwood sanctuary, singing their hymns of praise to the Father of mercies for the return of spring. The nests of the females being already built, they had nothing to do but be happy, anticipating the time when they themselves should be the "dealers-out of some small blessings" to their own dear helpless broods. As to their mates, they were about as independent, restless and noisy as might be expected, very much as any rational man would be who was the husband of a young and beautiful wife.

But the open fields to-day have super-abounded with pictures to please and instruct the mind. I know not where to begin to describe them. Shall it be at the very threshold of our farm-house? Well, then, only look at those lilac trees in the garden, actually top-heavy with purple and white flowering pyramids. The old farmer has just cut a number of large branches, and given them to his little daughter to carry to her mother, who will distribute them between the mantel-piece, the table, and the fireplace of the family sitting-room. But what ambrosial odor is that which now salutes the senses? It comes not from the variegated corner of the garden, where the tulip, the violet, the hyacinth, the blue bell, and the lily of the valley are vieing to outstrip each other in their attire; nor, from that clover-covered lawn, besprinkled with buttercups, dandelions, strawberry blossoms, and honeysuckles; but from the orchard, every one of whose trees are completely covered with snow-white blossoms. And from their numberless petals, emanates the murmur of bees, as they are busy extracting stores of honey. Oh, what an abundance of fruit—of apples, cherries, peaches, and pears, do these sweet blossoms promise! But, next week there *may* be a bitter *frost*; and this is the lesson which my heart learns. Now that I am in the springtime of life, my hopes,

in number and beauty, are like the blossoms of trees, and
I know not but they may even on the morrow be withered
by the chilly breath of the grave. But let us loiter farther
on. The western slope of this gentle hill is equally divided,
and of two different shades of green; one is planted with
rye, and the other with wheat. The eastern slope of the
hill has lately been loosened by the plough, and is of a
sombre color, but to my eye not less pleasing than the
green. And this view is enlivened with figures besides—for
a farmer and two boys are planting corn, the latter opening the bed with their hoes, and the farmer dropping in the
seed (which he carries in a bag slung at his side), and
pushing it with his foot. And now, fluttering over their
heads is a roguish bob-o-link, *scolding* about something
in their *wake*, at a *respectful* distance, and hopping along
the ground are a number of robins, and on the nearest
fence a meadow-lark and bluebird are "holding on for a
bite." But there is no end to these rural pictures; . . .

A mountaineer, who is to take this letter to the post-
office, is waiting for me below, and I must close,—hoping
that the country pictures I have endeavored to sketch may
have a tendency to make you feel a portion of that joy,
which has characterized this delightful Spring Day.

A Good Word for Winter

The rediscovery of nature was in a sense part of the rediscovery of the outdoors in general. People were finding that all four seasons could be fun. The wholesome pleasures of a New England winter make the subject of an essay in the second volume of the *Lowell Offering*. Prepared by a contributor signing herself "Ego," the piece has a genuine Down-East charm. The recipes for enjoyment are explicit and sensible, and—much to the point—they are inexpensive. Throughout, "Ego" has all the enthusiasm of a missionary seeking converts. If Lowell's next winter seemed livelier to the mill girls, "Ego" doubtless deserved some of the credit.

Three elements in her essay ought to be emphasized. One is her observation that Americans of the 1840s still clung, whenever possible, to the comforts of being indoors during brisk weather. As "Ego" notes, "There is not probably a nation in the world whose people exercise so little in the open air as ours." It should be added that exercise in the evenings still suffered from the prejudice against "night air" which would continue long after the 1840s ended. Bedroom windows stayed shut after dark except in balmy weather. Another element is the observation that amusements could now be the province of all the people—not only of the well-to-do but also of the mill workers and their friends. "Ego" was right; the pleasures of outdoor life could be enjoyed more readily now because people did not have to work as long or hard as they had to before. The 1840s were good times. The last element is the presence, here as almost everywhere else, of American practicality. Exercise is worth while not merely because we enjoy it but also because it builds us up. Outdoor exercise keeps us strong.

SOURCE: "Ego," "Winter Amusements," *Lowell Offering*, II (? 1842), 59–62.

Winter Amusements

Mr. Editor: I wish to call the attention of your fair readers to winter recreations. I mean out-of-door amusements—for of in-door pleasures we have already quite a variety. Of course, sleigh-rides (I mean in large companies, and in an elegant new-fashioned vehicle,) would be quite popular, if they were more easily managed. But besides the expense, there is much labor requisite in arranging and directing a large party, in the short time which usually elapses from a snow-storm to a thaw. Every thing must be done in a hurry-flurry, and nobody likes to be hurried or flurried; and then there are large bills for the gentlemen to pay, and often injured dresses for the ladies to replace, and a great many unpleasant "after-scenes;" but there might be other and cheaper amusements, in which all who wished, could easily participate.

There is not probably a nation in the world whose people exercise so little in the open air as ours. Our climate, I acknowledge, is variable; but exposure would render us less vulnerable to its local diseases, and inure us to all its changes. These very sudden and frequent alternations of heat and cold, of wet and dry, are arguments in favor of constant, though not careless, exposure. With proper precautions, we may be enabled to defy our barbarous winters; our dreary, drizzling, drenching springs; our debilitating, melting, scalding summers, and our shivering, though more equal and healthy, autumns.

We should not wait for pleasant days and unclouded skies, but walk and run and slide and skate in any weather, when we can do so without abusing our constitutions and tempting disease. Few are probably aware how much judicious, careful exposure to all weathers, can do towards strengthening a constitution.

I have mentioned sliding and skating, although they are not usually classed with female recreations, or exercises. But in some countries the prejudice against them is unknown; and among the Russians, Hollanders, and more northerly nations, they are frequent amusements. Even in England, they are occasionally practised; and it is probable that if some English actress, or French *danseuse*, should endeavor to revive the custom here, our fashionables would be enraptured with the idea. Oh, how I have sometimes wished that I could pretend to be a foreign princess, or some such body, and set fashions in dress, manners, domestic habits and every thing else. How very useful I *might be,*—but it is of no use to repine at fortune or circumstances.

"But we might do all these things," some one will say, "if they are not customary or fashionable." True, we might; but we do not wish to come home from a happy party, looking as if we had been away, stealing sheep, or robbing hen-roosts, or doing some such mean tricks. We wish to have public opinion corrected upon this subject, and all acknowledge that we are right; and that out-door amusements are far preferable, even in winter, to sitting in crowded rooms, gossiping about each other or flirting with the beaux. Not that we approve of girls going out of doors when old Boreas is holding forth with one of his most terrible blasts, or when the clouds are "pouring down pitch-forks," and all such sharp things, as the little boys say. But we think that as

> Too much confinement fades the fair,
> A pleasant slide in open air,
> With pleasant company, at night,
> When the moon shines, will set all right.

Now we cannot conceive of a more pleasant amusement for a clear, cold, frosty winter night, than for a bevy of brave young men and fair young maids to go out, when the sparkling stars and brilliant moon are glittering upon the icicled trees and snow-crusted earth, and taking some hand-sleds, "half-a-dozen more or less," according to the number of the party, and betaking themselves to some steep hill, draw up their sleds and drive up their bodies; and then, after all have gained the summit, arrange themselves in complete order, and, by a well-directed jerk, impart a momentum to each vehicle, which will soon carry it pleasantly and safely to the bottom of the hill.

It is, to be sure, a sad pity that there should be such a drawback to the pleasure, as having to drag the sleds up hill; but it is so with all the pleasures of this earth. There is some abatement to every felicity, and dregs to every cup of bliss. But when the company is large, sleigh-bottoms might be used. These hold more, and are equally as convenient to handle. But as the burden of their conveyance, and the trouble of assisting the ladies, would both come upon the "nobler sex," the females need suffer but little, unless through the exercise of sympathy—which some one says is no suffering at all.

Then there is the skating—equally as pleasant as the sliding, if only well managed. As much time and practice are requisite to render any one an expert skater, the ladies might obviate this difficulty by the following plan: Let a gentleman provide himself with two pairs of skates, one for himself and the other for his partner. Having well secured them to their feet, she could take fast hold of the skirts of his coat, and if he was a dexterous glider, and she maintained a firm position, a gay time she could have of it, enjoying all the pleasure without incurring any of the fatigue of this exercise.

But besides the health, vigor and buoyancy imparted to the constitution, there would be another important advantage in this amusement. In the near proximity of lads and lasses which would be unavoidable, and especially at a time when the spirits were wildly exhilerated, and glad feelings bursting forth in sounds of merriment, how easily would hand meet hand, and heart respond to heart, and

PLATES 20 THROUGH 36

PLATE 20. *Croton Water Celebration* 1842. Issued by J. F. Atwill. Courtesy of the Harry T. Peters "America on Stone" Lithography Collection, the Smithsonian Institution.

PLATE 21. *A Pic-Nic on the Wissahickon*. Drawn by W. Croome and engraved by Rawdon, Wright & Hatch. From *Graham's Magazine*, XXV (October 1844), opposite p. 184. Courtesy of the Library of Congress.

PLATE 22. Sugaring Off. Drawn by T. H. Matteson and engraved by S. A. Schoff. From *Columbian Magazine*, VIII (July 1847), frontispiece. Courtesy of the Library of Congress.

PLATE 23. *The Angler*. Painted by William James Hubard, 1846.
Courtesy of the Corcoran Gallery and Mr. George Katsafouros.

PLATE 24. Rural Pastime. Drawn by T. Allom and engraved by Henry Smith. From *Columbian Magazine*, VIII (October 1847), frontispiece. Courtesy of the Library of

PLATE 25. *Capt. Dampier on Ascension Island.* Engraving by Ellms.
From *American Magazine,* II (January 1842), 20. Courtesy of the
Library of Congress.

PLATE 26. *The Victor in the Tournament.* Painted by A. Deveria and engraved by S. H. Gimber. From *Columbian Magazine*, I (May 1844), frontispiece. Courtesy of the Library of Congress.

PLATE 27. *Schiller*. Drawn by S. Carse and engraved by A. L. Dick. From *Columbian Magazine*, VII (May 1847), frontispiece. Courtesy of the Library of Congress.

PLATE 28. *Little Red Riding Hood*. Painted by Edwin Landseer and engraved by A. L. Dick. From *Arthur's Magazine*, II (November 1844), frontispiece. Courtesy of the Library of Congress.

PLATE 29. *Elements of National Thrift and Empire.* Drawn by J. G. Bruff and lithographed by E. Weber & Co., 1847. Courtesy of the Library of Congress.

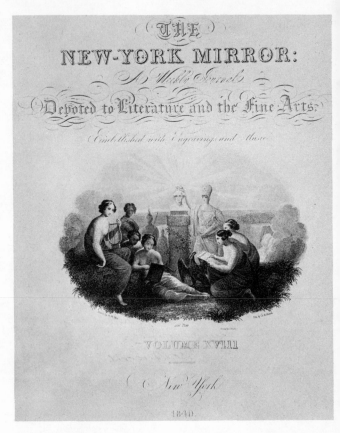

PLATE 30. The New-York Mirror: A Weekly Journal, Devoted to Literature and the Fine Arts, Embellished with Engravings and Music. Drawn by R. W. Weir and engraved by A. B. Durand. From New-York Mirror, XVIII (1840), title page. Courtesy of the Library of Congress.

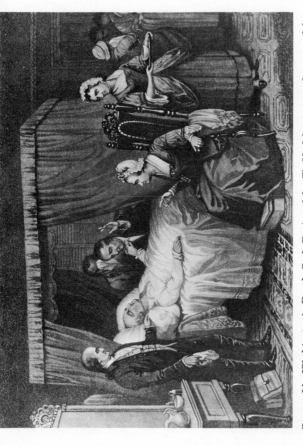

PLATE 31. *Washington's Death Bed.* Designed by T. H. Matteson and engraved by H. S. Sadd. From *Columbian Magazine*, V (May 1846), frontispiece. Courtesy of the Library of Congress.

PLATE 32. *Captain Smith & Pocahontas*. Drawn by J. Morton and engraved by H. S. Sadd. From *Columbian Magazine*, II (November 1844), frontispiece. Courtesy of the Library of Congress.

PLATE 33. *The Emigrants*. Drawn by J. A. Dallas(?). Poetry by Henry Hirst(?). From *Illustrated Monthly Courier*, I (September 1848), 36. Courtesy of the Library of Congress.

PLATE 34. One of the "Upper Ten Thousand." Drawn by S. E. Brown. From *Broadway Journal*, March 1, 1845. Courtesy of the Library of Congress.

PLATE 35. *Gang of Slaves Journeying to be Sold in a Southern Market.* Drawn by W. H. Brooke and engraved by F. Holl(?). From James Silk Buckingham, *The Slave States of America,* 1842. Courtesy of the Library of Congress.

PLATE 36 (Above and on facing page). *Black and White Slaves.* Drawn by E.W.C. and issued by A. Donnelly, 1844. Courtesy of the Harry T. Peters "America on Stone" Lithography Collection, the Smithsonian Institution.

soul commingle with soul; and, in their unrestrained felicity, how readily would they resolve to toil together in all the up-hills, and slide merrily the down-hills, and skim gaily over the smooth places of life; and thus many very nice young people might be saved from a life of single blessedness.

And then should a lady, incautiously venturing upon a thinner sheet of ice, unfortunately (?) fall through, how romantic it would be for her partner to dive after her, and save her! and then the papers would ring with the incident, or acccident, and the printers would say that the life thus preserved, they doubted not, would be consecrated to the gallant deliverer; and a hint would be given to remind them that the printer's "imp" is very fond of wedding cake, &c.

But we have said enough to convince all who are convincible, of the utility of these pleasures, and hope our good word will not be spoken in vain.

DOCUMENT 32

The Taste of Humor

It is an article of the American creed that we are endowed with a sense of humor. We take our endowment so seriously that we become outraged when charged with lacking it. We are supposed to have this valuable asset to so great an extent, as a matter of fact, that it not only contributes to our enjoyment but also— American practicality again—helps us in life. It gives us aid as well as comfort. It armors us against the effects of injury; it provides us with weapons against insult.

During the 1840s American humor in the form of the anecdote, the tall tale, and the joke existed in abundant measure, judging from reports of the time. Certainly stories were told much more often than they were written down; but unfortunately only the published word endures, so we must depend on printed rather than oral humor for our samples. A smaller amount of humor in print for the 1840s has survived than one might imagine. Even the longer tales, the sort composed by the few professional comedians willing to write, failed to reach print except in rare cases. In the 1850s the chronicles of American humor would be rich and the names of the main humorists would become well known. As the 1850s ended, everyone would hear, in particular, about Artemus Ward. In the 1840s pickings were slim, however.

Yet we have enough examples to risk some generalizations. We find, for instance, that a good deal of the humor of the 1840s ran to satire and burlesque. Pomposity proved to be a favorite American target. But as a rule nothing was safe from the comedian except religion. There was even an occasional satire on so sensitive a subject as slavery, with fun being poked at both

sides, at the enemies of slavery as well as at its friends.
Other subjects, however, gave readier results, among
them two that are still favorites, the American female
and the American school. Paying his respects to both,
William B. Fowle (1795–1865) composed one of his
best and most raucous skits, "The School Committee."
He put it first in his comic volume *Familiar Dialogues*
and it is reprinted here.

SOURCE: William B. Fowle, *Familiar Dialogues and Popular Discussions* (Boston, 1841), pp. 7–14.

The School Committee

MRS. VESTRY, the Minister's Wife.
MRS. BLUNT, the Deacon's Wife.
MRS. BRIEF, the Lawyer's Wife.
MRS. PILL, the Doctor's Wife.
MRS. SQUASH, a Farmer's Wife.
MRS. LUG, a Widow Lady, rather deaf.
MISS PRIM, an ancient Maiden, once a School-Mistress.
MISS SNAP, a satirical young Lady.
MISS FAIRMAN, the Candidate for the Village School.

[*All present but Miss Fairman.*]

Mrs. Vestry. LADIES, we are all assembled, and the
young lady who has applied for the village school is in the
next room. Shall I invite her in?

Mrs. Blunt. Is she handsome? I have no *idee* of employing any beauty, to be running after the boys when she
should be teaching the children.

Mrs. Vestry. She makes no pretensions to any other
beauty than that of the mind, I believe.

Mrs. Blunt. Let her come in, then.

[*Mrs. V. introduces Miss Fairman to Mrs. Brief,
who takes her by the hand, and says,*]

Mrs. Brief. Allow me to introduce you to Mrs. Pill,
the lady of our physician;—to Mrs. Blunt, the wife of our
worthy deacon—

Mrs. Blunt. And as well entitled to be called *lady* as the best of you, let me tell you! *Wife!* forsooth!

Mrs. Brief. I plead not guilty, as we lawyers say, of any intentional disrespect. [*She then goes on introducing Miss Fairman.*] This is Miss Prim, who may be called a fellow-laborer with you in the field of education.

Miss Prim. No longer so, I desire to be thankful! I left the profession before *every* body entered it.

Miss Snap. You left it when your pupils left you, I have been told; but it was so long ago, I do not remember the circumstances.

Miss Prim to Miss Snap. A few more years would be of infinite service to *some* folks.

Mrs. Brief. Miss Fairman, this is Miss Snap, whom you will find a ready assistant in *cutting* such twigs as you may not be able to bend. [*She lets go Miss Fairman, whose hand Mrs. Vestry takes, and says,*]

Mrs. Vestry. Let me introduce you, miss, to Mrs. Squash, the wife of one of our richest parishioners; and Mrs. Lug, who is rather hard of hearing, but whom you will find zealously interested in the cause of education.

Mrs. Blunt. You had better take *cheers*, ladies, and *set* down while the examination goes on. [*All sit.*] Young woman, come here. I warn you that you will have a severe examination; for we ladies have complained so much of former schoolma'ms, that the men have made us a committee to examine applicants, and suit ourselves; and we are going to do the thing thoroughly. Pray, what's your name, young woman?

Miss Fairman. Susan Fairman, madam.

Mrs. Blunt. How old are you?

Miss Prim. I object to that question, as an improper one. I would not tell my age to any one.

Miss Snap. The young lady may not have the same objection.

Miss Fairman. I shall be eighteen in a few days.

Mrs. Lug, [*holding her hand up to her ear as a deaf*

person does.] Did you say you were *eighty* years old, miss?

Miss Fairman. No, madam; only eigh*teen.*

Mrs. Squash. Why, you have hardly left off tires! Pray, can you make a *punkin* pie?

Miss Snap. If she can't, I dare say she can make one of *squash.*

Mrs. Squash. I should like to have my questions answered by the *gal* herself.

Miss Fairman. Madam, I never made a pie of the kind you name.

Mrs. Squash. A pretty farmer's wife you'd make!

Miss Fairman. Madam, I applied for a school, and not for a husband.

Mrs. Lug, [*holding her hand to her ear.*] What! does she want a husband! Why, there's Jonathan Squash, *jest* old enough for her.

Mrs. Vestry. Ladies, let us not wander from the purpose of our meeting. Miss Fairman, will you be good enough to inform the committee where you were educated, and the extent of your studies.

Mrs. Blunt. Ay, ay; where were you *eddicated?* what do you know? Come, I'll question you, myself. In what state were you born into the world?

Miss Fairman. In Massachusetts, madam.

Mrs. Blunt. In Massafiddlestick!

Miss Snap. Mrs. Blunt expected you would say you were born in a state of sin and misery. She is a sound divine, but no geographer.

Mrs. Vestry. Please to inform us, Miss Fairman, of such particulars as we may need to aid us in our judgment.

Miss Fairman. I have had a good school education, ladies, but pretend to nothing more than is necessary to qualify me to teach the common branches in a common village school, which is all I understand yours to be.

Miss Prim. That will never do for Smartville: we must have something more than *common.* In *my* day, no teacher with such pretensions would have dared to apply for a school. Have you ever studied algebra?

Miss Fairman. Never. I did not know that it was taught in a common village school.

Miss Prim. It is not; but it is the basis of a good education. No *lady* should be ignorant of algebra.

Mrs. Lug. What! don't the *gal* know there is such a thing as a *zebra?* [*Holding her hand up to her ear.*]

Miss Snap. This knowledge would be of more use to her than algebra. Pray, Miss Prim, did you ever study algebra yourself?

Miss Prim. Yes; I spent two weeks upon the delightful science, and almost made myself mistress of it.

Mrs. Pill. Did you ever make any use of it afterwards?

Miss Prim. I came to examine, but not to be catechized, madam.

Miss Snap. When a stocking was *minus* a foot, did your algebra ever make it *plus?*

Mrs. Lug. What! does the *gal blush?* Well, I like to see young folks blush.

Mrs. Pill. Pray, Miss Fairman, have you ever learned Latin?

Miss Fairman. No, madam; my father did not think it so important for females as their own language; and he never encouraged the study of it by his daughters.

Mrs. Pill. He was a dolt. Why, Latin, miss, is the basis of every learned profession; and my husband, Dr. Pill, says he could not prescribe without it.

Mrs. Squash. The more is the pity; they only use Latin to hide the *pison* names of their nasty drugs. My husband once took it into his head that every good farmer must know Latin, that he might know the *larned* names of vegetables; and so every *single* tree was called an *Arbor* after that; and every squash, an *Iguana-falciforma-peripatetica*, or some such nonsense. For my part, I hope to hear a squash called a squash as long as I bear the name.

Mrs. Vestry. Ladies, let us not forget the object of

our meeting. Miss Fairman, may I ask at what school you were educated?

Miss Fairman. At the Female Monitorial School, madam, in Boston.

Mrs. Lug. What school is that? A *tory* school! that will never do, miss; we are all *wigs* here.

Mrs. Squash. I really believe the *gal* is a Jacksonman in disguise.

Miss Fairman. Ladies, you mistake the *nature* as well as the name of the school. It is called monitorial, because the elder pupils, who assist the teacher, are called monitors.

Miss Prim. Ay, ay; this is one of the new-fangled notions that have made instruction so vulgar an employment that I can not endure it. When *children* take up the ferule, it is time for *us* [*drawing herself up*] to lay it down.

Mrs. Blunt. You don't intend to introduce any such notions here, miss?

Miss Fairman. I hoped, madam, that a judicious use of monitors would not be objected to.

Mrs. Squash. What! do you mean to set other children to teach my *darters?*

Miss Fairman. I should like to employ the more advanced pupils, whosever children they may be, in instructing those who know less than themselves.

Mrs. Brief. Then Mrs. Cowyard's brats may be set to teach our children, Mrs. Vestry!

Mrs. Vestry. I have no objection to that, if her children know more than ours. My husband says we should always be willing to receive instruction from any source however humble.

Miss Prim. I dare say Mr. Vestry would even allow that children are competent to *teach* children. Preposterous idea!

Mrs. Vestry. I know he would allow it, for I have often heard him say, that men are only children of a larger growth; and there was no more difference between *his* attainments and those of his parishioners, than there is be-

tween some children and others. He considers himself as
a monitor amongst his brethren.

Mrs. Brief. If he is only a *monitor*, pray, who is our
teacher? or have not we any?

Mrs. Vestry. He is accustomed to call the Savior the
great Teacher. But I think we had better ascertain how
the young lady has been instructed, and what she has
learned, before we condemn her system utterly.

Mrs. Pill. I should like to ask her one question. Pray,
miss, if one of your pupils should cut her finger badly, what
would you do?

Miss Snap, [*aside to Miss Fairman.*] Tell her you
should send for her husband, Dr. Pill, and you will make
her your friend forever.

Miss Fairman. I should probably send her home,
madam.

Mrs. Blunt. Come, come, let *me* put her a serious question. Young woman, how many *comman-de-ments* are
there?

Miss Fairman. Ten were given by Moses, madam.

Mrs. Lug. How many did she say?

Miss Snap. Ten.

Mrs. Lug. Ay, ay; that's right; the *gal's* right for once.

Mrs. Blunt. Now tell me how much of the Primer
you know by heart. What comes next *arter* "The cat doth
play, and after slay."

Miss Snap, [*aside to Miss F.*] Tell her, "Whales in
the sea, great fish they be."

Miss Fairman. I must confess my ignorance, madam.

Mrs. Blunt. Young woman, I don't know what my
husband, Deacon Blunt, would say, to find you so ignorant
of the first principles of religion.

Miss Fairman. Madam, I would respectfully remark,
that I have been taught to draw the principles of my religion from the Bible, and not from the Primer.

Mrs. Blunt. Yes, that is one of Mr. Vestry's notions;
but every body learned the *Primer* when I was a *gal.* I
could say it backwards as well as *forruds.*

Miss Prim. Will the young *la*-dy be good enough to inform the committee whether she has studied botany?

Miss Fairman. I have, madam.

Miss Prim. Did you study the philosophical part of the science, which treats of the loves and the language of plants?

Miss Fairman. No, madam, I have only studied their structure and uses.

Miss Prim. I supposed you had neglected the only *ethereal* part of the science. This comes of your new-fangled *system*, I suppose.

Miss Fairman. No, indeed, madam. Nonsense can be taught by the monitorial plan as well as by any other. The subjects taught depend upon the teacher, and not upon the system.

Mrs. Blunt. I have seen enough of the *gal.* She will never do for me. She don't even know her Primer.

[*She dashes out.*]

Miss Snap. "The eagle's flight is out of sight."

Mrs. Brief. Mr. Brief will never suffer his children to be taught by Mrs. Cowyard's brats. [*Exit.*]

Miss Snap. "Out, out, *Brief* candle!"

Mrs. Pill. I cannot swallow her ignorance of Latin.

[*Exit.*]

Miss Snap. Because she could not swallow your pills, I suppose.

Mrs. Squash. I can never vote for a miss so young that she cannot make a *punkin* pie. I thought, at first, she *might* do for my son Jonathan. [*Aside.*] [*Exit.*]

Miss Snap. So, because she can't cook a *punkin*, she is not allowed to become a Squash!

Miss Prim. I must withhold my approbation from one who has no soul for the loves and language of flowers, and who has never studied algebra.

Miss Snap. And whose charms being *plus*, would render yours a negative quantity.

Miss Prim. *My* children—I mean my neighbors', for I desire to be thankful that I have none of the nasty things

—shall never go to a monitorial school with my consent. Monitorial, indeed!   [*Exit.*]

Mrs. Lug. Who did she say was dead?

Miss Snap. Your tories, I suppose.

Mrs. Lug. Well, I am sorry for them; I had rather they had repented; but they sha'n't get foothold in our village while I am on the committee. Good bye.   [*Exit.*]

Miss Snap. A good riddance to them all! Now, Miss Fairman, let me congratulate you upon escaping from such patrons.

Mrs. Vestry. Give me your hand, my dear. You have borne the trial modestly and patiently. My husband has been applied to for a preceptress of an academy, and I am sure that, after he has heard the result of this meeting, he will confer the situation upon my young friend. Come, let us find him.

Social and Solitary

Foreign travelers often remarked, wincing slightly, that the Americans were a social, a gregarious people. They loved to gather in groups. They were forever organizing new clubs and societies or joining old ones. This observation by our visitors had a considerable measure of truth. We obviously had many societies. There were some for business, some for pleasure, some for profit of various kinds, some simply for enjoyment. In the 1840s those designed for business and financial advantage were not yet as popular as they later would be. The ancestors of Rotary and Kiwanis had only begun to appear; the associations of merchants, of craftsmen, of professional men, though more numerous, were only a promise of what they would become in succeeding decades. Societies for pleasure, however, abounded. So did the societies which adroitly mixed something useful with the pleasure. Of these the best example was certainly the lyceum. Throughout each winter it presented weekly lectures. It put on its platform a mixture of local luminaries, traveling spellbinders, and prominent intellectuals. Emerson, for one, lectured to hundreds of lyceums during his long career. Though the lyceum movement's original aim was to educate, by the 1840s the lyceum entertained more than it informed. But American gregariousness included much more than belonging to organizations. It showed itself in the myriad social pleasures of the time: the parties, picnics, church festivals, holiday celebrations, and so on, right through to the impromptu gathering of a few neighbors in a parlor or on a front porch.

The ultimate in American gregariousness can be seen in the splendid print of the Croton Water Celebration published by J. F. Atwill. The scene is New York, already our most crowded city; people gather in the park and cluster on the sidewalks to watch the parade; and the parade itself is made up of organization after organization, rank after rank of militiamen, firemen, and such. According to accounts of the event, many different societies marched, from ward clubs to mutual-benefit guilds, though they cannot be identified in the picture. The next picture, "A Pic-Nic on the Wissahickon," shows a more frequent if less striking social occasion. Here a group of Philadelphia ladies and gentlemen relax, despite their formal dress, and enjoy the delights of the outdoors. The pleasant woods and stream contribute to their gaiety. The picnickers include that most typical American comedian, the man who becomes the life of the party by putting on a woman's hat.

The country had its social pleasures as well as New York or Philadelphia. The rural pleasures as a rule were more useful than the urban kind but that did not seem to diminish their attractiveness—quite the reverse. The husking bee and quilting bee constitute excellent examples. The sweetest of such rustic recreations must have been the sugaring-off party. In "Sugaring Off" we see the succulent maple sap being boiled, cooled, and consumed.

Although American gregariousness showed itself in the social enjoyments of life, all enjoyments certainly were not social. The pleasures of solitude also made their claim. Whether active or passive, enjoyed indoors or out, they were increasingly important. The American of the 1840s already displayed an ambivalence about society and was beginning to evidence it in his recreations. The joys of being alone, he realized more and more, had their proper place in his world. Among active outdoor enjoyments, fishing was already recognized as one of the best ways for a man to get away from it all. From the little boy with his improvised pole to the adult angler with his more costly equipment, they all attested to the lure of a secluded scene in which the fisherman was the only human being. "The Angler" shows the painter Charles Lanman, who wrote the essay on "A Spring Day" reprinted earlier in this section. It is worth noting that he has more to occupy him than a rod and reel, for his hand rests on an open book. He represents an interest in the passive as well as the active enjoyment of life. In "Rural Pastime" too there is only a single human figure. A lady sits sketching a scene from nature. Wood, water, and mountain all look peaceful. Tranquillity is the keynote.

Of the solitary pleasures reading was the most frequent. Often it was for escape. The crude picture of "Capt. Dampier on Ascension Island" exemplifies the interest in the exotic, the far-off. Travel books were highly popular through the 1840s. Many a reader relished the recurring accounts of journeys to the jungle, of voyages to unexplored lands. Escape could come in time as well as place. For an America generally obsessed with the present, the past offered a tempting refuge for relaxation. The Middle Ages proved most popular, particularly as painted in the romantic fiction of Sir Walter Scott. They were likewise popular in art; in point, "The Victor in the Tournament," from the *Columbian Magazine*, with its medieval pomp and pageantry.

The two remaining pictures in this group represent opposites. The engraving "Schiller," also from the *Columbian Magazine*, attests to the growing awareness of European culture in general and European literature in particular. The works of the great German poet-dramatist were finding their way to this country, both in original and translation, while an influential cluster of American teachers and critics was engaged in making the public realize the riches of continental European civilization. On the other hand, the engraving "Little Red Riding Hood" reminds us of the folk contribution to the enjoyment of life. The fables and simple tales of childhood were passed on from generation to generation. There were not as many printed versions in the 1840s as there would be later but oral transmission made them unnecessary.

With others or by himself, the American was learning to enjoy life increasingly. He no longer had to fight for a living in the way he was forced to before. In the progressive 1840s the struggle for existence had eased

off. Moreover, the old Puritan attitude toward recreation was being modified. By today's standards leisure
was still rare, the workday forbiddingly long, and the
enjoyment of life limited. But to the men and women
of that decade it was a time when the fresh spice of
pleasure was seasoning their otherwise businesslike lives.

PLATE 20. *Croton Water Celebration 1842*. Issued by
J. F. Atwill.

SOURCE: The Harry T. Peters "America on Stone" Lithography
Collection, the Smithsonian Institution.

This lively lithograph has many things to say. It tells us
about the growing sense of municipal responsibility, for
here in a dramatic demonstration of civic pioneering is
the city of New York now piping water from a reservoir
nearly forty miles off. It tells us about other civic advances
which are dependent on an ample, cheap water supply,
such as better fire protection and improved sanitation. It
tells us about the development of technology which permitted so impressive an engineering feat. And, most important for our present purpose, it tells us about the
Americans themselves at a moment of civic celebration.
Here is all the American gregariousness and vitality that
foreign observers reported. The scene is crowded with
people. The massed ranks of marchers, with their bands,
gay uniforms, and big placards, are seen on three sides of
the picture. Most of the watchers stand on one side of the
street or the other; the rest lean out of their windows to
take in the spectacle. In the lower left- and right-hand
corners of the picture two small groups of well-dressed
New Yorkers enjoy themselves simply by talking with one
another. The men posture negligently while the women
stand in ladylike attitudes. In the center of the lithograph
a crowd clusters around the fountain, which sends up its
broad plumes of water. A holiday atmosphere suffuses
the scene.

Technically, the lithograph is an interesting mixture of the quaint and the sophisticated. The design is so symmetrical that it is awkward. The dark lines of the fence in the center converge on the fire cart, with its length of hose along its side, but the cart and the riders are weakly drawn and do not hold our attention. However, the massive fountain rises boldly in the middle of the composition; it has the emphasis it deserves. The chiaroscuro is effectively if simply handled. The light tones of the fountain are enclosed by the dark ones of the foliage; the gray masses of the marchers are enclosed in turn by the white walls of the buildings. The drawing though crude is animated. And the over-all impression has a good deal of charm to it.

PLATE 21. A *Pic-Nic on the Wissahickon*. Drawn by W. Croome and engraved by Rawdon, Wright & Hatch.

SOURCE: *Graham's Magazine*, XXV (October 1844), opposite p. 184. Library of Congress.

The social pleasures of the outdoors grew as did America's leisure. As more Americans began to live in cities and towns, the parks and woods became increasingly desirable for purposes of recreation. The picnic party of Philadelphians depicted here is obviously enjoying the escape from the city. The couple in the foreground relax by flirting mildly; the man lounges on the grassy bank while the lady makes a chaplet of leaves. At the couple's left a little amiable tussling is taking place. At the right, on the river, a boat full of merrymakers moves along. One lady in it fails, however, to be amused. She has been deprived of her bonnet and looks with annoyance at the flute player in the bow who has appropriated it.

The treatment of the subject is in the Romantic vein. The foliage is dense and mostly dark. As usual there is some water. The composition is carefully varied. At the center of the scene the two tree trunks converge to point at the seated couple. The group on the left of them is highlighted and is framed by the surrounding trees. The occupants of the boat are outlined against the far bank. Up above them at the top of the picture there is an area of light intended to set off the umbrage immediately below. In this light area stands a house, which provides an artistic balance for the flirting couple, serves as an added point of technical interest to the viewer, and epitomizes the confined civilization from which the picnickers have temporarily emerged.

PLATE 22. *Sugaring Off.* Drawn by T. H. Matteson and engraved by S. A. Schoff.

SOURCE: *Columbian Magazine*, VIII (July 1847), frontispiece. Library of Congress.

Sugaring off can symbolize all the rural activities that meant social enjoyment. Country dwellers had learned from the frontier the advantages of co-operation; the pleasures of co-operation promptly made themselves felt too. The neighbors from miles around gathered to help in a barn-raising or to take part in a husking bee, recognizing that along with the labor would come gossip, flirtation, shop talk, good food, comic stories, and all the other things we associate with festivity. Here we see a folk festival; its occasion is the sweet sap of a tree.

The sugar maple could be found in two-thirds of the United States as it was in 1840, but then as now the best places were Vermont and northern New York State. The tapping of the maple tree constituted one of the rites of spring. In this engraving most of the steps in making maple sugar are shown. The pails for carrying it, the large iron pots for boiling it, and the pans for cooling it all appear. The party is taking place at night, partly because the sap flowed more freely then and partly because the party-goers would be busy during the day.

The effect of firelight gives a strong pattern to the composition. Sharp lines of force are lacking but the areas of light and shade have been strikingly contrasted. The play of light is quite unrealistic but artistically sound. The focus of attention is the prankster in the middle of the engraving. Four of the other people in the party watch him while he blows heartily away. The central group shades off into dark, and then light plays again over the other two couples in the lower left-hand corner and the two syrup-sippers at the far right. The picture has a sense of vivacity, even though the movement is rather limited and the characters give the appearance of being posed.

PLATE 23. *The Angler.* Painted by William James Hubard, 1846.

SOURCE: The Corcoran Gallery. Courtesy of Mr. George Katsa-fouros.

This contemplative sportsman, seated with a book, might have been the great Izaac Walton himself, who was known for his thoughtful serenity as well as for his fisherman's skill. The subject is, however, the painter and writer Charles Lanman as seen by his friend and fellow painter Hubard. Hubard has posed him in salient outline against a bold sky which occupies the top two-thirds of the canvas. The bottom third is a landscape conceived in the usual Romantic manner. We see a bosky grove and some other trees, the customary water with a bridge across it, and a bank and part of a tree trunk looming on the right. The face and figure of Lanman have been slightly romanticized, though by no means as much as the wooded background. Hubard's brushwork is careful and precise. The tones of the face look natural; the painting of the coat lapels is especially adroit technically. The atmosphere of the whole composition is gentle without being soft.

"The Angler" is emblematic of the interest in the 1840s in nature, in the outdoors in general, and in enjoyment by oneself. But its subject is too polished to be typical and so should be balanced by a conception of the proverbial barefoot boy fishing with a bent pin hung from a string on a stick. That should help to strike the American average.

PLATE 24. *Rural Pastime*. Drawn by T. Allom and engraved by Henry Smith.

SOURCE: *Columbian Magazine*, VIII (October 1847), frontispiece. Library of Congress.

The sketcher smiles faintly as she draws a scene in the countryside. Once again we have a picture in the fashionable Romantic mode. This one mingles the beautiful with the sublime in its composition, for there are not only the expected leafy trees and placid water but also the steep cliffs and waterfall that we associate with the sublime. The customary cows stand reflectively in the middle of the stream; a dog lies curled at the sketcher's feet. But she is the sole human being in the picture and evidently enjoys the fact. In the middle distance, framed by two clumps of trees, there is even a ruin, that badge of the Romantic interest in the medieval.

"Rural Pastime" is notable for three reasons. It suggests through its choice of subject that some people, at any rate, tried to create art as well as appreciate it. Sketching had been one of the traditional accomplishments of the lady and so fitted in well with the rising interest in art during the 1840s. She could draw pictures as well as buy them. And "Rural Pastime" in its technique and tone illustrates one of the many changes rung on the Romanticism which marked the temper of this period. Its mingling of the beautiful and sublime would become especially attractive to the artist who moved toward the grander scenery of the West for his material. Lastly, it reminds us of the continued existence of the English influence in our Romanticism. By the 1840s English Romanticism was past its prime, but the Romantic movement in this country was still strong and would show itself in, among other things, the *Columbian Magazine's* choice of "Rural Pastime," the work of an English painter, to reproduce.

PLATE 25. *Capt. Dampier on Ascension Island.* Engraving by Ellms.

SOURCE: *American Magazine,* II (January 1842), 20. Library of Congress.

The recreational reading that Americans did during the 1840s included an abundance of travel literature. Every part of the world seemed to interest them, though the reasons varied according to region. Europe was apt to be attractive because of its cultural richness, its storied past. The East was attractive no doubt because it represented a variety of ways of life, all different from our own. Africa fascinated us by its gaudy savagery. And the South Seas enthralled us with their promise of an exotic, sensuous existence. They established themselves in our interest in the 1840s and have remained alluring, especially for the male reader, ever since. For him the carefree love of a beautiful, brown-skinned girl apparently has a permanent appeal.

Some of the favorite accounts of voyaging in the South Seas could be found in the books by the British buccaneer and discoverer, William Dampier. Though written over a century before, they maintained their place in the 1840s as classics of travel literature. On one of his voyages Dampier was marooned for more than a month with his crew on Ascension Island. In the crude woodcut reproduced here, he is searching for water, which seems almost within reach, while the island's famous goats look bored.

PLATE 26. *The Victor in the Tournament*. Painted by
A. Deveria and engraved by S. H. Gimber.

SOURCE: *Columbian Magazine*, I (May 1844), frontispiece.
Library of Congress.

For an America all too involved in the present, reading
about the past offered a tempting relief. It was not yet
the heyday of the costume novel but a sprinkling of such
novels could already be found on the publishers' lists. The
great exemplar, throughout the nation but especially in the
South, was *Ivanhoe*. To many a delighted reader its high
point was the tournament scene in which Wilfred of Ivanhoe dashed down the wicked Brian de Bois-Guilbert. Here
and there in the South, in emulation, local groups sponsored an occasional tourney themselves; today in Maryland
at least one still exists. To the reader of the 1840s the
valor and prowess of the knights, the beauty and virtue of
the ladies, the humble devotion of the peasants, and the
richness of the pageantry made a varied and considerable
appeal. These romantic reflections of the past could be
discovered not only in the novels but also in the short
stories and poems being read during this decade, and in
the art. The magazines besides printing fiction and verse
about the Middle Ages not infrequently published pictures, especially by English artists, showing chivalry in all
its trappings.

Invariably the artist's treatment of a medieval subject
was sentimentalized. "The Victor in the Tournament" provides a case in point. Each face, whether male or female,
looks pretty; each expression if not empty is vapid. Here,
as a matter of fact, all the faces even appear to have the
same sweet features—liquid eye and Roman nose—so that
we feel that somehow we have come to the reunion of one
large family. The figures form a tableau with attitudes so
stagy that they might derive from a popular melodrama.
We can easily imagine that the page, for instance, on the

far left has just been directed to hold his pose and that the trumpeters have been firmly reminded not to let their trumpets become parallel. The center of interest for the composition lies of course in the knight in shining armor and the Queen of Love and Beauty who bends over him. We find little to attract us in most of the other figures in spite of the artist's palpable attempt to give them something to do, such as pointing a finger or waving a scarf. Both topic and treatment are the kind that would draw loud laughter from Mark Twain after the Civil War. Notwithstanding, both before and after the war, many an American vicariously enjoyed adventuring in the days of chivalry.

PLATE 27. *Schiller*. Drawn by S. Carse and engraved by A. L. Dick.

SOURCE: *Columbian Magazine*, VII (May 1847), frontispiece. Library of Congress.

Gazing soulfully aloft and surrounded by scenes from his writing, the great Friedrich Schiller sits before us. He is an eloquent representative of the European culture which was opening up for the 1840s. In the America of that time Schiller's reputation stood even higher than Goethe's. For one thing, his Romantic temper fitted the American mood much better than Goethe's elegantly Classical one. For another, Schiller's works were regarded as having higher moral standards than Goethe's. The sexual sensationalism of *Faust* was suspect; nothing in Schiller seemed as censurable. Longfellow, the most persuasive advocate of German literature our country had, preferred Schiller to Goethe on both these counts. He found in Schiller a more idealistic moral atmosphere and also a closeness to the heart of humanity. Longfellow was convinced that the poet should write for the multitude who feel, as well as the few who think; and so he favored Schiller in spite of Goethe's astonishing genius.

The present engraving commemorates not Schiller's dramas but his poems. The subjects shown here come mostly from his romantic, idealistic ballads. At the upper left, the first scene refers to "The Song of the Bells," the one below it to "The Alpine Hunter." The three scenes at the bottom derive from "The Struggle with the Dragon," "The Gods of Greece" (probably), and "Pegasus in the Yoke." The next one, above, illustrates "The Journey to the Foundry" and the last "The Veiled Picture of Sais" (an ancient Egyptian city). The subjects of the vignettes, different from one another as they appear, have in common a Romantic feeling and action; nothing is businesslike, contemporary, or matter-of-fact. The artist's treatment is in the Romantic mode too and gives full scope to the elaboration that the 1840s relished.

PLATE 28. *Little Red Riding Hood.* Painted by Edwin Landseer and engraved by A. L. Dick.

SOURCE: *Arthur's Magazine,* II (November 1844), frontispiece. Library of Congress.

At the basic level of American culture lay a common stock of stories. They were the tales that people learned as children and could never forget because of their immense popularity. Some came from American history and literature: Washington at Valley Forge, for instance, or Rip Van Winkle asleep in the mountains. These were the newest. Some came from our heritage of English culture: for instance, *Mother Goose* (probably first published in London in 1760); some came from more foreign folk tales and legends. Almost all were modified at least slightly by the sentimentalism of the 1840s. Here, in point, is Little Red Riding Hood, the appealing heroine of her grisly old fable. Her story seems to have started in France, had a happy ending added to it in Germany by the brothers Grimm, and entered America in a translation of the

German version as early as the start of the nineteenth century. And here the artist is English.

In our engraving the selection of scene from the story and the treatment of subject are both purest sentimentality. Many places in the story exist where the child could have been portrayed but the artist chose the tense moment when she opens her grandmother's door. The treatment of the little girl's face—tiny mouth, enormous eyes, apprehensive expression—is a masterpiece of the popular pathetic. The pudgy little hands clutching the cloak also are designed to add to the appeal. The anticipation of danger is there; but the American child could be reassured, for her version unlike the early French one ended happily.

PART VI

Comprehending Our Country

Glorious Columbia

In the 1840s we loved our country more and loved it more openly than we do now. No one can measure the change exactly but there seems little doubt that it took place. The pride and affection of those youthful years manifested themselves in many directions. They can be seen most vividly in the popular literature and art. In her poem "Our Country" Mrs. L. H. Sigourney (1791–1865) lavishes praise on the United States to an extent that would embarrass a present-day American. No poet of any standing would currently let himself be caught publishing a paean as artless and unblushing as hers. Admittedly Mrs. Sigourney ranks as a hack poet but the homage she paid in this poem could be found, more subtly expressed, in the work of numerous better writers of her time.

"Our Country" is reprinted below because it perfectly epitomizes the assertive innocence of young America in its own view. All is excellence. Though slavery was the most formidable of facts, Mrs. Sigourney along with most of her countrymen tried to shut her eyes to its grim implications. She could not quite, however, and the thought of it does impel her to hint her fear of secession and voice her hope for continued unity.

From the Atlantic to the Pacific, whatever Mrs. Sigourney observes strikes her as good. She apostrophizes America: "fair land! free land! / How glorious art thou!" Then, in the bulk of the poem, she proceeds to touch on and overpraise much in American life that we have seen described in this book. She looks through the rosiest of spectacles. To her the farmer is sturdy, happy, and productive. The laborer is strong and thrifty. Education exists in this utopian land for its own sake. Art deftly

fulfills itself. Transportation is ceaseless, communication
swift. The immigrant is always welcome. Congress is
sagacious, industrious, and—thank heaven—united. The
entire country, personified as Columbia, is Christian.
Columbia is the mother of an ample brood. Her strength
lies most in the youth and in the clergy but the teacher
also is of great importance. "These are thy strength, my
land!" Mrs. Sigourney asserts, "These are thy hope."

Having painted the American scene in glowing colors, Mrs. Sigourney comes to the end of her poem; and
now we hear the muted echo of her single earlier apprehension, the fear of disunion. She says in her final
sentence, "God keep thee perfect in thy many parts, /
Bound in one living whole."

Mrs. Sigourney's language is as full-blown as her
eulogies. No noun exists comfortably without the support of adjectives; no idea can be stated properly unless
decorated with metaphor. The blank verse is the kind
that lends itself all too well to schoolroom recitation.
The total result is a very good example, technically, of
bad American poetry.

SOURCE: Mrs. L. H. Sigourney, *Illustrated Poems* (Philadelphia,
1849), pp. 382–85.

Our Country

Land of broad rivers and of ocean-lakes,
Sky-kissing cliffs and prairies prank'd with flowers,
That, seated on thy mountain-throne, dost hear
The Atlantic and Pacific's mighty surge
Battling against thy coast, and throw to each
Thy snow-white sails, that visit every clime
And kindred under heaven,—fair land! free land!
How glorious art thou!

                 Mid thy cultured vales
The sturdy reapers sing, garnering the corn
That feedeth other realms besides their own.
—Toil lifts his brawny arm, and takes the wealth
That makes his children princes; Learning wins

By studious lamp the better gold, that dreads
Nor rust nor robber's wile; Art deftly brings
Tissue and tincture and the fretted stone;
Strange steeds of iron, with their ceaseless freight,
Tramp night and day; while the red lightning bears
Thy slightest whisper on its wondrous wing.
—Proudly thou spread'st thine eagle-pinion o'er
The exiled, and the crush'd from every clime,
Giving them welcome. May no vulture beak
Transpierce thee for thine hospitality,
But sons of strangers build thy walls, and call
Thy gates salvation.
                                'Neath thy lofty dome
'Tis good to linger, where, in conclave high,
Convene the chosen from thy many States,
Sages, and men of eloquence, who stretch
Their line of travel through an empire's length
To pour their wisdom at thy shrine, and make
Thy union perfect. From the wind-swept hills,
To where the rich magnolia drinks the breath
Of fervid suns—from the great, beating heart
Of the young, giant West, to where the East,
Wrinkled with thought, doth nurse a nation's mind,
They come to do thee honor. There, to list
The grave debate, or catch the kindling thrill
With which impassion'd eloquence maintains
Thine equal laws, inspires the ardent prayer
Of patriot love, that God would hold thee safe,
And firmly knit thy children's hearts, to share
One home, one destiny.
                                A mighty wind
Doth shake the palaces of ancient time,
And voices mid the despot thrones are heard,
Crying, as in Jerusalem of old,
"Let us depart!" But thou, my blessed land,
Like some fair hearth which hovering angels guard,
Gather thine offspring round thee, and make bright
Their hallow'd chain of love. Warn them to bear

Each other's burdens, seek the common good,
Be pitiful to error, and repress
Each ruder breath that stirs to wrathful deeds.

Oh, beautiful and glorious! thou dost wrap
The robes of Liberty around thy breast,
And as a matron watch thy little ones
Who from their cradle seek the village school,
Bearing the baptism on their infant brow
Of Christian faith and knowledge, like the bud
That, at the bursting of its sheath, doth feel
Pure dews, and heavenward turn.

There is thy strength,
In thy young children, and in those who lead
Their souls to righteousness. The mother's prayer
With her sweet lisper, ere it sinks to rest—
The faithful teacher mid a plastic group—
The classic halls—the hamlet's slender spire
From whence, as from the solemn gothic pile
That crowns the city's pomp, ascendeth sweet
Jehovah's praise—these are thy strength, my land!
These are thy hope.

Oh! lonely ark, that rid'st
A tossing deluge, dark with history's wrecks,
And paved with dead who made not Heaven their help,
God keep thee perfect in thy many parts,
Bound in one living whole.

Document 35

America Made Plain

Samuel Goodrich (1793–1860) wrote both for children and adults. He proved to be remarkably prolific and enormously popular. As "Peter Parley" he achieved the distinction of becoming the nation's unofficial schoolmaster. Writing under that pen name, he published *Manners and Customs of the Principal Nations* in the middle 1840s. Throughout the book, because he is aiming at the young, he makes things clear—and trundles out truisms—in a way he would not have for an adult audience. That is precisely the value for us of the brief chapter "United States" reprinted below. Its observations are consistently so obvious for his time that they are justified only in a book for juvenile reading. They are not, however, after over a century always obvious to us. Most are, it is true, but having Goodrich announce them confirms our preconceptions. All his observations, whether new or not, somehow seem more official when couched in Goodrich's flat phrases.

The tone of the chapter is patriotic; Goodrich plainly feels that he must act the advocate to his young readers. Most of the good things he says about his country are the expected ones. Not always, though; when he extols Americans for speaking better English than do Englishmen, he passes even beyond the usual praise. But when he points out the freedom from distinctions of rank, the flourishing of humane learning as well as of business affairs, the absence of a burdensome military establishment, the freedom of religion, and the exceptional thrift and ingenuity of his countrymen, he is moving along well-traveled roads. With allowance for his patriotic zeal, his observations are reasonably sound; the things he says are true, if not always to the extent he makes

them out to be. There is one observation, however, that
he fails to make: he never says anything about slavery.

SOURCE: Peter Parley [Samuel Griswold Goodrich], *Manners and
Customs of the Principal Nations of the Globe* (Boston, 1845),
pp. 20–23.

United States

The mass of the people of the United States are the
descendants of English people who settled in the country
at various periods within the last two centuries. There
have, indeed, been settlements formed here from France,
Sweden and Holland, and emigrants from these countries,
as well as Ireland, Germany, and other portions of Europe, have been and still are pouring into the country.
Still, the nation is essentially English, the tide of emigra-
tion hardly serving to tinge, certainly not to change, the
general character of society.

One of the most striking peculiarities of this country,
is, that from Maine to Louisiana, the people all talk better English than can be heard from the mass, in the city
of London. For a space 1500 miles in extent, and among
15,000,000 of people, the traveller will hear nothing like
the provincial dialects of Lancashire, Northumberland,
Yorkshire, &c., which render it difficult for the people of
one county in England to understand those of another.
There is not, probably, on the globe, an example of another nation, so populous and so widely extended, that
speaks any language so correctly, and with such uniformity,
as do the Americans their English mother tongue.

The freedom from those distinctions of rank which
strike the traveller in other countries, is a peculiarity of
our manners. We have no privileged classes, and none of
the badges and liveries which follow in their train. All
classes dress alike; all travel in the same vehicles; all meet
on the same footing of equality before the law, and, for
the most part, before society. The tendency to exclusive-

ness is checked and repressed by public opinion, which is exercised more to secure equality than even liberty. For this reason, American life appears to foreigners to be uniform, flat and insipid; as in costume, we are deficient in those picturesque dresses, which please the eye of a painter, so in thought and feeling we are regarded as wanting those contrasts which give interest and dramatic effect to society in Europe. We are looked upon as all engrossed in the single pursuit of wealth, not allowing time for those reflections and emotions which dignify and refine society.

We are, doubtless, a busy, enterprising people; the ample fields of prosperity, which lie open before us, are calculated to urge us steadily forward in the race of life. It may be admitted too, that society wears an aspect of uniformity among us. But both of these points seem resolved into this —that we are an uninteresting people, because we are generally well off. We can easily afford to admit that we have no courtly standard of manners, and therefore are, perhaps, behind some classes, in European nations, in artificial refinements—while, as an offset, we may claim that we have few paupers, and no beggars, except those that come from foreign lands. When it is said, however, that we are wholly engrossed in the chase of money, we deny the charge, and challenge the world to produce another instance in history, in which so young a country has done so much for literature, learning, religion and humanity, as these United States.

One of the first things that strikes an American, in most foreign countries, is the constant appearance of military force in town and country. Such a thing would not be endured here. The few soldiers with us are confined to regular garrisons. The bristling of the bayonet, as a signal to the people, of their servitude and the necessity of their obedience, is revolting to every sentiment of an American bosom.

Another peculiarity of our country, is that we have no

national church, no connection between church and state. Every individual supports that worship which he prefers. It might have been supposed, that under such a system, religion would pass into neglect, but there is, probably, no part of the world where religion is better supported, and where it exercises a deeper influence upon society.

In dress, the people follow the fashions of Europe. Paris gives the law in millinery and mantua-making, and the tailors of London are dictators as to male attire. We have no provincial costumes; lawyers and judges wear neither wigs nor gowns. The Catholic and Episcopal clergymen dress as in Europe, but those of other sects wear a common black citizen's dress, and sometimes a black gown in the pulpit.

Our houses are chiefly of wood, and though the general arrangement is the same as in the houses of England, yet the aspect is very different. Mr. Dickens, accustomed to the heavy stone architecture and sombre hues of the houses in that country, was very much struck with the sharp outlines and white paint, of our New England dwellings.

The American people are generally admitted by foreigners to display great energy and enterprise, and a remarkable power of mechanical invention. They are, doubtless, what might be expected of an Anglo-Saxon race, placed in circumstances to call every thrifty faculty into full exercise. "The United States," says an able English writer, "was colonized a century later than Spanish America; but their brilliant and rapid progress shows, in a striking light, how much more the prosperity of nations depends on moral than on physical advantages. The North Americans had no gold mines, and a territory of only indifferent fertility, covered with impenetrable woods; but they brought with them intelligence, industry, a love of freedom, habits of order, and a pure and severe morality. Armed with these gifts of the soul, they have converted the wilderness into a land teeming with life and smiling with plenty; and they have built up a social system so preëminently calculated to promote the happiness and moral improvement of mankind, that it has become, truly, the envy of nations."

DOCUMENT 36

Hero of Heroes

Our choice of heroes tells us something about ourselves. For Americans of the 1840s there was a single figure in the center of their pantheon, George Washington. All others were much less important. We had no continuum of heroes; we had Washington and then far behind him Jefferson, Jackson, and the rest. Today his luster has dimmed and he is seldom invoked. In his place we have set Abraham Lincoln and recently another dead president, John Fitzgerald Kennedy. But throughout the antebellum decades the father of our country was enshrined in the memories of his countrymen.

They saw him as a brave, stubborn man of great moral stature. They saw him as a true leader, a selfless aristocrat who was not one of them but willing to serve to the utmost on their behalf. They did not see him as an intellectual, a diplomat, or a wit. They saw him fairly well in fact as he was. And when the man did not fit the image they wanted, they altered history to make him fit. For example: Washington was not literally and actually a devout Christian nor for that matter the absurdly noble character that Parson Weems made him in his fables. Nevertheless, the man in the street firmly believed that Washington was a dedicated church member. He believed that Washington sought the solace and guidance of prayer on every important occasion. Though this was untrue one of the widely circulated lithographs of the 1840s showed him kneeling in prayer on the snow at Valley Forge. The man in the street believed with equal firmness that Washington could never tell a lie and that the moral fables that Parson Weems fabricated were all of them correct.

Above all, his countrymen venerated him, consciously

and undoubtedly unconsciously, as the father of his country. "Adelaide," writing in the second volume of the *Lowell Offering*, expresses her veneration in a cemetery ode of some technical skill and loftiness of tone. Her stanzas are in the neo-classical tradition; the measures are stately. She rings her changes on the refrain "He lies in pomp" and reminds us that in his greatness Washington remained an essentially simple man. The pomp, she states, is not one of surface show but is rather the outward evidence of his inner virtues.

SOURCE: "Adelaide," "The Tomb of Washington," *Lowell Offering*, II (? 1842), 79–80.

The Tomb of Washington

"He sleeps there in the midst of the very simplicities of Nature."

There let him sleep, in Nature's arms,
  Her well-beloved, her chosen child—
There 'mid the living, quiet charms
  Of that sequestered wild.
  He would have chosen such a spot,
'Twas fit that they should lay him there,
Away from all the haunts of care;
  The world disturbs him not.—
He sleeps full sweet in his retreat—
  The place is consecrated ground,
It is not meet unhallowed feet
  Should tread that sacred mound.

He lies in pomp—not of display—
  No useless trappings grace his bier,
Nor idle words—they may not say
  What treasures cluster here.
  The pomp of nature, wild and free,
Adorns our hero's lowly bed,
And gently bends above his head
  The weeping laurel tree.

In glory's day he shunned display,
   And ye may not bedeck him now,
But Nature may, in her own way,
   Hang garlands round his brow.

He lies in pomp—not sculptured stone,
   Nor chiseled marble—vain pretence—
The glory of his deeds alone
   Is his magnificence.
   His country's love the meed he won,
He bore it with him down to death,
Unsullied e'en by slander's breath—
   His country's sire and son.
Her hopes and fears, her smiles and tears,
   Were each his own.—He gave his land
His earliest cares, his choicest years,
   And led her conquering band.

He lies in pomp—not pomp of war—
   He fought, but fought not for renown;
He triumphed, yet the victor's star
   Adorned no regal crown.
   His honor was his country's weal;
From off her neck the yoke he tore—
It was enough, he asked no more;
   His generous heart could feel
No low desire for king's attire;—
   With brother, friend, and country blest,
He could aspire to honors higher
   Than kingly crown or crest.

He lies in pomp—his burial place
   Than sculptured stone is richer far;
For in the heart's deep love we trace
   His name, a golden star.
   Wherever patriotism breathes,
His memory is devoutly shrined
In every pure and gifted mind;
   And history, with wreaths

Of deathless fame, entwines that name,
　　Which evermore, beneath all skies,
Like vestal flame, shall live the same,
　　For virtue never dies.

There let him rest—'tis a sweet spot;
　　Simplicity becomes the great—
But Vernon's son is not forgot,
　　Though sleeping not in state.
　　There, wrapped in his own dignity,
His presence makes it hallowed ground,
And Nature throws her charms around,
　　And o'er him smiles the sky.
There let him rest—the noblest, best;
　　The labors of his life all done—
There let him rest, the spot is blessed—
　　The grave of WASHINGTON.

American Civilization

To see ourselves as others see us is one of the best, and sometimes one of the most startling, ways to self-knowledge. As a matter of fact, the American psychiatrist Harry Stack Sullivan has argued that the picture others have of us is the true one and that when we see ourselves differently we err. Sullivan never extended his theory from the individual to the nation but that is another possible application of it. At any rate, the foreign observer has often painted our picture in strokes so bold that they have both interested and irritated us.

In helping to understand the 1840s, the visitors from abroad played various roles and showed various degrees of perception in their reports. The superficial observer usually commented on our quaint customs, noted that we bragged and spat, and remarked on the bumptious pride of our womenfolk. The more discerning one was apt to search for our scale of values and to describe our democratic institutions. The most thoughtful observer devoted himself, more than once, to an inquiry on the shaping of the American mind and the molding of the American spirit.

Among our many foreign visitors it is difficult to pick out one to represent the rest. Tocqueville is the obvious selection and a very good one, but his judicious views are well known and easily accessible. Most of the others, however honest their intentions, erred in one direction or another. Many summed us up with condescension. A few such as Francis Grund were too much impressed and portrayed us as better than we deserved. Most were hasty; only a few gave us the benefit of a careful appraisal. Among the few one of the shrewdest was a Scot, George Combe (1788–1858).

He scrutinized us with a searching eye. A good part of the resulting observations and judgments are exceptionally sound. Only in a single respect did he prove untrustworthy. He was a noted apostle of phrenology and in anything he says involving that pseudo-science he is suspect. In the present selections, from the chapter "American Civilization" in the third volume of Combe's *Notes on the United States*, the phrenological patches have been cut out. So has some other material not to our purpose.

That purpose is to find out the factors which to Combe molded the American mind, to see where he thought they accomplished less than they should, and to look into the role of public opinion as the most striking of these factors.

At the opening of the chapter he quotes from the French historian Guizot to the effect that a nation is civilized when the external condition of man "is quickened and ameliorated" and the internal condition "is exhibited with lustre and grandeur." Combe quickly disposes of the problem of the external condition of man: in America it is literally the best in the world. Then he turns to the internal condition and, in particular, the influences that help to form the American mind. First he defines the internal organization of the mind. He considers it to be "endowed with animal propensities, moral and religious sentiments, and intellectual faculties." The first two are instinctual, the third rational. The "province of intellect is to study and to acquire knowledge, and, when enlightened by it, to direct, guide, and restrain all the impulsive powers." Having given his definitions, Combe considers the main means employed to develop the American mind. He sees five. They are domestic education, district schools, religious instruction, professional instruction, and political action. All are being used to cultivate the intellect of the masses. All are powerful engines for the purpose but none, as Combe sees it, is functioning quite as effectively as it should.

Domestic education, or family training, is marred by the parents' permissiveness and lack of culture. Public school education is marred by mediocre teaching and faulty educational psychology. Religious instruction is marred by the fact that our many sects disagree with one another in their teachings. Professional instruction, or the influence of technical training, is marred by an emphasis on material success instead of on cultural values. Political action, which for Combe means implementing the idea that all men are created equal, is a special case. The intention and accomplishment are both superb. The dedication to the utmost development of the individual is the "grand feature of American society." On the other hand, the weakness that mars it is the most threatening that we have. It is the vulnerability to public opinion.

Combe goes into the problem of public opinion at some length. He does not see it as bad in itself. In fact it is the great ally of individual development when it is controlled by the mind. But when public opinion is controlled by impulse, it becomes a tyrant, enforcing a ruthless conformity. Then we have the tyranny of the majority, and Combe asks questions about it that we have not answered yet.

Notwithstanding, we have in the concern for the individual's growth and in the four other great agents of cultural development the means for a splendid civilization. For us, for our nation, Combe concludes, "the race is ever onward."

SOURCE: George Combe, *Notes on the United States of North America during a Phrenological Visit* (Edinburgh, 1841), III, 247–60, 267, 287–90, 297–99.

American Civilization

In no country, probably, in the world is the external condition of man so high as in the American Union. The enterprise, intelligence, activity, and economical habits of the people have multiplied to an astonishing extent all the physical elements of human enjoyment. It was observed to me by a gentleman who is minutely and extensively acquainted with the United States, that in this country no man who is able and willing to work need to go supperless to bed. This far he stated the fact. Labourers here are rich compared with the individuals in the same class in Europe. Their food is wholesome and abundant; their dwelling-houses comfortable and well furnished; they possess *property*, and enjoy many of the luxuries which property, in a state of civilization, is capable of purchasing. The American cities contain great wealth; and reckoning the whole property, and the whole population of the Union, and dividing the value of the one by the sum of the other, my impression is that the product would shew a larger amount of wealth for each individual in the United States, than exists in any other country in the world, Great Britain alone probably excepted: In the United States this property is so equally diffused, that it is really national.

The formation of railroads and canals, the multiplication of steam-boats, ships, machinery, manufactories, and houses, the extension of the productive soil; in short, the advance of all that ministers to the well-being of "the external condition of man," proceeds in the United States on a gigantic scale, and with extraordinary rapidity. We must grant, therefore, that whatever other "imperfections" may exist "in the social state," this fundamental element of civilization abounds in a high degree.

The condition of the *"internal nature"* of man is the next index to civilization. The human mind is endowed with animal propensities, moral and religious sentiments, and intellectual faculties fitted for observation and reflection. The propensities and sentiments are blind impulsive powers, which inspire man with desires, and impel him to seek for their gratification; but they do not discern either the mode of obtaining their own objects, or the extent to which they may be advantageously indulged. The province of intellect is to study and to acquire knowledge, and, when enlightened by it, to direct, guide, and restrain all the impulsive powers. The mind of an individual is perfect in proportion as it is capable of extensive action, of regulating itself in accordance with the rules of duty, and of finding its way to good in every sphere of its existence. If its scope of action be narrow; if it need external guidance; or if it fail to accomplish its own permanent welfare, it is imperfect in the degree in which it comes short in any of these particulars. I apply these data to measure the condition of the *internal* man in the United States.

The Anglo-Saxon race, which chiefly has peopled the United States, has been richly endowed by nature with mental qualities. It possesses, in a high degree, all the faculties classed under the three grand divisions before mentioned; but, to attain their complete development, they need cultivation. In the United States the development of the mind of the mass of the people is accomplished by the following influences:—1*st*, By domestic education. 2*dly*, By district schools. 3*dly*, By religious instruction. 4*thly*, By professional instruction; and, *lastly*, By political action.

1*st, Of Domestic Education.*—The object of education in the family circle is to develope and regulate the affections, as well as to instruct the understanding. So far as a stranger can discover by observation, or learn by inquiries, the family education in the United States is exceedingly various, and depends for its character much more on the natural dispositions of the parents, than on any system of instruction. In general the parents are in easy circumstances, are happily matched, are good-natured, active, and frugal; and these qualities insensibly cultivate similar dispositions in the young; but there are of course numerous exceptions; and education has not advanced so far among the masses as to render domestic training systematic. Every family has its own manners, maxims, and modes of treatment. Speaking generally, the faculties of the child are allowed free scope in the family circle, without sufficient enforcement of self-denial, or of the subordination of the lower to the higher powers. The first useful lesson to a child is that of self-restraint, or of foregoing a present enjoyment at the call of duty, or for the sake of a higher, although more distant, good. Many American children appear to be indulged in their appetites and desires, and to be too little restrained in the manifestation of their propensities. Egotism, or the idea that the world is made for them, and that other persons must stand aside to allow them scope, is a feature not uncommonly recognised. The consideration of the manner in which their sentiments and modes of action, will affect other individuals of well regulated and well cultivated minds, is not adequately brought home to them. In short, the active manifestation of the moral sentiments in refined habits, in pure and elevated desires, and in disinterested goodness, is not aimed at systematically as an object in domestic training. I speak of the masses composing the nation, and not of the children of well educated and refined individuals.

In intellectual cultivation, domestic education is still more defective, because in the masses the parents themselves are very imperfectly instructed.

On the whole, therefore, the domestic training and instruction appear to me to be imperfect, viewed in relation to the objects of enlarging the mind's sphere of action, of conferring on it the power of self-restraint, and also the ability to discover and successfully to pursue its own permanent welfare.

2dly, Of Common School Education.—From the various remarks which have already been presented in these volumes, the reader will be prepared to draw the inference that, viewed in relation to the three objects before mentioned, the common school education in the United States is also imperfect; I should say very imperfect. The things taught (chiefly reading, writing, and arithmetic) are not in themselves education. If sedulously and wisely applied, they may enable the individual to obtain knowledge; but the common schools stop short of supplying it. They even communicate very imperfectly the art of acquiring it; for some of the teachers are themselves ill qualified; their modes of teaching are defective, and the attendance of the children at school is brief and irregular. The addition of a library to each school-district was dictated by a perception of the magnitude and importance of the deficiency in this department. It appears to me that besides great improvements in existing schools, still higher seminaries are wanted, in which the elements of natural, moral, and political science, with their applications to the purposes of individual and social enjoyment, may be taught to the whole people.

One, and probably the most important, element in an education calculated to fit an individual for becoming an accomplished member of the American democracy, is *training* the faculties to their proper modes of action. This can be accomplished only by calling them all into activity, and by communicating to the higher powers the knowledge and habit of governing the lower. Mere intellectual instruction is not sufficient for this purpose; the propensities and sentiments must be trained in the field of life. . . . This end will be best accomplished by communicating to children the knowledge of their own faculties, and of their spheres of use and abuse, by placing them in circumstances in which these may be called into action, and superintending that action in such a manner as to cultivate the powers of rapid judgment and steady self-control. The play-ground is an important field for conducting this branch of education. The principles and practice of it are explained in the works of Wilderspin and Stow already referred to. This department of education is in a very humble condition in the United States; and yet to them it is all-important. Every one of their citizens wields political and judicial power; he is at once the subject of the law and its pillar; he elects his own judges, magistrates, and rulers, and it is his duty to obey them. If ever knowledge of what is right, self-control to pursue it, and high moral resolve to sacrifice every motive of self-interest and individual ambition, to the dictates of benevolence and justice, were needed in any people, they are wanted in the citizens of the United States. A well *instructed* citizen will consider the influence of any law on the general welfare before he consents to its enactment, and a well *trained* citizen will not only obey that law when enacted, but lend his whole moral and physical energies, if necessary, to enforce its observance by all, until repealed by constitutional authority. An *ill instructed* citizen will clamour for the enactment of any law which promises to relieve *him* from an individual inconvenience, or to confer on him an individual advantage, without much consideration concerning its general effects; and an *ill-trained* citizen will seek to subject the magistrates, judges, and the law to his own control, that he may bend them in subserviency to his interest, his ambition, or his inclinations, from day to day, as these arise and take different directions. The *ill-trained* citizen takes counsel of his self-will; and self-will, uninstructed and untrained to the guidance of moral principle, leads to destruction. . . .

Lecturing to the people in lyceums is extensively practised in the United States, and as a mode of public instruction it is well calculated to advance their intelligence; but hitherto, owing to the defects of their education in the primary schools, it has not yielded half its advantages. As formerly mentioned, the lectures delivered in lyceums are generally of a miscellaneous character, developing no subject systematically, and sacrificing profound interest to variety and temporary excitement; yet no other lectures would attract persons of mature age, whose minds had not been opened up, in their elementary education, to the value of scientific knowledge. If the simpler elements of the natural sciences were taught in childhood, the mind, when it expanded into vigour, would long for fuller developments of their principles, and the lectures in the lyceums might then assume a high character of usefulness.

Viewing the object of education, then, to be to communicate knowledge by which the sphere of the mind's action may be enlarged,—to train each individual to self-control and the love of good,—and to enable him, by these means combined, to pursue successfully his own welfare,

the educational institutions of the United States appear
generally to be defective.

3dly, Of Religious Instruction.—The objects of religious
instruction are twofold; first, To obtain salvation in a future life; and, secondly, To conduce to practical virtue in
this world. I regard the first as belonging to the sphere
of theology, and as beyond the jurisdiction, equally of the
philosopher and the civil magistrate. By the principles
consecrated at the Reformation each individual has the
exclusive right of judging on this subject for himself, and
for those whose souls Providence has intrusted to his care.
I merely remark, that I perceive great differences existing
in the opinions of American sects regarding, first, the extent of the danger to which the human soul is exposed in
a future life; and secondly, the means by which this danger may be avoided; but that each sect exhibits a means of
salvation which it considers commensurate with its own
ideas of the danger. All profess to found their belief on a
sound interpretation of Scripture; and as only the Great
Judge of all can decide which has reached the largest portion of truth, we may hope that they may all prove essentially successful in accomplishing this important end. Instruction in the nature and extent of the danger, and in
the nature and use of the means to avert it, constitutes a
large portion of the religious education communicated to
the young. The clergy of the various sects appeared to
me to be most assiduous in the discharge of this duty;
and from the extensive attendance on religious worship
exhibited in every part of the Union which I have visited,
their teaching appears to have excited that deep interest
in the subject, which is the only legitimate proof, in this
world, of their success. The grand motive of the clergy of
all sects is, no doubt, the love of souls; but there is a
secondary consideration which is, probably, not without
some effect in securing their exertions, namely, the knowledge that the acceptance of their peculiar doctrines regarding salvation is the tie which binds the people to their
ministrations, and that the more successfully they impress

a firm conviction of their views on their flocks, the more secure do they feel in obtaining the means of their own subsistence, and the greater also are their power and influence over their people. This branch of religious instruction, therefore, appears to be in a salutary and satisfactory condition in the United States.

But religious instructors teach also the morality and religion which ought to regulate human conduct in this world. In the great outlines of secular duty, all the Christian sects are agreed; and the clergy of all sects teach them to their flocks. In the course of my attendance in the churches of the United States, I could not, however, avoid making two remarks on this subject; first, that, in proportion as the tenets of any sect represented the dangers of eternal perdition to be great and imminent, and the means of salvation to be difficult, the clergy of that sect taught their own doctrinal views on these points more zealously and more extensively, and the practical duties of Christianity relatively less frequently; and *vice versa*. Secondly, That the teaching of practical duties was in the vast majority of churches exceedingly general, rarely descending to specific instructions regarding the proper line of conduct to be pursued in the most momentous and difficult departments of life. . . .

4thly, Professional Callings.—The great majority of the people of the United States are engaged in arts, manufactures, commerce, navigation, agriculture, divinity, law, and medicine; and their pursuits are therefore useful, and productive of enjoyment. . . . As the paths of industry are rarely obstructed by bad laws or artificial obstacles, American civilization, in this department, will bear a favourable comparison with that of the most advanced nations. These avocations, however, do not fully develope the highest faculties of the mind. They cultivate Acquisitiveness, Self-Love, and the love of distinction, more than Benevolence, Veneration, Conscientiousness, and Ideality. They call the intellect into activity, but many of them do not necessarily direct it to moral objects. They are deserving of all praise as important elements of civilization, indeed as necessary to the very foundations of it; but in order to exhibit the "*internal* nature of man with *lustre* and *grandeur*," higher pursuits must be added to and mingled with them. The schools, colleges, and the pulpit, must supply the lustre and grandeur in which the avocations of common life are necessarily defective. Great improvements in professional attainments remain to be made in the United States. American divines are not in general so learned as those of England, but they appear to be more practical; while the professions of law and medicine in the rural districts, comprising nineteen-twentieths of the whole United States, stand in need of large accessions of knowledge to bring them to a par with the same professions in the enlightened countries of Europe. The improved education which I have suggested would render the practices of the professions in some degree scientific or philosophical pursuits, in which each individual would endeavour, in his vocation, to observe the laws which the Creator has established as essential to success, and the calm calculations of reason would, to some extent, regulate the impulsive and empirical movements which have hitherto been fraught with so much suffering to the people.

5*thly, Political Institutions.*—The American Declaration of Independence announces that "all men are created equal," a proposition which, however liable to be disputed in some respects, has (leaving out of view the African race) been practically adopted as the fundamental principle of all the institutions and legislation of the United States. It is the most powerful maxim for developing the *individual*, in all his faculties and functions, that has ever been promulgated, and it has certainly produced great results. It is probably the first abstract proposition that is clothed with an intelligible meaning in the mind of the American child, and it influences his conduct through life. It sends forth the young citizen full of confidence in himself, untrammelled by authority, unawed by recognised superiority in others, and assured of a fair field for every exertion. . . .

In short, the grand feature of American society is the fulness with which it develops *all* the faculties of its individual members, without impressing peculiar biases on any of them; and hence its heterogeneous aspect in the eyes of foreigners. There is no evil and no good which may not be predicated of it with truth. Numerous examples could be adduced in support of every picture representing good, better, best; bad, worse, worst, in American society. Perhaps the reader may suppose that the same may be said of society in every country; but certainly not to the same striking extent as in the United States. In Europe the different classes are cast in distinct moulds, and some of the faculties of the individuals constituting each class are suppressed, while others are highly developed, to fit them for their conditions. In the United States the individual man stands forth much more as Nature made him, and as freedom and equality have reared him. . . .

The dangers which individuals incur from braving public opinion in their personal habits or pursuits bear a relation to two circumstances—the extent of their own dependence on that opinion,—and if they be independent of it, on the degree of their own sensitiveness to disapprobation. In the case of clergymen, physicians, and lawyers, the dependence of the individual on public opinion is direct and striking, and in most mercantile pursuits, also, opinion may, to a considerable extent, influence individual prosperity. Besides, the example of bowing to it, set by the aspirants after public offices, who are generally the boldest, most active, and influential members of the community, generates and cultivates the habit of doing so in those who move in a private sphere; and the habit being once established, sensitiveness increases in proportion to its universal prevalence and duration, until at last, in many instances, it degenerates into a dread of public disapprobation, so powerful, that it paralyzes virtue, and deserves no milder epithet than that of moral cowardice.

This extreme sensitiveness is a peculiar characteristic of the Americans: But as I have already described the minds of the people to be developed by their institutions in all their faculties, each man according to his own nature, and as each may be discerned pursuing his individual objects with a predominating egotism, there appears to be a contradiction between these two portraitures of society. The representations wear the air of paradox; and, in point of fact, nothing struck me so forcibly in the United States as the inconsistency between one aspect of the character of the people and another. Phrenologically, I explain these anomalous appearances by the impulsive activity of *all* the faculties, undirected by any great land-marks either of established custom, sentiment, or reason. The faculties themselves are heterogeneous in their objects and feelings, and if they be manifested freely, one in one set of circumstances, and another in another, without a presiding guide, inconsistency will be evolved by Nature herself. Within the limits permitted by public opinion, an American will pursue his pleasure and his interest, as if no other being existed in the world; his egotism may then appear complete; but when he meets an opposing public opinion, he shrinks and is arrested. The state of manners allows a pretty wide latitude of self-indulgence, and foreigners reporting on this phasis of character describe the people as personifications of egotism; but when the limit of public opinion is reached, this egotist may be seen quailing before it, although virtue, honour, and religion, should call on him to brave it. Again, he will not pursue his self-indulgence so far as to give personal offence to his neighbour, because this would be resented. In short, he has that vivid regard to opinion, that he restrains himself whenever he incurs the risk of its condemnation; and if he act improperly, it is because opinion tolerates the wrong.

British authors, however, have in general erroneously

estimated the comparative influence of public opinion in their own country and in the United States. It appears to me to be pretty nearly as active and influential in Britain as it is in America, certain differences in its modes of operation being taken into consideration. In Britain . . . society is divided into a number of distinct classes, each of which has standards of opinion of its own. There is a public opinion peculiar to each class, and that opinion has acquired definite forms by the influence of ancient institutions. The opinions and modes of feeling of the individuals in each class, grow with their growth and strengthen with their strength, and in the maturity of life these conventional impressions appear to be absolutely natural. The differences between the grades of society produce corresponding differences in opinion and modes of action; and when an observer surveys individuals of each class acting according to their own perceptions of propriety, he may imagine that, because they differ, each is manifesting a fine moral independence, in following the dictates of his own judgment. But this is an error. In America all men are regarded as equal; there is no distinct separation into classes, with a set of established opinions and feelings peculiar to each. As society is young, and the institutions are recent, there are no great influences in operation to mould opinion into definite forms, even within this one circle, which nominally includes all American citizens. The proper contrast, therefore, is between the power of public opinion in an English grade and in the American single circle; and if so viewed, the difference will not be found to be so greatly against the Americans as is generally supposed. . . .

Far, therefore, from regarding the great power of public opinion in the United States as in itself an evil, I view it as a gigantic controlling influence which may become the most efficient ally of virtue. It is delightful to see the human mind, when emancipated from artificial fetters, evolving from its own deep fountains a mighty restraining power, far superior in force and efficacy for the accomplishment of good, to all the devices invented by the self-constituted guides of mankind. At present, this power is operating in the United States essentially as a blind impulse; many of the artificial standards erected in Europe by monarchy, aristocracy, feudalism, established churches, and other ancient institutions for its direction, have been broken down, and no other standards have yet been erected in their place. No manners or maxims have yet received the stamp of general acceptation, to enable opinion to settle on them with security.

That this is the true theory of the phenomena of public opinion, is rendered probable by the fact that its mighty influence is of recent growth. For many years after the Revolution, it was not felt to the same extent as at present,—opinion continued to be modified by the monarchical feelings in which the people had been educated, long after they became their own rulers. It is only within these five and twenty years that the people have discovered and chosen to wield their own sovereign authority; and as if for the very purpose of controlling them, public opinion has within the same period developed its stupendous powers. The ground is gradually becoming cleared of the antiquated posts and rails that directed public sentiment into particular paths; and the question occurs, what is destined to supply their place? Christianity will readily occur, as the most desirable guide; but at present, and for some generations, its influence will be limited by the conflicts existing between the different sects. Besides, the pulpit still devotes too little of its attention to secular affairs, and there are yet too few instances of combination among Christians of all denominations to accomplish general practical good, irrespective of their several doctrinal views. May not some aid be obtained from the maxims of moral and political science, founded on a sound interpretation of the nature of man and of the external world, and of their reciprocal relationship? If the mere forms of monarchy, aristocracy, feudalism, and religious establishments, often at variance with reason and the best interests of mankind, have become fetters with which opinion has been bound as in adamantine chains, why may not the dictates of God's wisdom, when developed to the understanding and impressed upon the moral sentiments from infancy, produce as powerful and a much more salutary effect? The United States must look to instruction in moral and political science, aided and sanctioned by religion, for the re-erection of standards and guides of opinion; and to the accomplishment of this object the new philosophy will constitute a valuable assistant.

One distinct cause of the fear of individuals to oppose public opinion, when wrong, is the want of reliance on the moral tendency of the public mind, and on its inclination to correct its own errors, and to do justice to those who have braved its disapprobation in defence of truth. The vivid excitement under which opinion is formed, is one element in producing this terror; but another unquestionably is the uncertainty which is felt regarding both the principles and motives by which, at any moment, it may be swayed. The public intellect is practical and direct, and it neither investigates principles nor embraces distant or comprehensive views; while the public feeling is composed of a confused jumble of selfish and moral impulses, the course of which, on any particular emergency, often defies calculation. Nevertheless the race is ever onward; there is little looking back, little calm reflection, little retracing of steps once taken, unless some unsurmountable obstacle presents itself, which, from its magnitude and immovability, deflects the public mind, or makes it recoil upon itself.

DOCUMENT 38

Natal Day

The national morale was high, the country's optimism almost unbounded. Pride in the achievements of the past combined with confidence in the future. The one day in the year, above the rest, when it seemed particularly proper to express all this was the national birthday, the Fourth of July. A birthday means more to a child than to a man, sometimes more to a young country than to an older one. At any rate, in the 1840s the Fourth stood out as our most sanguine festival, celebrating much that it does not now. Today we mark a shrunken Fourth, one that has lost its oratory, parades, and waving banners; one that now reflects our uneasy role in a world we never made. But in the 1840s we celebrated our national awareness on the Fourth. With pride and fireworks we showed what it meant to be American.

Paying homage to the day and everything it represented, the Reverend George Bethune (1805–62) wrote more stirringly than usual in "The Fourth of July." The long lines of verse move to the sound of marching music. Their contents help us to comprehend the America of the 1840s through the ideals they contain: freedom, courage, hospitality and generosity, reverence. Throughout the poem the tone is jubilant; only at the end, in the prayer to God to keep our country one, do we sense the threat of slavery and disunion.

SOURCE: George W. Bethune, *Lays of Love and Faith, with Other Fugitive Poems* (Philadelphia, 1848), pp. 87–91.

The Fourth of July

MAINE, from her farthest border, gives the first exulting
    shout,

And from NEW HAMPSHIRE'S granite heights, the
    echoing peal rings out;

The mountain farms of staunch VERMONT prolong the
    thundering call;

MASSACHUSETTS answers: "Bunker Hill!" a watch-
    word for us all.

RHODE ISLAND shakes her sea-wet locks, acclaiming
    with the free,

And staid CONNECTICUT breaks forth in sacred har-
    mony.

The giant joy of proud NEW YORK, loud as an earth-
    quake's roar,

Is heard from Hudson's crowded banks to Erie's crowded
    shore,

NEW JERSEY, hallowed by their blood, who erst in bat-
    tle fell,

At Monmouth's, Princeton's, Trenton's fight, joins in the
    rapturous swell.

Wide PENNSYLVANIA, strong as wide, and true as she
    is strong,

From every hill to valley, pours the torrent tide along.

Stand up, stout little DELAWARE, and bid thy volleys
    roll,

Though least among the old Thirteen, we judge thee by
    thy soul!

Hark to the voice of MARYLAND! over the broad Chesa-
    peake

Her sons, as valiant as their sires, in cannonadings speak.

VIRGINIA, nurse of Washington, and guardian of his
    grave,

Now to thine ancient glories turn the faithful and the
    brave;
We need not hear the bursting cheer this holy day in-
    spires,
To know that, in Columbia's cause, "Virginia never tires."
Fresh as the evergreen that waves above her sunny soil,
NORTH CAROLINA shares the bliss, as oft the patriot's
    toil;
And the land of Sumter, Marion, of Moultrie, Pinckney,
    must
Respond the cry, or it will rise e'en from their sleeping
    dust.
And GEORGIA, by the dead who lie along Savannah's
    bluff,
Full well we love thee, but we ne'er can love thee well
    enough;
From thy wild northern boundary, to thy green isles of the
    sea,
Where beat on earth more gallant hearts than now throb
    high in thee?
On, on, 'cross ALABAMA'S plains, the ever-flowery glades,
To where the Mississippi's flood the turbid Gulf invades;
There, borne from many a mighty stream upon her might-
    ier tide,
Come down the swelling long huzzas from all that valley
    wide,
As wood-crowned Alleghany's call, from all her summits
    high,
Reverberates among the rocks that pierce the sunset sky;
While on the shores and through the swales, 'round the
    vast inland seas,
The stars and stripes, 'midst freemen's songs, are flashing
    to the breeze.
The woodsman, from the mother, takes his boy upon his
    knee,
To tell him how their fathers fought and bled for liberty;
The lonely hunter sits him down the forest spring beside,

To think upon his country's worth, and feel his country's
    pride;
While many a foreign accent, which our God can under-
    stand,
Is blessing Him for home and bread in this free, fertile
    land.
Yes! when upon the eastern coast we sink to happy rest,
The Day of Independence rolls still onward to the west,
Till dies on the Pacific shore the shout of jubilee,
That woke the morning with its voice along the Atlantic
    sea.
—O GOD! look down upon the land which thou hast
    loved so well,
And grant that in unbroken truth her children still may
    dwell;
Nor, while the grass grows on the hill and streams flow
    through the vale,
May they forget their fathers' faith, or in their covenant
    fail!
God keep the fairest, noblest land that lies beneath the
    sun;
"Our country, our whole country, and our country ever
    one!"

DOCUMENT 39

The Chosen People

Part of our confidence during the 1840s came from
the conviction that we were predestined by the Deity
for an especially noble role on this planet. We had only
to look back in the past and then around us in the
present to see manifold marks of divine regard. The
first settlers entering New England sometimes likened
themselves to the Israelites, the Chosen People, coming
to conquer Canaan for Jehovah. Two centuries later
George Bancroft, when writing his much applauded
volumes on the history of the United States, still saw
the hand of God guiding our country's actions. He saw
it more clearly early in our history than late, but none-
theless he saw it. His unquestioning belief was shared
by a host of lesser men. One was the Reverend George
B. Cheever (1807–90), a New York clergyman who
published *God's Hand in America* in 1841. In a fore-
word another clergyman, named Skinner, exclaims,
"That Hand has been progressively revealing itself from
our commencement as a people." Cheever believes in
our great good fortune. But he also shows himself aware
of the responsibilities that go with God's favor, for he
finds plenty of space in which to point out our shortcomings. Though he stresses our chief blemish, slavery,
he does not fail to remind us of other signs of our im-
perfection. All these, he says, we must try prayerfully
to remove.

Most of chapter IX is reprinted here. It is preceded
by a synopsis which sums up the whole matter: "Interest
and Grandeur of the Divine Experiment with us as a
People.—Conditions of Success.—Causes at Work to Dis-
turb and Thwart it."

SOURCE: George B. Cheever, *God's Hand in America* (New York and London, 1841), pp. 139–48, abridged.

Chapter IX

We cannot conceal from ourselves, nor would we wish to do it, that the responsibilities of every kind resting upon this country are mightier than those which belong to any other nation in the world. Especially is this the case with the religious responsibilities of a Christian church which God has so remarkably blessed. If we redeem them, it will be glorious for us and glorious for the world. It is good for us, on this mount of vision, commanding on all sides an immense moral view, to call to mind our multiplied responsibilities, and see what sublime motives animate us onward. We stand upon a lofty and imposing situation. We are compassed about by a great cloud of witnesses, being made a spectacle, not only to the world, but to an innumerable company of angels and the spirits of the just made perfect. It may be no dream of the imagination, but an undoubted reality, that higher orders of intelligences are watching our movements with intense interest, and that Paul, and Peter, and John, and all the beloved apostles of our Saviour, and all who have since trod in their footsteps, and through toil and pain and death inherited the promises, are looking down upon us, and waiting, I had almost said with painful anxiety, the result of this mighty experiment. It seems as if Heaven had placed our country in this situation to try us; to see whether we would faithfully use the incalculable power in our hands for speeding forward the world's regeneration, and if not, how many accumulated blessings we could waste and reject.

In contemplating the picture of our happiness in a course of national piety, and in making such an enumeration of our national talents for a wide moral influence, we are not to forget that it is only through a probation of severe and holy discipline, that we can hope to arrive at the attainment of such glory. Nor must we for a moment let the remembrance pass from our minds, that it is "not by might, nor by power, BUT BY MY SPIRIT, SAITH THE LORD OF HOSTS," that the great work is to be accomplished. We may have had the noblest and most pious ancestry on earth; we may possess the freest institutions, the strongest physical power, the most inexhaustible wealth, the highest foreign influence and reputation; we may enjoy the most universal diffusion of knowledge; and what is more than all, the Spirit of God may be poured out upon us for a time in accumulated revivals of religion; and yet we may turn every one of our vast capabilities to ruin, except God keep us humble, and preserve in us a spirit of deep contrition and dependance on him.

Besides, there is another and a widely different view of our whole subject. There is a gloomier prospect in the probabilities of our country's future destiny. There is at least one dark spot in our moral and political horizon. Yet we cannot suffer ourselves to believe that God will permit, with the growth of our nation in populousness and power, the continuance of the enormous evil of SLAVERY, the indulgence of that great sin, which would inevitably prove the destruction of all our hopes of usefulness and glory. If he should do this, and give us over, like his ancient people, to our own heart's lusts then we should indeed become a signal and terrible example of God's holy indignation. Then, in the prophetic language of Milton, and with allusion to our past extraordinary history, "as if God were weary of protecting us, *we shall be seen to have passed through the fire, that we might perish in the smoke.*" For we cannot ourselves remain free, and yet persist in imposing bondage on others. "And it usually happens," (that great writer profoundly remarks in his Second Defence of the People of England,) "by the appointment, and as it were retributive justice of the Deity, that that people which cannot govern themselves, and moderate their passions, but voluntarily crouch under the slavery of their lusts, should be delivered up to the sway of those whom they abhor, and made to submit to an involuntary servitude." But if after all our lofty privileges and excitements to glory, we do deny God, and turn from following his pleasure, to follow our own depravity, and fill up the measure of our iniquities, then our fall and punishment must be a second Jewish tragedy on a wider and more awful scale, and all the curses written in the book of the law cannot but descend upon us. . . .

Though this be all hypothetical and visionary, yet we do not know that there is any thing in the record of prophecy to conflict with the supposition or the possibility of such an additional scene in the great instructive drama, which God is permitting to be played in this world, and which he will suffer to be played out without interruption. At any rate, however far the designs of God's providence may seem manifested and in process of execution in regard to ourselves, and however important the instrumentality of a nation and a church so trained and disciplined might appear in the midst of a world so depraved and degraded, it becomes us to remember that as God out of the stones in the streets of Jerusalem could have raised up children unto Abraham, so he can now just as easily accomplish his purposes and his prophecies without our aid.

DOCUMENT 40

(PLATES 29–34)

The American Image

There was no perfect mirror for Americans. At best they saw a distorted image, flawed and cracked, its surface crazed. Yet here and there they could catch glimpses of themselves and so build up a picture, a picture far from faultless but not without a certain amount of fidelity.

Among the pictorial documents of the 1840s which help to do this, one of the most revealing is an 1847 lithograph "Elements of National Thrift and Empire." Through the selection of the elements it includes, it suggests much of American thinking and feeling of the time. The title itself is unusually telling, to us, for it focuses on "Thrift," with its connotations of a frugal, industrious, now-outmoded, way of life, and on "Empire," with its grandiose and seemingly undemocratic political associations. We were democratic of course but at the same time we were more and more convinced that it was our "manifest destiny" (the term was first used in 1845) to rule the continent. The range in this broad scene is from the ample symbols of government down to the modest scrolls in a corner entitled "Science & Art" and "Charter of the Smithsonian Institution."

To remind ourselves, consequently, that comprehending our country involves some understanding of high culture as well as mass culture, we have the ornate title page of the *New-York Mirror: A Weekly Journal, Devoted to Literature and the Fine Arts, Embellished with Engravings and Music*. In the picture on the page, Columbia and the bust of Washington watch with solemn approval the activities of a group of the muses. Once again, we were democratic but we nevertheless were engaged in building a culture of literature, music, and art which involved the elite as well as the masses. In fact the elite came first, more often than not.

Another side of ourselves emerges in the lithograph "Washington's Death Bed." Here we have tokens of our veneration for our first President (our father as well as the nation's) and of our respectful yet realistic attitude toward death, which is today under as great a cultural taboo as sex was in the 1840s. We glimpse ourselves in relation to our country and to life and death likewise. Washington was one kind of symbol; he stood for the classic republican past. The pioneer was another; he represented the wave of the future, the rough, hardy migrants pushing to the West. He is hymned in "The Emigrants." His energy, his stoical endurance, his determination to improve his lot were all characteristics that the times were beginning to attribute to the highly varied men, and women, taking part in the westward movement.

As the waves of pioneers moved through the West, more waves of migrants from Europe came into the Atlantic ports to take their place. The largest amount of immigration would not arrive till after the Civil War but even before that it rose each year. In 1840 we received over 80,000 immigrants from the far side of the Atlantic and in 1849 over 286,000. With native-born Americans moving to strange territory and foreign-born Americans increasing in number every year, the need for maintaining our national identity grew great. The public schools were our prime cultural agent but they were not alone. Literature, art, and music were enlisted in the cause. So were the modest ancestors of today's so-called mass media. What all these agents tried to do was to preserve a common culture, a common body of American experience and tradition. George Washington and the American Revolution were its most prominent features but it went back to the Pilgrims and their early struggles and still further back, to Captain John Smith and Pocahontas. They and others became the figures in an American mythology. Almost every child learned about them; they became part of the civilization he shared unquestioningly with other Americans.

Any time that an American analyzed himself one characteristic was sure to appear. It was a sense of humor. In "One of the 'Upper Ten Thousand'" we have a prize example. First of all, the artist recognizes that class distinctions exist even in the egalitarian 1840s, and that they are common knowledge. The poor are the poor and they are less powerful than the rich. But the rich are not to be taken too seriously. They offer as inviting a target for satire as any penniless Paddy from Erin. So here we have a strutting New York swell looking at us with slit-eyed and comic condescension.

In the 1840s America was growing up. One sign was a new self-consciousness. We were engaged in defining ourselves, in comprehending our country, in sensing the many places where we agreed as well as the few where we differed.

PLATE 29. *Elements of National Thrift and Empire.* Drawn by J. G. Bruff and lithographed by E. Weber & Co., 1847.

SOURCE: Library of Congress.

To understand American ideals is to understand American actualities better. Here we see the things that the artist selected out of many to include in his partly allegorical, partly realistic panorama; here we see the good America as he conceived it. There would be a certain risk in taking his selections too seriously—we might well ask if they were representative—except that we know, first, that his lithograph was popular and, secondly, that it was only one of a number coming out at this time with the same general idea and similar development. The terms "Thrift" and "Empire" determine of course the content of the composition. "Thrift" connotes both the American frugality and industry so persuasively preached by Benjamin Franklin and the capitalistic enterprise, the wide-ranging industrial and agricultural operations, that would reach a peak after the Civil War. "Empire" is a bold, provocative term.

This is indeed Manifest Destiny; this is the eagle scream-
ing. The mid-1840s were a period of imperial expansion
for the United States and the lithograph illustrates the
fact. Yet art softens reality, for there are no soldiers shown.

The vast scene, nominally the city of Washington, is full
of the symbols of government. On the far left stands the
White House; in the center is the Capitol; between the
two stretch other government buildings. In the foreground
Columbia gazes at Ceres while holding up Washington's
picture. Nearby, dramatically dividing the lithograph,
stands the Washington Monument. Striking though it is in
the composition, it was actually still a dream; it had not
yet been erected. To the right is religion, in the shape of
an impressive Washington church, probably a glorified version of St. Patrick's.

The bounteous growth of the American economy is suggested in numerous ways. The artifacts of agriculture
abound: plough, sickle, axe, sheaves, and so forth. Stock
grazes in the fields; there are even two beehives near the
bottom of the picture. The appurtenances of industry and
transportation are scattered throughout: for industry, factories, cogwheels, millstones; and for transportation, ships,
canal boats, horses, covered wagons—but railroads only in
the symbol of a scroll.

"Elements of National Thrift and Empire" represents a
mingling of the American dream with American reality,
suggesting to us not only what Americans thought that they
were but also what they wanted to be. The artist had no
hesitation in drawing the Washington Monument in spite
of the fact that no stone of it had yet been shaped. He
felt sure that he could count on the future.

PLATE 30. *The New-York Mirror: A Weekly Journal, Devoted to Literature and the Fine Arts, Embellished with Engravings and Music.* Drawn by R. W. Weir and engraved by A. B. Durand.

SOURCE: *New-York Mirror*, XVIII (1840), title page. Library of Congress.

Though the cultural side of life was certainly not the dominant one in the civilization of the 1840s, its importance was steadily rising. The calls for an American literature, an American music, an American art rose, swelled, and were heeded. An American high culture began to appear. One token is the title page of the *New-York Mirror*. True, the *Mirror* never reached the multitude but as journals go it lasted a long time. Its first number appeared in 1823, its final one in, apparently, 1857. Throughout its lengthy career the *Mirror* maintained its interest in Americana. Its initial statement read that "the character of this work is intended to be, literally and emphatically, *American*"; and the passage of time never modified the statement much. During the middle 1840s Poe acted briefly as its editor, giving the journal additional weight.

Other indications of our awareness of culture included, above all, our avowed interest in education. It was already an American fetish. Besides the concern with education, there were such signs—mentioned before—as the increase in published books, magazines, and newspapers; the augmented sale of sheet music; the rise of the art-unions; the mass distribution of lithographs and engravings; and the vogue for lyceum lectures. A new day was dawning. Culturally it was brightest on the East Coast, especially in New York, Boston, and Philadelphia but not without its gleams as far away as New Orleans and St. Louis.

This culture combined the old with the new, the ancient with the modern. In the *Mirror's* title page the bare-breasted muses of classic Greece appear in the same composition with Washington and prim Columbia; in the background Indians loom on one side and the wonders of Niagara Falls are glimpsed on the other.

PLATE 31. *Washington's Death Bed.* Designed by T. H. Matteson and engraved by H. S. Sadd.

SOURCE: *Columbian Magazine,* V (May 1846), frontispiece. Library of Congress.

It can be argued that we understood life better a century ago than we do now, because then we comprehended death. We accepted it and honored it with an experienced solemnity. Here is a picture from a popular magazine which today would have no parallel. Even if President Kennedy's death had been peaceful, it would scarcely have become the subject of magazine art. But in those days the decease of a great man was dwelt on because it gave death an added dimension. It reminded us that the end awaited everyone, the great and the small, the humble and the renowned. It seemed, as a result, entirely proper to reproduce such a picture as "Washington's Death Bed" not only as an adornment to a magazine but also with the idea that it might be framed to hang, for instance, on a bedroom wall.

In this composition the light shines on the dying, or already dead, President. Martha, who has been watching somberly, sits at the foot of the bed. His devoted secretary Tobias Lear holds Washington's hand, which he has just pressed to his heart in a despairing gesture. His longtime physician Dr. Jonas Craik watches sadly with his hand on Washington's pillow. Servants stand around sorrowfully, including his faithful body servant, the Negro Christopher. The artist has attempted to make the drawing as faithful as the history but with limited success. The general draftsmanship is laborious, the handling particularly of the faces is far from deft. Yet this heavy, gloomy lithograph has a certain impressiveness. Form matches content despite the artist's technical shortcomings. This is a picture to remember and perhaps to keep.

The picture testifies again to the pre-eminence of Washington in our national tradition. Already an American legend by the 1840s, the career of Washington from beginning to end provided us with important ethical standards. At the beginning Washington taught us, through the fabrications of Parson Weems, never to tell a lie. At the end he taught us fortitude in the face of death. And in between he gave us a wealth of instruction in patriotism, probity, and unselfishness.

PLATE 32. *Captain Smith & Pocahontas*. Drawn by J. Morton and engraved by H. S. Sadd.

SOURCE: *Columbian Magazine*, II (November 1844), frontispiece. Library of Congress.

In the American legendary, our idolized Washington lacked only one thing. It was love. Americans have always loved love and esteemed the sacrifice which a romantic young man or woman made for it. That is, if the sacrifice was a moral one. We had no relish for heartbroken fancy women or dedicated adulterers. In our mythology the love we admired was best symbolized, perhaps, in the self-sacrificing devotion of the Indian princess Pocahontas for her swashbuckling captain.

The episode gave us what we wanted. It did not matter that scholars said waspishly that it may never have happened. Nor that Pocahontas later married someone else. We believed John Smith when he wrote that the angry Powhatan was ready "to beat out his brains" when his desperate daughter intervened by putting Smith's head in her arms and laying "her own upon him to save him from death." Here in *Captain Smith & Pocahontas* the hero offers us a classic example of manly resignation while the heroine is the personification of selfless love. It should probably be added that American mythology has not found it necessary to include a complementary episode in which an Anglo-Saxon lady pleaded for the reprieve of her dusky chief.

As art for the many, this lithograph ranks fairly high. The light and shade have been boldly handled. The white smoke outlines the one executioner and his club; the weapon of the other marks one edge of the smoke. Pocahontas and Smith stand out against the dark masses of the braves. The composition is a rather interesting alternation of diagonals and horizontals. Two primary horizontals define the picture. One is at the bottom; the other is formed by the tops of the Indians' heads. But the top one is dramatically broken by the rising smoke, which introduces the diagonals of the peaked roof and of the figures of Smith and Pocahontas. The pyramidal structure of the center is accentuated by the lines of the two weapons. They tend in fact to draw too much of our attention. The artist has probably sensed this because he has introduced one more important horizontal, Powhatan's extended forearm and hand, which points directly at the kneeling pair and so focuses our interest where it ought to be. We look at the scene with satisfaction, knowing that love counts above all. We enshrine the episode in our tender hearts.

PLATE 33. *The Emigrants.* Drawn by J. A. Dallas [?]. Poetry by Henry Hirst [?].

SOURCE: *Illustrated Monthly Courier*, I (September 1848), 36. Library of Congress.

Americans still think of themselves as pioneers. The designation is a flattering one, with its implications of bold American innovation as opposed to tired European traditionalism. America ventures into the new; Europe clings to the old: that is the feeling. And it is in its way accurate enough. However, it is worth noting that we were ready to romanticize about it only when most of us were beginning to be comfortable if not metropolitan. As a nation we praised the pioneer only after many of us stopped our personal pioneering. While four-fifths of the country was still to be entered, subdued, and settled—that is, in our early days as a nation—the pioneer was not universally admired. Tart old Timothy Dwight in his *Travels in New-England and New-York* (1821) wrote of the pioneers of his time: "These men cannot live in regular society. They are too idle, too talkative, too passionate, too prodigal, and too shiftless." But a generation later a poet could write admiringly that "god sustains the Emigrant, His Pioneer below."

This was the view that time would see prevail. The poet could rhyme the nobility of the pioneer, his hardships, and his bravery. Here in the picture "The Emigrants" he and his family are shown stopping at a water hole somewhere in the Rockies. The artist has tried hard to enlist our sympathy in his subject. The father stands, weary but determined, next to his wife. She holds a child in her arms. A little boy perches unconcernedly on the horse's back while he holds a rifle. A dog, favorite symbol of American warmth, looks moodily into the distance. The artist's technique is unpolished, his pyramidal composition too simple; but his message is clear enough.

Today the western pioneer symbolizes one whole side of America for the world. He is celebrated in television shows, cheap novels, and motion pictures. He stars in the mass media, ranking second only to the ubiquitous cowboy, his liveliest descendant. He shines in our western mythology. French and German children, among many others, now put on their imitation buckskin suits and fire briskly at the oncoming Indians. Timothy Dwight would have been astounded.

PLATE 34. *One of the "Upper Ten Thousand."* Drawn by S. E. Brown.

SOURCE: *Broadway Journal*, March 1, 1845. Library of Congress.

With national awareness there developed an appreciation of national foibles and hyperboles. The best butts for American humor came either from the top or the bottom of the economic ladder. At the bottom were the frontier ranter, the Negro, and the immigrant Irishman: their comic possibilities were considered great. The frontier ranter usually appeared in the form of "half-horse, half-alligator" and the comedy lay either in his grotesque exaggerations or else in the difference, later to be immortalized by Mark Twain, between his surface bravado and barely hidden cowardice. The Negro appeared as the prime character in the developing minstrel shows, in cheap lithographs, and in a host of stories. The favorite formulations were his slyness and his aping of white peculiarities. The Irishman was shown as drunken, quarrelsome, shiftless, and droll. Very near the top of the ladder stood the ostentatious New Rich. Their artless attempts to achieve social status, their gauche extravagances, and their surface smugness all attracted the American humorist. At the top itself stood the members of the "Upper Ten Thousand."

They were the ancestors of the Four Hundred; they were the New York elite. The phrase the "Upper Ten Thousand" began to be current in the 1840s and remained popular for decades, spawning a number of variants including "Uppertendom." Here we have a drawing of one of its prize specimens. He minces along, splendidly dressed and pouting like a pigeon. The artist has saved his best efforts for the facial expression. The narrowed eyes and small, tight-lipped mouth show a superlative disdain. Here is wealth personified—and comic.

PART VII

Epilogue and Prologue: Slavery

Universal Emancipation

It is a safe guess that a majority of Americans in the 1840s did their earnest best to wish slavery away, to pretend that it was not there. Not an overwhelming majority, true, but a majority. They wanted to ignore the problem and were apt to respond with irritation if not anger when someone persisted in forcing it on their attention. It did not matter whether it happened to be a fire-eating defender of slavery from the South or an ardent abolitionist from the North. A plague on both their houses: that was the view of the moderate majority.

Although slavery played a minor role in the consciousness of most of the country, this was of course not true in the South. But in the 1840s even the South desired for the most part simply to take slavery for granted. For the Southern temper had not yet hardened and there was still some distance between the average white Southerner and his political leaders. In the next decade those leaders, and the brute logic of events, would urge the South into an obsession about the defense of slavery. But not yet.

On the Northern side the man who tried hardest in the 1840s to raise slavery to an issue of supreme importance was William Lloyd Garrison (1805–79). He became the spearhead of the abolition movement in New England and, by default, throughout the rest of the North. He fought with incendiary word and deed to free the slaves. He tolerated no compromise on a matter which the majority of his fellow citizens hoped to compromise. The speeches he made and the articles he wrote were passionate, often, and historically important. Time has preserved them. His poems, on the other hand, though often equally fervent are now forgotten. Yet they were impelled by the same antislavery drive. Its force can be felt in the verses under their elaborate nineteenth-century rhetoric. His *Sonnets and Other Poems* appeared in 1843. Typical titles are "Hope for the Enslaved," "Liberty for All," and "Universal Emancipation," which is reprinted below.

Two elements in this poem make it especially representative of the period. One is Garrison's assertion, which he was still willing to see published at this time, that freedom for the slaves would come without war. The other is his complementary conviction that emancipation would occur through God's will—and would occur soon.

SOURCE: William Lloyd Garrison, *Sonnets and Other Poems* (Boston, 1843), pp. 9–11.

Universal Emancipation

Though distant be the hour, yet come it must—
    Oh! hasten it, in mercy, righteous Heaven!
When Afric's sons, uprising from the dust,
    Shall stand erect—their galling fetters riven;
    When from his throne Oppression shall be driven,
An exiled monster, powerless through all time;
    When freedom—glorious freedom, shall be given
To every race, complexion, caste, and clime,
And Nature's sable hue shall cease to be a crime!

Woe if it come with storm, and blood, and fire,
    When midnight darkness veils the earth and sky!
Woe to the innocent babe—the guilty sire—
    Mother and daughter—friends of kindred tie!
    Stranger and citizen alike shall die!
Red-handed Slaughter his revenge shall feed,
    And Havoc yell his ominous death-cry,
    And wild Despair in vain for mercy plead—
While Hell itself shall shrink, and sicken at the deed!

Thou who avengest blood! long-suffering Lord!
  My guilty country from destruction save!
Let Justice sheath his sharp and terrible sword,
  And Mercy rescue, e'en as from the grave!
  Oh, for the sake of those who firmly brave
The lust of Power—the tyranny of Law—
  To bring redemption to the perishing slave—
Fearless, though few—Thy presence ne'er withdraw,
But quench the kindling flames of hot, rebellious War!

And ye—sad victims of base Avarice!
  Hunted like beasts, and trodden like the earth;
Bought and sold daily, at a paltry price—
  The scorn of tyrants, and of fools the mirth—
  Your souls debased from their immortal birth!
Bear meekly—as ye've borne—your cruel woes;
  Ease follows pain; light, darkness; plenty, dearth:
So time shall give you freedom and repose,
And high exalt your heads above your bitter foes!

Not by the sword shall your deliverance be;
  Not by the shedding of your masters' blood;
Not by rebellion—or foul treachery,
  Upspringing suddenly, like swelling flood:
  Revenge and rapine ne'er did bring forth good.
God's time is best!—nor will it long delay:
  Even now your barren cause begins to bud,
And glorious shall the fruit be!—Watch and pray,
For, lo! the kindling dawn, that ushers in the day!

DOCUMENT 42

The Problem for the Polity

Today the mind almost automatically rejects any rationale for slavery and so it is difficult to represent the Southern point of view in terms that we can respond to. However, the presentations of John C. Calhoun (1782–1850) are probably as persuasive as any. His "Remarks on Presenting his Resolutions on the Slave Question" were made in the United States Senate on February 19, 1847. To his colleagues on the floor of the Senate he describes in grave, responsible tones the dilemma of the South. In the foreseeable future he discerns nothing but dwindling power for his part of the country and so he appeals to the Senate to support the South. And speaking over the heads of his fellow Senators he appeals to the rest of the country.

He bases his remarks on his conviction that ours is a federal constitution. The states, he asserts, are the constituents, not the people. Consequently, each state has inalienable rights, among them the right to take its property into any other state or territory. That property includes slaves. Any law that prohibits slavery in any present or future state of the Union is unconstitutional. "Let us," he demands, "go back and stand upon the constitution!" At the end he presents his resolutions. They are specifically directed against what historians call the "Wilmot Proviso," which was a move the year before by a Pennsylvania Congressman, David Wilmot, to amend an appropriation bill so that it would bar slavery from all territory taken from Mexico. "Mr. President," begins Calhoun as he addresses the presiding officer of the Senate.

SOURCE: *Speeches of John C. Calhoun*, ed. Richard K. Cralle (New York, 1854), in *Collected Works*, IV, 340-49.

Remarks on Presenting His Resolutions on the Slave Question

Mr. President, it was solemnly asserted on this floor some time ago, that all parties in the non-slaveholding States had come to a fixed and solemn determination upon two propositions. One was,—that there should be no further admission of any States into this Union which permitted, by their constitutions, the existence of slavery; and the other was,—that slavery shall not hereafter exist in any of the territories of the United States; the effect of which would be to give to the non-slaveholding States the monopoly of the public domain, to the entire exclusion of the slaveholding States. Since that declaration was made, we have had abundant proof that there was a satisfactory foundation for it. We have received already solemn resolutions passed by seven of the non-slaveholding States—one-half of the number already in the Union, Iowa not being counted —using the strongest possible language to that effect; and no doubt, in a short space of time, similar resolutions will be received from all of the non-slaveholding States. But we need not go beyond the walls of Congress. The subject has been agitated in the other House, and they have sent up a bill "prohibiting the extension of slavery" (using their own language) "to any territory which may be acquired by the United States hereafter." At the same time, two resolutions which have been moved to extend the compromise line from the Rocky Mountains to the Pacific, during the present session, have been rejected by a decided majority.

Sir, there is no mistaking the signs of the times; and it is high time that the Southern States—the slaveholding States, should inquire what is now their relative strength in this Union, and what it will be if this determination should be carried into effect hereafter. Already we are in a minority

—I use the word "we" for brevity's sake—already we are in a minority in the other House,—in the electoral college,—and I may say, in every department of this Government, except, at present, in the Senate of the United States—there for the present we have an equality. Of the twenty-eight States, fourteen are non-slaveholding and fourteen are slavehold-ing,—counting Delaware, which is doubtful,—as one of the non-slaveholding States. But this equality of strength exists only in the Senate. One of the clerks, at my request, has furnished me with a statement of what is the relative strength of the two descriptions of States, in the other House of Congress and in the electoral college. There are 228 representatives, including Iowa, which is already rep-resented there. Of these, 138 are from non-slaveholding States, and 90 are from what are called the slave States—giving a majority, in the aggregate, to the former of 48. In the electoral college there are 168 votes belonging to the non-slaveholding States, and 118 to the slaveholding, giv-ing a majority of 50 to the non-slaveholding.

We, Mr. President, have at present only one position in the Government, by which we may make any resistance to this aggressive policy which has been declared against the South; or any other that the non-slaveholding States may choose to adopt. And this equality in this body is one of the most transient character. Already Iowa is a State; but owing to some domestic difficulties, is not yet represented in this body. When she appears here, there will be an addition of two Senators to the representatives here of the non-slaveholding States. Already Wisconsin has passed the initiatory stage, and will be here the next session. This will add two more, making a clear majority of four in this body on the side of the non-slaveholding States, who will thus be enabled to sway every branch of this Govern-ment at their will and pleasure. But, if this aggressive policy be followed—if the determination of the non-slave-holding States is to be adhered to hereafter, and we are to be entirely excluded from the territories which we already possess, or may possess—if this is to be the fixed policy of

the Government, I ask what will be our situation hereafter?

Sir, there is ample space for twelve or fifteen of the
largest description of States in the territories belonging
to the United States. Already a law is in course of passage
through the other House creating one north of Wisconsin.
There is ample room for another north of Iowa; and another north of that; and then that large region extending,
on this side of the Rocky Mountains, from 49 degrees down
to the Texan line, which may be set down fairly as an area
of twelve and a half degrees of latitude. That extended
region of itself is susceptible of having six, seven, or eight
large States. To this, add Oregon which extends from 49
to 42 degrees, which will give four more, and I make a
very moderate calculation when I say that, in addition to
Iowa and Wisconsin, twelve more States upon the territory already ours—without reference to any acquisitions
from Mexico—may be, and will be, shortly added to these
United States. How will we then stand? There will be but
fourteen on the part of the South—we are to be fixed,
limited, and for ever—and twenty-eight on the part of the
non-slaveholding States! Double our number! And with
the same disproportion in the House and in the electoral
college! The Government, Sir, will be entirely in the hands
of the non-slaveholding States—overwhelmingly.

Sir, if this state of things is to go on—if this determination, so solemnly made, is to be persisted in, where shall
we stand, as far as this Federal Government of ours is
concerned? We shall be at the entire mercy of the non-
slaveholding States. Can we look to their justice and regard
for our interests? I ask, can we rely on that? Ought we to
trust our safety and prosperity to their mercy and sense of
justice? These are the solemn questions which I put to
all—this and the other side of the Chamber.

Sir, can we find any hope by looking to the past? If
we are to look to that—I will not go into the details—we
will see, from the beginning of this Government to the
present day, as far as pecuniary resources are concerned—as

far as the disbursement of revenue is involved, it will be found that we have been a portion of the community which has substantially supported this Government without receiving any thing like a proportionate return. But why should I go beyond this very measure itself? Why go beyond this determination on the part of the non-slaveholding States,—that there shall be no further addition to the slaveholding States,—to prove what our condition will be?

Sir, what is the entire amount of this policy? I will not say that it is so designed. I will not say from what cause it originated. I will not say whether blind fanaticism on one side,—whether a hostile feeling to slavery entertained by many not fanatical on the other, has produced it; or whether it has been the work of men, who, looking to political power, have considered the agitation of this question as the most effectual mode of obtaining the spoils of this Government. I look to the fact itself. It is a policy now openly avowed as one to be persisted in. It is a scheme, which aims to monopolize the powers of this Government and to obtain sole possession of its territories.

Now, I ask, is there any remedy? Does the Constitution afford any remedy? And if not, is there any hope? These, Mr. President, are solemn questions—not only to us, but, let me say to gentlemen from the non-slaveholding States, to them. Sir, the day that the balance between the two sections of the country—the slaveholding States and the non-slaveholding States—is destroyed, is a day that will not be far removed from political revolution, anarchy, civil war, and wide-spread disaster. The balance of this system is in the slaveholding States. They are the conservative portion —always have been the conservative portion—always will be the conservative portion; and with a due balance on their part may, for generations to come, uphold this glorious Union of ours. But if this scheme should be carried out—if we are to be reduced to a handful—if we are to become a mere ball to play the presidential game with—to count something in the Baltimore caucus—if this is to be the result—wo! wo! I say, to this Union!

Now, Sir, I put again the solemn question—Does the constitution afford any remedy? Is there any provision in it by which this aggressive policy (boldly avowed, as if perfectly consistent with our institutions and the safety and prosperity of the United States) may be confronted? Is this a policy consistent with the Constitution. No, Mr. President, no! It is, in all its features, daringly opposed to the constitution. What is it? Ours is a Federal Constitution. The States are its constituents, and not the people. The twenty-eight States—the twenty-nine States (including Iowa)—stand, under this Government, as twenty-nine individuals, or as twenty-nine millions of individuals would stand to a consolidated power! No, Sir. It was made for higher ends. It was so formed that every State, as a constituent member of this Union of ours, should enjoy all its advantages, natural and acquired, with greater security, and enjoy them more perfectly. The whole system is based on justice and equality—perfect equality between the members of this republic. Now, can that be consistent with equality which will make this public domain a monopoly on one side—which, in its consequences, would place the whole power in one section of the Union to be wielded against the other sections? Is that equality?

How, then, do we stand in reference to this territorial question—this public domain of ours? Why, Sir, what is it? It is the common property of the States of this Union. They are called "the territories of the United States." And what are the "United States" but the States united? Sir, these territories are the property of the States united; held jointly for their common use. And is it consistent with justice—is it consistent with equality, that any portion of the partners, outnumbering another portion, shall oust them of this common property of theirs—shall pass any law which shall proscribe the citizens of other portions of the Union from emigrating with their property to the territories of the United States? Would that be consistent—can it be con-

sistent with the idea of a common property, held jointly for
the common benefit of all? Would it be so considered in
private life? Would it not be considered the most flagrant
outrage in the world—one which any court of equity would
restrain by injunction, or any court of law in the world
would overrule.

Mr. President, not only is that proposition grossly inconsistent with the constitution, but the other, which un-
dertakes to say that no State shall be admitted into this
Union, which shall not prohibit by its constitution the
existence of slaves, is equally a great outrage against the
constitution of the United States. Sir, I hold it to be a
fundamental principle of our political system, that the
people have a right to establish what government they may
think proper for themselves; that every State about to become a member of this Union has a right to form its government as it pleases; and that, in order to be admitted
there is but one qualification, and that is, that the Government shall be republican. There is no express provision to
that effect, but it results from that important section,
which guarantees to every State in this Union a republican
form of government. Now, Sir, what is proposed? It is proposed, from a vague, indefinite, erroneous, and most dangerous conception of private individual liberty, to overrule this great common liberty which a people have of
framing their own constitution! Sir, the right of framing
self-government on the part of individuals is not near so
easily to be established by any course of reasoning, as the
right of a community or State to self-government. And yet,
Sir, there are men of such delicate feeling on the subject
of liberty—men who cannot possibly bear what they call
slavery in one section of the country—although not so much
slavery, as an institution indispensable for the good of both
races—men so squeamish on this point, that they are ready
to strike down the higher right of a community to govern
themselves, in order to maintain the absolute right of
individuals, in every possible condition to govern themselves!

Mr. President, the resolutions that I intend to offer present, in general terms, these great truths. I propose to present them to the Senate; I propose to have a vote upon them; and I trust there is no gentleman here who will refuse it. It is manly, it is right, that such a vote be given. It is due to our constituents that we should insist upon it; and I, as one, will insist upon it that the sense of this body shall be taken; the body which represents the States in their capacity as communities, and the members of which are to be their special guardians. It is due to them, Sir, that there should be a fair expression of what is the sense of this body. Upon that expression much depends. It is the only position we can take, that will uphold us with any thing like independence—which will give us any chance at all to maintain an equality in this Union, on those great principles to which I have referred. Overrule these principles, and we are nothing! Preserve them, and we will ever be a respectable portion of the Union.

Sir, here let me say a word as to the compromise line. I have always considered it as a great error—highly injurious to the South, because it surrendered, for mere temporary purposes, those high principles of the constitution upon which I think we ought to stand. I am against any compromise line. Yet I would have been willing to acquiesce in a continuation of the Missouri compromise, in order to preserve, under the present trying circumstances, the peace of the country. One of the resolutions in the House, to that effect, was offered at my suggestion. I said to a friend there, "Let us not be disturbers of this Union. Abhorrent to my feelings as is that compromise line, let it be adhered to in good faith; and if the other portions of the Union are willing to stand by it, let us not refuse to stand by it. It has kept peace for some time, and, in the present circumstances, perhaps, it would be better to be continued as it is." But it was voted down by a decided majority. It was renewed by a gentleman from a non-slaveholding State, and again voted down by a like majority.

I see my way in the constitution; I cannot in a compromise. A compromise is but an act of Congress. It may be overruled at any time. It gives us no security. But the constitution is stable. It is a rock. On it we can stand, and on it we can meet our friends from the non-slaveholding States. It is a firm and stable ground, on which we can better stand in opposition to fanaticism, than on the shifting sands of compromise.

Let us be done with compromises. Let us go back and stand upon the constitution!

Well, Sir, what if the decision of this body shall deny to us this high constitutional right, not the less clear because deduced from the entire body of the instrument, and the nature of the subject to which it relates, instead of being specially provided for? What then? I will not undertake to decide. It is a question for our constituents, the slaveholding States—a solemn and a great question. If the decision should be adverse, I trust and do believe that they will take under solemn consideration what they ought to do. I give no advice. It would be hazardous and dangerous for me to do so. But I may speak as an individual member of that section of the Union. There is my family and connections; there I drew my first breath; there are all my hopes. I am a planter—a cotton-planter. I am a Southern man and a slaveholder—a kind and a merciful one, I trust—and none the worse for being a slaveholder. I say, for one, I would rather meet any extremity upon earth than give up one inch of our equality—one inch of what belongs to us as members of this great republic! What! acknowledged inferiority! The surrender of life is nothing to sinking down into acknowledged inferiority!

I have examined this subject largely—widely. I think I see the future. If we do not stand up as we ought, in my humble opinion, the condition of Ireland is prosperous and happy—the condition of Hindostan is prosperous and happy—the condition of Jamaica is prosperous and happy, compared with what must be that of the Southern States.

Mr. President, I desire that the resolutions which I now send to the table be read.

[The resolutions were read as follows:—

"*Resolved*, That the territories of the United States belong to the several States composing this Union, and are held by them as their joint and common property.

"*Resolved*, That Congress, as the joint agent and representative of the States of this Union, has no right to make any law, or do any act whatever, that shall directly, or by its effects, make any discrimination between the States of this Union, by which any of them shall be deprived of its full and equal right in any territory of the United States, acquired or to be acquired.

"*Resolved*, That the enactment of any law, which should directly, or by its effects, deprive the citizens of any of the States of this Union from emigrating, with their property, into any of the territories of the United States, will make such discrimination, and would, therefore, be a violation of the constitution and the rights of the States from which such citizens emigrated, and in derogation of that perfect equality which belongs to them as members of this Union, —and would tend directly to subvert the Union itself.

"*Resolved*, That it is a fundamental principle in our political creed, that a people in forming a constitution have the unconditional right to form and adopt the government which they may think best calculated to secure their liberty, prosperity, and happiness; and that, in conformity thereto, no other condition is imposed by the Federal Constitution on a State in order to be admitted into this Union, except that its constitution shall be republican; and that the imposition of any other by Congress would not only be in violation of the constitution, but in direct conflict with the principle on which our political system rests."]

I move that the resolutions be printed. I shall move that they be taken up to-morrow; and I do trust that the Senate will give them early attention and an early vote upon the subject.

Scripture and Slavery

John Calhoun, most thoughtful of the Southern leaders, appealed vigorously to those of his fellow citizens in the North who were open-minded. His greatest barrier was the overpowering weight of the evidence, once it was gathered and measured, against slavery. Once a serious evaluation of the merits of the case was attempted, there was only one answer: abolition. Yet attempts were made both in the North and South by persons of many different backgrounds to give an honest appraisal of the problem. There were not only politicians and humanitarians, there were merchants, artisans, educators, and—an unusually influential group—clergymen.

The role of the Christian denominations in the gradually growing debate over slavery was important. By force of tradition and circumstance the clergy were the keepers of our conscience as well as, in a considerable number of cases, our temporal spokesmen. The problem of whether they were to take a position and, if so, what one, troubled a good number of them. In the 1840s most of the major denominations did their best to steer away from the reefs of the slavery question. But two of the most active split apart during the decade. The Baptists and the Methodists of the South withdrew from their national organizations to form their own regional ones.

A representative of the clergymen who tried hard to see both sides of the question can be found in the person of the Reverend Albert Barnes (1798–1870). In his perplexity he went to Scripture, to the Bible as a guide. Many another did too but Barnes was distinguished by the thoroughness and systematic nature of his search.

In the growing discussion about slavery the Bible was invoked by both sides. Citations from it, and arguments based on those citations, were frequently used both to attack and to defend the "Peculiar Institution" of slavery. Midway between the defenders and attackers stood a large group of people who looked to the Bible for help with this vexed question. One was Barnes, a Presbyterian minister from Philadelphia. A professed student of Scripture for twenty years, he felt it his duty to go through the Bible in an orderly manner and with an open mind in order to determine what it really said about slaveholding. He himself inclined against it, he said, but he did his best to be fair; and we can judge that he succeeded reasonably well. He carefully assembled his data and then presented it with heavy documentation. His work abounds in biblical chapter and verse.

The book was published in 1846 as *An Inquiry into the Scriptural Views of Slavery*. Judicious though Barnes was, he found no substantial evidence in the Bible for the pro-slavery side. The excerpts reprinted below are from the section headed "The principles laid down by the Saviour and his Apostles are such as are opposed to Slavery, and if carried out would secure its universal abolition."

SOURCE: Albert Barnes, *An Inquiry into the Scriptural Views of Slavery* (Philadelphia, 1846), pp. 344–55.

The Principles Laid Down

The Christian religion teaches that "God hath made of one blood all the nations of men for to dwell on all the face of the earth," (Acts xvii. 26,) and that as the children of the common Father they are regarded as equal. All the right which one human being has ever been supposed to have over another, in virtue of any superiority in rank, complexion, or blood, is evidently contrary to this doctrine of the Bible in regard to the origin and equality of the human race. The *common nature* which man has,

is not affected, in any respect, by the colour of his hair
or his skin, by the difference of his stature, by national
physiognomy, or by any ethnographical distinctions in the
form of the skull. This common nature, as distinct from
the brute creation, remains the same under every external
appearance, and every form of intellectual and moral development. A man may be wiser or less wise than I am;
he may have more or less property; he may have a more
richly endowed, or an inferior mental capacity, but this
does not affect our common nature. He is in every respect,
notwithstanding our difference in these things, as completely a human being as myself; and he stands in precisely the same relations towards the Creator and Father
of all. He, like myself, has an immortal soul, and is placed
in a state of probation, as a candidate for everlasting happiness or everlasting wo. He has an intellect capable of an
endless progression in knowledge; and God has given him
the right to improve it to the utmost. He is endowed with
a conscience, which, like his immortal intellect, for ever
constitutes an impassable line between him and the inferior races of the animal creation. In virtue of this endowment, it is his right and privilege to seek to know the will
of God, and to act always with reference to the future
state on which he is soon to enter. He is a sinner, and,
as such, is placed in substantially the same circumstances
with all others before God, in reference to the rewards of
heaven or the pains of hell. It was with reference to this
common nature that redemption was provided. It was our
common nature which the Son of God assumed when he
became incarnate, and, *in* that assumption, and in all his
sufferings for man, he regarded the race as having such a
common nature. He was not a *Jew*, except by the accident
of his birth; but he was a *man*, and in his human frame
there was as distinct a relation to the African and the
Malay, as there was to the Caucasian. The blood that
flowed in his veins, and that was shed on the cross for
human redemption, was the blood of a human being—a
descendant of Adam—and had as much reference, when it

warmed his heart with benevolence, and when it was shed on the cross, to a descendant of Ham as to the posterity of Japheth or Shem. Every human being has a right to feel that when the Son of God became incarnate he took *his* nature upon him, and to regard him as the representative of that common humanity. It is on the basis of that common nature that the gospel is commanded to be preached to 'every creature,' and any one human being has a right to consider that gospel as addressed to him with as specific an intention as to any other human being whatever. It is on the basis of that common nature also that the Holy Spirit is sent down from heaven to awaken, convict, and convert the soul; and any human being, no matter what his complexion, may regard the promise of the Holy Spirit to be as much addressed to him as to any other one—though that other one may have a more comely form or complexion; may be clothed in the imperial purple, or may wear a coronet, or a crown. In *all respects* pertaining to our common origin; to our nature as distinct from the brute creation; to the fall and to redemption; to the rights of conscience and to the hopes of glory, the human race is regarded in the Bible as on a level. There is an entire system of things which contemplates *man as such* as distinguished from the inferior creation; not one of which pertains to a brute, however near the brute may seem to approximate a human being, and each one of which is as applicable to one human being as to another.

If these views are correct, then all the reliance which the system of slavery has ever been thought to derive from the supposed fact that one class of human beings is essentially inferior to another, is a false reliance. At all events, such views will find no support in the Bible, and they must be left to be maintained by those who recognise the Christian Scriptures as of no authority. A man acting on the views laid down in the Bible on this subject, would never *make* a slave; a man acting on these views would not long *retain* a slave: and Christianity, by laying down this doctrine of the essential equality of the race, has stated a doctrine which *must* sooner or later emancipate every human being from bondage.

(2.) The gospel regards every human being as invested with such rights as are inconsistent with his being held as a slave; that is, these rights, as recognised in the New Testament, always have been violated where slavery exists; are liable to be violated at any time; and there is no way of effectually guarding against such violation, for the power to violate them enters into every proper conception of slavery. In other words, it is involved in the notion of the system that the slaveholder has power to violate what are undoubted laws of God, and to interfere with and annul the arrangements which he has instituted for the good of man. If this be so, it will be conceded that the New Testament does not contemplate slavery as right, or as an institution to be perpetuated for the good of society.

Among those rights which are liable to be violated at the pleasure of the slaveholder, and against the violation of which from the very nature of slavery, it is impossible to guard, are the following:—

(*a*) The rights involved in the marriage relation. The master necessarily holds the power of preventing its being formed, or of annulling it at his pleasure. This results from the very nature of slavery, and never has been forbidden, and never can be, while slavery retains its essential features. It results from the right of *property*; for the right to buy a thing implies a right to sell it again; and as a man in purchasing one slave is under no obligation to purchase another, though it be the wife or child of the former, so it is in regard to the sale. As in procuring slaves originally, whether by the conquests of war, by kidnapping, or by purchase, no respect was had to the relations which they might sustain to their families, or any duties which might grow out of such relations, so there is no reference to any such duties or relations in the tenure by which they are held. On this very obvious principle all the laws pertaining to slavery in this land are founded. The right to separate husband and wife, parent and child, and brother and sister, is nowhere forbidden, and this power is constantly acted on. It is not known that an *attempt* has ever been made to regulate this by law, and the only influence by which it is sought to control it is by an appeal to the humanity of masters. There are doubtless thousands of cases where the master *would not* separate a husband from his wife by selling one without the other, but this does not prove that the law does not regard them as having the power, and is not to be taken into the account in estimating the character of the system.

Even supposing, moreover, that the husband and wife are not actually separated from each other, and the marriage bond wholly disregarded, still there are duties enjoined in reference to this relation in the New Testament which the recognised power of the master wholly sets aside. In the New Testament, the husband is declared to be the "head of the wife, as Christ is the head of the church," (Eph. v. 23, 1 Cor. xi. 3,) and as such has a right to rule in his family. The wife, *as such*, is commanded to be subject to her husband; to recognise his authority; to obey him; to love him; to submit to him in all things. "As the church is subject to Christ, so let the wives be to their own husbands in every thing." Eph. v. 24. Comp. Eph. v. 33; Titus ii. 4, 5; 1 Pet. iii. 1. Now this command is practically nullified in every case where slavery exists. The *master*, not the *husband*, possesses supreme authority in relation to every slave, male or female, and *his* will is to be obeyed, and *not* that of the husband, if they ever come in conflict. The master, too, by the laws of *all* slaveholding communities, has the power of *enforcing* obedience by punishment, even when it is against every wish and will of the husband. This power extends to her manner of employing her time; to her whole domestic arrangements; to her hours of labour and of rest; to her food and raiment; to her habitation, and to every comfort. Even when the husband is *sick*, there is no power of enforcing any right which the wife has by the laws of marriage in the Bible, to attend on him, and soothe his sorrows; and

though it may be that the duties which a wife owes to
her husband in such cases may not often be prevented by
an absolute interference on the part of the master, yet
the fact that it is not, is not to be traced to any mercy in
the institution of slavery, or the laws, but to the mercy of
our common humanity. Nothing *prevents* the master from
setting at naught the whole law of God on the subject.

(*b*) Slavery interferes with the natural right which a
father has over his children. This results, too, from the
nature of *property* implied in the relation. The primary
and the controlling notion is, that the child is *owned* by
the master, not that he is placed under the control and
authority of his father. The master, not the father, is
supreme. The Bible recognises certain duties as growing
out of the relation of a father and child, which are never
acknowledged in the code of slavery; and enjoins certain
duties which the father can never perform, except at the
pleasure of the master. The father is displaced from the
position where God has assigned him, and the master is
substituted in his place. The Bible has laid down certain
duties as binding on the parent, as such, and which properly
grow out of the relation of parent and child. The parent
is to "command his children and his household after him,"
(Gen. xviii. 19;) he is to "bring them up in the nurture
and admonition of the Lord," (Eph. vi. 4;) he is to "provide for his own, and specially for those of his own house,"
(1 Tim. v. 5;) he is to instruct them in the ways and
duties of religion, to lead their devotions, to seek to prepare them for heaven, to be their counsellor and adviser
in regard to the perplexities and duties of life. Children,
on the other hand, *all* children, are to 'honour their father
and mother, that their days may be long in the land,'
(Ex. xx. 12;) they are to 'obey their parents *in all things*,'
(Col. iii. 20;) they are to 'obey their parents in the Lord,'
(Eph. vi. 1.) Now, it is impossible to secure the discharge
of these duties under the system of slavery. The whole
question whether a father *may* perform these duties at all,
rests with the master. The father's own time is not at his

disposal; he is at liberty to select and appoint no hours when he will instruct his children; he has no right to designate any time when he will even *pray* with his family; and the whole business of 'providing for his own' is entirely taken out of his hands. The master provides, and is the agent appointed by the laws to do it. The father is under no obligation by the laws even to *attempt* it. It is not presumed that he *can* do it. It is not understood that he ever *will* do it. He violates none of the obligations contemplated by slavery, if he makes *no provision whatever* for his children while he himself shall live, or after he is dead; if he leaves them to suffer without one sympathizing look or word; if he provides no physician for them in sickness, or even if he does not see them decently buried when they are dead. Food and raiment; medicine and physicians; shrouds, coffins, and graves are to be provided by the master. It is not contemplated by the law that the slave can ever be the owner of *property* enough to furnish his child a coffin or a grave. So also in the whole duty of training the child for heaven. If time is to be taken for that, it is to be at the pleasure of the master; if a religious teacher is to be employed, it is only at his pleasure, and under his direction.

The law of God is perhaps still more entirely nullified, in regard to the duty which the child owes to its parent. Here it is impossible for him to obey the command of God requiring subjection to his parent, if the will of the master comes in conflict with his. It is not designed that *the parent* shall be obeyed. The master has the absolute authority, and has the right to counteract any of the requirements of the father. The master, not the parent, directs in regard to the employment of the time, and appoints every task that is to be performed. The master has authority in the whole matter of discipline, and punishment is administered, not because the laws of a father have been disregarded, but because the will of the master has been disobeyed. The spirit of the whole institution is, not that the *father* is to be obeyed, but the *master*;

and if the father is *not* obeyed, the law lends no help to secure the respect and obedience of the child. The law has displaced the father from the position which God gave him, and has substituted the authority of another.

(*c*) Slavery interferes with the natural right which every human being has, to worship God according to his own views of what is true. That this right is recognised in the Bible, it would be needless to attempt to prove. See Acts iv. 18–20, v. 29; John v. 39; 1 Cor. x. 29; 1 Thess. v. 21; 1 John iv. 1; Prov. iv. 13; Luke xi. 52; Deut. x. 12, xiii. 4. The right to do this is everywhere now conceded, and is regarded as one of the great and inalienable principles of Protestantism and of liberty. It is the most important position which society has taken in its progress toward that state of perfectness which it is destined to attain; the last point which society is to reach in this direction—the *ultima Thule* of human hopes and prospects on this point. To establish this principle has cost more than any other which enters into just notions of liberty—for it is the result of discussions and inquiries pursued for ages; of all the persecutions and martyrdoms that have been endured; of all the self-denials and sacrifices in the cause of freedom. To maintain and enjoy the right of the undisturbed privileges of religion; the right to worship God unmolested; the right to hold what opinions they pleased; to worship God where, and when, and however they pleased; our fathers came to this western land, and endured all the sacrifices incident to the perilous voyage across the deep, and the peopling of what was then a vast and inhospitable wilderness. There is no other right for which an American citizen, at the North or the South, would more cheerfully lay down his life; none from which he would not sooner part.

And yet this right, so invaluable, is practically denied to the slave wherever the institution exists. The abundant quotations which I have made, in the former part of this work, from the laws of the Southern states, show, that, whatever kindness there may be on the part of many masters, this great right, so far as the slave is concerned, is denied him. Every thing pertaining to the worship of God —the time, the place, the manner—is entirely in the hands of the master; and there is not a company of slaves in the land that, according to the laws, can act *freely* in the worship of their Maker. The condition in which the early Puritans were placed in England, in the times of Elizabeth, James, and Charles I.; the condition in which the Nonconformists and Quakers were, in the time of Charles II.; the condition in which the Pilgrim Fathers were, in England and Holland—a condition so severe, that they sought the inhospitable shores of New England, in the dead of winter, rather than endure it—all these are nothing, when compared with the absolute right which the master has over his slaves in the Southern states. The world, even in the worst times of civil oppression, has never seen any thing worse than this; any thing which more entirely interferes with every sacred right of conscience.

And can any man believe, that it was the design of God to sanction such a system, or that it is in accordance with the principles of the New Testament, and is to be perpetuated for the good of society? Can it be believed, that God meant to put the authority to regulate entirely the manner in which he should be worshipped, into the hands of any man? The whole chivalry of the South would be in arms, if an attempt were made, from any quarter, to impose on them the same restrictions in regard to the worship of God which the laws make necessary respecting the slaves; and there is not on earth a class of men that would be more ready to shed their last drop of blood in opposition to such an attempt, and in defense of the very principles which are set at naught by their own laws respecting three millions of human beings—as free, by nature, to worship God in the manner which they prefer, as themselves.

(*d*) Slavery interferes with the rights of *property*. If any principle is clear, not only from reason, but from the

Bible, it is, that a man has a right to the avails of his
own labour. This is founded on the right which he has
to *himself*, and of course to all that he himself can honestly earn. If any portion of this is taken away by taxes
for the support of government, it is not on the principle
that another *man*, though at the head of the government
and ruling over him, has any right to it, but it is, that he
himself is *represented* in that government; and that it is,
to all practical purposes, an appropriation by himself, of
his own property, to make himself, his family, and the
remainder of his property more secure. It is not taken
from him; it is committed *by* him to others, to be employed in his own service, and in the protection which he
receives there is a full equivalent for all that is rendered to
the government. He is still regarded as the lawful owner,
and as having a right to all the avails of his own industry,
until it is thus surrendered to other hands.

This right, while it enters into all our notions of liberty,
and while the denial of it led to all the sacrifices which
secured American Independence, is abundantly recognised
in the Bible. An attempt to prove it is scarcely necessary;
but the following passages show what are the current statements of the Scriptures on the subject: "Wherefore I perceive that there is nothing better than that a man should
rejoice in his own works; for that is his portion: for who
shall bring him to see what shall be after him." Eccl. iii.
22. "Behold that which I have seen: it is good and comely
for one to eat and to drink, and to enjoy the good of all
his labour that he taketh under the sun all the days of
his life, which God giveth him: for that is his portion."
Eccl. v. 18. "Behold the hire of the labourers who have
reaped down your fields, which is of you kept back by
fraud, crieth; and the cries of them which have reaped are
entered into the ears of the Lord of Sabaoth." James v. 4.
"Thou shalt not defraud thy neighbour, neither rob him;
the wages of him that is hired shall not abide with thee
all night until the morning." Lev. xix. 13. "Rob not the
poor because he is poor; neither oppress the afflicted in

the gate: for the Lord will plead their cause, and spoil the soul of those that spoiled them." Prov. xxii. 22, 23. "For I the Lord love judgment, I hate robbery for burnt-offering." Isa. lxi. 8. "The people of the land have used oppression, and exercised robbery, and have vexed the poor and needy; yea they have oppressed the stranger wrong-fully. And I sought for a man among them that should make up the hedge, and stand in the gap before me in the land, that I should not destroy it: but I found none. Therefore have I poured out mine indignation upon them; I have consumed them with the fire of my wrath; their own way have I recompensed upon their heads, saith the Lord God." Ezek. xxii. 29–31. "Wo unto him that buildeth his house by unrighteousness, and his chambers by wrong; *that useth his neighbour's service without wages, and giveth him not for his work.*" Jer. xxii. 13.

Now it is unnecessary to attempt to prove, that this essential principle of the right of property is wholly at variance with slavery as it exists in this land, and indeed with all proper notions of its nature, wherever it exists. It is a fundamental doctrine in the idea of slavery, that the slave can be the legal owner of no property; can have no right to the avails of his own labour. This has been abundantly demonstrated in the quotations which have been made from the laws of the slaveholding states. The slave can own neither farm, nor house, nor ox, nor ass, nor any thing which his hands can earn. He can own no copyright of a book, and claim none of the avails of a book. He can buy nothing, and can sell nothing. He can contract no debt that could be collected of him; he can collect no wages from another for services rendered; he can make no will that the law would recognise as valid. There is even no little memento of kindness, which he may have received from his master or from others, which he can claim as his own; there is no such token, which the master might not legally appropriate to himself. The slave has no right to any portion of the corn or the cotton which his own hands have raised; nor can he ever look on a tree, a rosebush, or a flower, and say, legally, that it is his own.

Now, if the principles of the Bible on the subject of property are permanent principles, it is clear that the system of slavery is not in accordance with the word of God, and that it is not the intention of Christianity to perpetuate the system in the world. The fair application of these principles would soon bring the system to an end. Can it be believed that the New Testament sanctions the power of making void the marriage relation; of abrogating the authority of parents; of nullifying the command which requires children to obey their parents; of interfering with the right which every man has to worship God according to his own views of duty and truth; and of appropriating to ourselves entirely the avails of the labour of another man? Whatever may be the abstract views which any man may defend on the subject of human rights, yet no one can seriously maintain—I know not that any one has ever attempted to maintain—that these things are sanctioned by the New Testament. And yet, they are *essential* to the system. Slavery, in the proper sense of the term, never has existed without some or all of these things; it never can.

DOCUMENT 44

For the Defense

We may think of William Lloyd Garrison as representing both the polemical and logical attack on slavery. John C. Calhoun can stand for its most thoughtful defenders. The methodical and fair-minded Albert Barnes can represent the many Northerners who, once being brought to examine the institution of slavery, found it indefensible. But one large group remains to be represented, the Southerners who felt to their marrow that slavery was right. Of these an obscure Mississippian is an illuminating example.

Matthew Estes of Columbus, Mississippi, published *A Defence of Negro Slavery* in 1846. More nearly than many a more popular book it represented the primal feelings of the Deep South. Much of Estes' little book is concerned with the grimmest nonsense—Negro bones are poorer than white bones, for instance—but it also presents some of the frequent social and economic arguments for slavery. And, looking straight at his peers, he concludes his volume with a chapter on "Duties of Masters."

Perhaps the clearest index to Estes' attitude can be found in the final sentence of the *Defence*: "I know several Negroes that possess a degree of piety that but few white people can ever expect to equal." Here kindness mingles with classic condescension; ignorance is laced with light.

SOURCE: Matthew Estes, A Defence of Negro Slavery as it Exists in the United States (Montgomery, Alabama, 1846), pp. 63, 65–68, 154–57, 162–64, 168–70, 253–60.

A Defence of Negro Slavery

There is less beauty in the general form and outline of the Negro than in that of the white man. He has a flat, ugly foot; evidently designed, like the foot of the camel, to tread upon the sands of the great tropical deserts. There is, in all the works of God, a harmony and adaption of the parts to each other, which evince the highest possible degree of wisdom and goodness. The Negro has a black, thick skin, which emits a disagreeable odor; thick, woolly hair; a large mouth; ugly features; thick lips; a small calf to his leg, situated near the knee; a projecting shin bone. In a word, there is in the whole outline of the Negro, much less of symmetry and beauty than in that of the white man. . . .

But the Negro has other physical peculiarities which fit him for the situation that he occupies on this continent, and which I shall now proceed to mention.

Every one has observed at the inner corner of the eye of fowls, a semi-lunar membrane, which moves with great rapidity over the eye, when exposed to the solar rays. This has been called by naturalists, the *nictitating* membrane. It is designed to direct the course of the tears, and to protect the eye from the intense rays of the sun. In the eye of the white man, this membrane is very small, and seems only to direct the tears into a *sac* situated behind and below a small prominence at the inner *canthus* of the eye. In the Negro, this membrane is greatly expanded; and serves, in addition to the purpose of directing the tears, as in the white man, to protect the eye, as in the case of fowls, from the effects of the solar rays.

This membrane serves as a protection to the Negro

against the effects of the hardships, necessarily incident to the condition of Slavery.

"The Master," says Dr. CARTWRIGHT, of Natchez, "may forget or neglect to provide his Slaves with a covering for the head, to shield the eyes from the brilliancy of the sun, while laboring in the fields. Such neglect would greatly increase the irksomeness of labor, under a tropical sun, if GOD, in his goodness, had not provided the race of Canaan, whom he has doomed to Slavery, with the above-mentioned anatomical contrivance, or membranous wing, to protect the eyes against the brightness of the solar rays."

The difference between the Negro and the white man extends even to the intimate structure of their organs. The brain proper—that is, the *cerebrum*—in the Negro, is about ten per cent smaller than it is in the white man: and in texture it is coarser, more watery and flabby. When put into a dish it sinks loosely down, instead of standing firm and erect, as in the case of the higher orders of white men. The head of Lord Byron was small; and was, in consequence, said to contradict one of the fundamental principles of phrenology, viz: "that size, *ceteris paribus*, is a measure of power;" but after the death of his lordship, his brain was taken out and weighed—and to the astonishment of all, was found heavier than most brains of the largest size. The brain of the Baron Cuvier, though in appearance one-third larger, was only one or two drachms heavier. This great weight of the brain of his lordship, was owing to its extreme density. Its whole texture was firm and solid, the fibres compact, and the whole organ exceedingly free from water. When put into a dish, the parts firmly adhered together: so much so that it would have answered for dissection, without the usual process of hardening. Now the same difference that exists between the brain of Lord Byron, and those of ordinary individuals, exists between the white and black races of men. The power of Byron lay in the density of his brain; and the mental superiority of the white over the black race, is owing to the superior size and density of the brain.

Whatever may be said of phrenology in all its details, one position I consider established beyond controversy, viz: "that the brain is the seat of mind." This principle being true, it follows that the efficiency and power of the mind must depend on the efficiency and power of the brain. The inferiority of the Negro is thus clearly manifest.

But the difference between the white and black races does not end here; there is a considerable difference even in the bones. This extends not only to the general outline, but to their intimate structure. In general outline, the bones of the white man are much more elegant, smooth and symmetrical; all the protuberances are rounder, smoother, and the angles less abrupt than those of the Negro. The bones of the Negro are of a more dingy color, more spongy in structure, and coarser grained, than those of the white man. Among the higher orders of the white race, the bones have almost the appearance of ivory. I have a large cabinet of skulls and other bones, both of animals and men; and hence my opportunities are good to make observations. I find a great difference in the texture of these bones; those of the higher orders have almost the whiteness and density of ivory. Among the number is the skull of a French nobleman, and a number belonging to the race of Canaan. The former is handsome in all its parts, the processes all handsomely rounded, and the texture dense, firm, and white, like ivory. On the contrary, the bones belonging to the Negro are coarse-grained, spongy in texture, dingy and rough. The base of the skull, inside, has the appearance of being hewed out with a foot-adz. It is said that the skull of Byron, when sawed across to take out the brain, had very much the appearance of ivory.

A skillful observer can distinguish temperament from the bones alone. This I have so frequently observed, that no doubt can exist upon the subject. . . .

The reader will please call to mind a fact already men-

tioned, viz: that the constitution of the Negro peculiarly
fits him for a hot climate: that in such a climate he is in
his proper element, whilst the white man, on the contrary,
is adapted to a more northern climate, and cannot bear
extensive exposure at the South, without great risk of injury to his constitution. It must be admitted as a fact,
then, that without Negro labor, the larger and more fertile
portion of the South would be left uncultivated. I take
it for granted that the Negroes must be in a state of
Slavery; for if it were otherwise, free black labor could
never be commanded to the extent necessary to cultivate
the soil as at present. The history of the world contains
abundant proof that people in the condition of our blacks
will never labor to any extent, unless driven to it by necessity or by authority: hence so long as we have such a
boundless extent of unsettled country, we could not reasonably expect the Negroes to labor unless they were driven
to it by the authority of the Master. The institution of
Slavery, then, is the source of vast benefits to the country;
destroy it, and you ruin Southern agriculture, with all the
numberless blessings that flow from it. But for the sake of
perspicuity, I will use a little system:

1st. *Slave Labor improves the Health of the Country.*
—In every country—in every southern country in particular, there are extensive sources of disease, as ponds,
marshes, &c. New-Orleans, Charleston, and other Southern towns and cities, are built upon marshes, which have
been filled up by Slave labor. Our Southern climate
being unfriendly to the constitution of the white man, he
could never be induced voluntarily to undertake the removal of such sources of disease. The Negro, on the
contrary, can perform such labor without the slightest injury to his constitution. In Spain, Italy, Mexico, and in
some of the South-American Republics, where Negro Slavery does not exist, the causes of disease have accumulated
to an extent which renders the climate in the highest
degree unfriendly to the constitution of the white man.
Negro Slavery, as we have it here, under the guidance of

intelligent white men, would make those now desolate
countries blossom as the rose. Sources of disease would be
removed and man would soon regain his true position in
the scale of being.

2d. The cotton, tobacco, rice, and sugar of the South,
all the products of Slave labor, constitute the basis of
much of the wealth of this country, North and South,
and also of Europe. Destroy the production of cotton at
the South, and you will almost ruin Europe and America;
for all other portions of the world, it has been ascertained,
could not supply the demand for this article. Since the
acquisition of Texas, the South enjoys a monopoly of the
cotton lands of the world: for all efforts to grow cotton
in the East Indies have proved utterly fruitless; and the
supply from Brazil and Egypt is quite too small to meet
the present demand of the world. The world, then, is indebted to the Slave labour of the South, for a supply of
this very important article. The benefits resulting to the
world from this single article, are incalculable. Millions
of persons, here as well as in Europe, are engaged in the
production, transportation, and manufacture of this article: and the various articles manufactured from it have
become indispensable to the comfort of every country.
Cloths made of cotton are now used by the people of
every country. Shirts, table-cloths and various other articles, are made of cotton. More than one-half of the manufacturing establishments of this country and of England
are engaged in the manufacture of cotton goods. Thus it
appears, that in different ways, the cotton raised at the
South by our Slaves, gives employment to a larger number
of individuals—contributes more to the comfort of mankind generally, than any other single, nay, any other five
articles of trade, commerce, or agriculture. We make annually between two and three millions of bales, worth in
the raw state from sixty to seventy millions of dollars.
When manufactured, this cotton is worth almost an incalculable sum. . . .

But I have not as yet enumerated all the advantages of Slavery:

3d. *Slavery adds security and strength to the South, in a Military point of view.*—I am aware that the South, in case of war, is considered the most vulnerable part of the Union. This conclusion has resulted from a belief that our Slaves, like the down-trodden masses of England and other countries, would avail themselves of the first opportunity to throw off the yoke of Slavery: and hence it has been inferred by the less informed of our opponents, that our Slaves would be ready to join any foe that might invade our shores. Acting on this impression, the attempt has been several times made to stir up insurrection among our Slaves. Seventy years ago, Lord Dunmore, Governor of Virginia, offered liberty to the Slaves of Virginia, if they would join the British forces against their Masters. This they refused to do, notwithstanding the many tempting offers that were made them: they preferred adversity with their Masters, to freedom and gold without them. During the late war, several attempts were made to induce the Negroes to abandon their Masters; but this they always refused, though circumstances were highly favorable to the success of any attempt of the kind. Some years ago, when hostilities were apprehended with France, the plan of invading the Southern States, and of stirring up insurrection among the Negroes was instantly devised: and it is said that a British officer of high distinction, some years ago, deliberately planned the invasion of the Southern States at several points, with a view of stirring up our Slaves to insurrection. And very lately, we have been threatened with a black regiment from the West Indies, thinking that our Slaves would unite with them against the whites. Mr. Adams has said that in case of war, the South would be the Flanders of America. But notwithstanding all this, the South has nothing to fear. During the long period of seventy years, in which various attempts have been made to stimulate the Slaves to insurrection, there has never been any serious disturbance among them. A few disturb-

ances have occurred in particular neighborhoods, in which
a few white persons have been killed, but they have all
been easily suppressed and peace restored. There is not a
country under Heaven, where as few domestic disturb-
ances have occurred within the same period, as in the
Slave States of this Union. . . .

4th. *Slavery will tend to preserve the purity of our Republican Institutions.*—I agree with Mr. McDuffie, that
"Slavery is the corner stone of our republican edifice." In
a republican government like ours, the right of suffrage
must extend to all freemen who have reached the age of
twenty-one years; at least, such is the case in most of the
States of this Union. Such being the fact, the non-
slaveholding States must have a larger proportionate
number of unenlightened voters than the Slaveholding
States. The reason of this is very obvious: it is this: the
great body of those who perform the drudgery of society
at the South, are Slaves; and in consequence, are excluded
from the ballot-box—whilst at the North, the whole mass,
though but little superior to our blacks, many of them,
enjoy the right of suffrage. I do not wish to be understood
as intimating that all labor is incompatible with mental
culture—far otherwise—for some of the most intelligent
men in our land are laborers. In point of literary attainments, Burritt, the blacksmith, has but few equals in
this, or any other country. I do, however, maintain, that
there is, in the present state of the world, a certain kind
of drudgery, that is wholly incompatible with high mental
culture. A man engaged in incessant toil during the day
and part of the night, exposed to the sun, the rain, and
every change of weather, has but little leisure, and less
disposition, to improve his mental faculties. The small
portion of time allowed him is much more likely to be
employed in rest, which is necessary to repair his ex-
hausted energies; or if not, in something more amusing
than solitary study to such a mind. Some resort to the
bottle, and spend their leisure hours in revelry and mirth.
I need not be reminded that occasionally, men engaged in

the severest toil, excel in mental improvement: there are exceptions to all rules, but exceptions constitute no objection to the rule itself. I should be pleased to see a larger number of those engaged in severe toil, engaged in the laudable effort to improve their minds; but this cannot be expected to the fullest extent, until we have made still further advance in labor-saving machinery. . . .

BEFORE closing this work, it will be proper to sketch briefly the duties that Masters owe their servants. . . .

1st. *Masters are bound to supply all the necessary wants of their Slaves.*—This is implied in the apostolic injunction that Masters should render unto their servants *"that which is just and equal."* As the servant is the property of the Master, and his whole time is devoted to his service, it is imperative on the Master to supply his servants with an abundance of food and clothing, suitable for them in their situation as servants. The wants of the sick, the young, and the aged, should be specially attended to.

But servants are not only attended when sick, but their wants are liberally supplied when in health. My acquaintance among the Slaveholders is extensive: with many of them it is intimate. Enjoying these opportunities, I have spared no pains to ascertain how they treat their Slaves; and the result of the whole is decidedly favorable.

As to food, they are amply supplied: bacon, pork, beef, corn bread, potatoes, peas, cabbage, turnips, and many other articles, they receive in abundance. Many of the planters measure out weekly the provisions for the Negroes, but others simply provide them daily with a sufficiency to supply their wants. I have no acquaintance with any planter, that fails to supply his Slaves liberally with food: there may be individuals of this class; and if so, they should be severely rebuked by an enlightened community. No man that half feeds his Negroes, should be countenanced by the community: on the contrary, he should be scouted from all decent society. In fact, such is the case: I have occasionally heard of men that did not feed well, and I have always heard them condemned by the community. They are looked upon as monsters, who are not entitled to the respect and confidence of society. Our country is becoming too democratic to be swayed by wealth, in the absence of virtue and intelligence.

2d. *Masters are bound to provide suitable houses for their Slaves.*—This is necessary, not only as a matter of humanity and Christian duty, but as a matter of interest; for by providing suitable houses for their servants, much expense is often saved in the way of doctors' bills, and other expenses: even the lives of the Slaves may be preserved in this way. From the observations which I have made, I am induced to think that much improvement is needed in this particular; and that it is possible to effect this improvement with but very little outlay of expense. . . .

3d. *Masters are bound not to exact more than a reasonable amount of service from their Slaves.* I have before commented upon a peculiarity in the Negro character, viz: an obstinate resistance to every effort to force him to the performance of more than a reasonable amount of service. The Negro is the most obedient Slave in the world, and will as readily perform a reasonable service; but any attempt to force him beyond this, will be met by obstinate, mulish resistance. The mild, obedient Slave is converted into the obstinate, reckless rebel against his Master's authority, fearing nothing, feeling nothing, and caring for nothing. A knowledge of this trait in the Negro character has its due influence upon all Slaveholders. They scarcely ever require of them more than a reasonable service, for they are fully aware that a contrary course would result in more trouble and expense than a little. . . .

4th. *Masters are required to govern their Slaves with dignity and mildness, but with inflexible firmness.* A passionate, ill-tempered man, not being able to govern himself, cannot of course be expected to govern others. Such persons are unfit to govern any one; they always govern their families badly, and their Negroes are always turbulent, disobedient, and unruly. The passions of the Master arouse the passions of the Slave; this takes place on the principle of sympathy, a law of our nature which is now well understood. A Master, to command obedience, must be calm, firm, and dignified. . . .

5th. *Masters are required to attend to the moral condition of their Slaves.* Duty and interest both dictate this; a moral upright Slave is much more valuable than an immoral one. Slaves should be kept from the use of intoxicating drinks; at least, they should always be corrected when they indulge to excess. But this is a point that Masters are not backward in attending to; they generally keep a strict watch over their Slaves in this particular, for they are well aware that a drunken Slave is almost worthless. I have known a few drunken Slaves, and only a few; and they were almost worthless to their Masters. . . .

6th. *Masters are required to attend to the religious condition of their Slaves.* By this I mean, that they should allow them every facility for attending Divine service. I know of no Master that neglects this duty; our Negroes all enjoy ample privileges in this particular, as far as my knowledge extends. Most of our Negroes have the privilege of attending preaching once or twice a week; and besides, they hold religious meetings of their own as often as they wish. Among the 3,000,000 of Negroes at the South there are probably not less than 600,000 communicants. Most of these are orderly, correct members of the Church, and have in reality, more earnestness and zeal than the whites themselves. I know several Negroes that possess a degree of piety that but few white people can ever expect to equal.

DOCUMENT 45

(PLATES 35–36)

The Two Faces of Slavery

Vision lies in the eye of the beholder, we sometimes hear. When it came to seeing slavery in the South, it all depended on who was doing it. The artists and illustrators who favored slavery painted it as a benign institution which gave the master the labor he needed and the slave the security and sustenance he would have perished without. The artists who opposed slavery dipped their pens in acid to depict little but miserable chattels and brutal owners.

The defenders of slavery found English criticism of the Peculiar Institution especially obnoxious. In the first place, it was none of England's business that we continued to keep our slaves after she had freed hers. In the second, Britain's starveling wage slaves, victims of a heartless capitalism, were far worse off than any American slave sheltered and safe in his plantation cabin. "Black and White Slaves" makes that point vividly. On the other side was the inescapable fact that human beings under slavery were pieces of merchandise, to be bought and sold at will, to be protected or abused as the owner wished. The tentative subtitle of *Uncle Tom's Cabin* had been "The Man that was a Thing." The point was sound. And whatever the conditions, to most observers there was something innately evil in the idea of one man owning another. The illustration "Gang of Slaves Journeying to be Sold in a Southern Market" appeared in the book of an English journalist who wanted to like the South but could not avoid dwelling on the corruptions of slavery. The picture would tell its bitter story even if the artist had not heightened his effects.

PLATE 35. *Gang of Slaves Journeying to be Sold in a Southern Market*. Drawn by W. H. Brooke and engraved by F. Holl (?).

SOURCE: James Silk Buckingham, *The Slave States of America*, 1842. Library of Congress.

At first glance the scenery in this composition appears to be almost of the standard Romantic kind. But the artist has tempered it to fit his grim subject. The water is no placid pool but a fall and then a rapids, if not deep still turbulent. The trees show less foliage and more trunk than is usual, and the trunks are gnarled. Furthermore, they are not firmly set in the soil; they look ready to lean or slide. The most salient modification of the more gentle Romantic mood, however, lies in the treatment of the whitish tree trunk at the upper right. Its withered lower limb is pointed like a stern and gigantic finger at the Negroes about to feel the white man's whip. The whole trunk in fact suggests an accusing figure. The angle of the whip parallels the line of the limb as does the one slave's upraised arm. The whole constitutes a powerful, unified gesture.

As we would expect in the work of a trained artist, the chiaroscuro is handled with sophistication. The composition is well organized, keeping its elements within itself and always drawing the viewer's eye back to the central scene the tree limb points at. And in the upper center, outlined in a tiny patch of light, two small figures stand watching—and make their own comment.

PLATE 36 (on two pages). *Black and White Slaves*. Drawn by E. W. C. and issued by A. Donnelly, 1844.

SOURCE: The Harry T. Peters "America on Stone" Lithography Collection, the Smithsonian Institution.

All is lightness and air in the scene on American slavery, while the darkness of the hovel broods over the dismal English scene. In one of the South's favorite defenses the artist has arranged a signal contrast between the two pictures. He has kept the compositions similar in technique and pattern in order to underline the difference in content. In each scene there is a large diagonal on the upper left to help frame the grouped figures and on the lower right stands the master-figure who comments on the situation before him. The captions at the top of each picture continue the symmetry—and in content could not contrast more.

The grateful old Negro is saying, "God bless you massa! you feed and clothe us. When we are sick you nurse us, and when too old to work, you provide for us!" The kindly owner reflects, "These poor creatures are a sacred legacy from my ancestors and while a dollar is left me, nothing shall be spared to increase their comfort and happiness." In the other panel the starving millworker's meditations are full of despair: "Oh heaven! in this boasted land of freedom to be starving for want of employment! No relief from the purse-proud aristocracy whose bloated fortunes have been made by our blood and toil!" The only response he receives from the bloated British plutocrat facing him is a peremptory, "Come pack off to the work house! that's the only fit asylum for you."

The propaganda appeal of the pair of pictures is patent. And, we should remember, it was not always confined to the South alone. In point, the lithograph we are discussing originated in New York.

Secondary Sources

Books about the 1840s are few. Meade Minnigerode's *The Fabulous Forties* (1924) is social history told with a light touch. It deals with private and public life both. E. Douglas Branch's *The Sentimental Years* (1934) covers the period from 1836 to 1860. It offers a broad view of antebellum life, describing among other things the literature, fine arts, reform movements, and religious trends of the time. Carl Bode's *The Anatomy of American Popular Culture, 1840–1861* (1959) takes up the fine arts one by one and the various kinds of printed works popular during the period, describes them, and suggests their relationship to the American character.

Selected portions of four other books are useful for background. Oliver Larkin's *Art and Life in America* (1949) is a panoramic work with a section, pages 147–231, on the years from 1830 to 1870. Frank Luther Mott's *Golden Multitudes* (1947) and James Hart's *The Popular Book* (1950) are both studies of American best sellers. Pages 76–142 in Mott and 85–139 in Hart contain some information about popular works of the 1840s. Carl Bode's *The American Lyceum: Town Meeting of the Mind* (1956) approaches the period through its lecturing; he examines the relation of the lyceum to other elements in antebellum cultural history.

ANCHOR BOOKS